Redesigning the American Dream

REVISED AND EXPANDED

Redesigning the American Dream

The Future of Housing, Work, and Family Life

REVISED AND EXPANDED

Dolores Hayden

W. W. Norton & Company
New York • London

FOR PETER MARRIS
AND
LAURA HAYDEN MARRIS

For information about permission to reproduce selections from this book, write to Permissions, W. W. Norton & Company, Inc., 500 Fifth Avenue, New York, NY 10110

The text of this book is composed in Transitional
with the display set in Helvetica Neue Light
Composition and book design by Silvers Design
Manufacturing by Edwards Brothers Incorporated
Production manager: Leeann Graham

Library of Congress Cataloging-in-Publication Data

Hayden, Dolores.
    Redesigning the American dream: the future of housing, work, and family life/
    Doloes Hayden.—Rev. and expanded.
cm.
                    Includes bibliographical references and index.
                        ISBN 0-393-73094-8 (pbk.)
        1. Housing—United States—History. 2. Architecture, Domestic—United States—History. 3. City planning—United States—History. 4. Feminism—United States—History. I. Title.

HD7293 .H39 2002
    363.5'0973—dc21   2002066504

W. W. Norton & Company, Inc., 500 Fifth Avenue,
New York, N.Y. 10110
www.wwnorton.com

W. W. Norton & Company Ltd., Castle House, 75/76 Wells St., London W1T 3QT

0 9 8 7 6 5 4 3 2 1

Contents

PART III. Rethinking Public Life 191

Preface

to the 2002 Edition

Eighteen years ago, when I wrote *Redesigning the American Dream*, I argued that American architects and planners needed to rethink the architecture of gender. The single-family houses produced after World War II for returning veterans did not fit late-twentieth-century families. I suggested that Americans needed new kinds of housing and neighborhoods to serve diverse households. Returning to the topic in 2002, I remember the annual conferences on women's issues run by the Urban Planning Program at UCLA between 1980 and 1984. Scholars and practitioners came from across the United States and Canada to tackle housing, transportation, and economics, as well as architecture and urban design. When I wrote *Redesigning the American Dream*, the book reflected the intense excitement we all felt about creating cities to promote women's equality.

Since then, I've had much more experience with housing and urban preservation as well as years of parenting. As the mother of a fourteen-year-old daughter, I've enjoyed the pleasures of family life harnessed to the challenges of full-time work. Along with my husband, I've worked the double day (parenting and earning) on the East Coast and the West Coast, within city limits and way outside them. The two-earner family is the predominant American household type, yet the solution to American housing and childcare needs is still nowhere in sight. As an urban historian and an architect, I welcome a chance to update the book—in print until recently—and review how American life has changed, or not changed, in the past eighteen years.

Throughout the United States, a broad debate about the design of better neighborhoods emerged in the 1990s. Many environmentalists, architects, and planners have challenged suburban sprawl and proposed alternatives. "Green" architects save energy, recycle materials, and minimize ecological damage. "New Urbanist" designers rediscover the porch, widen the sidewalk, and narrow the street, while considering neighborhood scale and public transit. Renewed attention has been focused on metropolitan regions. In the 2000 elections, many local and state contests were fought around "Smart Growth" issues.

There is a curious silence about women in all of the anti-sprawl literature. No new ideals of neighborhood or sustainability can prevail without critical reexamination of attitudes toward women as earners and nurturers. In both the United States and Europe, women's second shift of nurturing has been the subject of many new analyses by economists, sociologists, and policy planners, but little of this analysis extends to architecture. The book remains in print because I have linked social and economic conditions to spatial ones. The United States still has a housing crisis of disturbing complexity, one that continues to evolve as affluence brings bigger houses for some, politicians resist assistance to women workers, and the gap between rich and poor Americans widens, despite prosperity. A feminist critique of housing policy still points to the interlocked disadvantages of class, race, and gender. Poor women of color and their children remain those with the least access to decent housing.

In 1984, I set up an extended comparison between the home as haven (the American strategy), the industrial strategy (typical of the former USSR or China), and the neighborhood strategy (typical of social democratic societies such as Sweden or Denmark). In successive chapters, I explored the social, economic, and architectural forms advocates of each strategy had adopted. Since 1984, the American home as haven has been propped up by more commercial services, such as fast food, and new technologies, such as the home computer. Women's involvement in the paid labor force has continued to rise, but basic supports—decades overdue—have still not arrived. The United States remains the only major nation without a child-care policy. It has the weakest parental-leave policy of any advanced country. While some large private employers provide paid maternity leave, many don't. Ignorance about these issues is appalling. The "price of motherhood" remains contested, even as economists calculate it more accurately. "Family values" has been seized as a slogan of the extreme right wing.

During the same years, the industrial strategy has lost credibility with the dissolution of the USSR. A revival of the neighborhood strategy has occurred in Europe, with campaigns by women—including professionals, trade union members, and housewives—for better urban design. The European Charter of Women in the City, drafted in 1994, and sponsorship of demonstration projects throughout the European Community, are heartening. Recent projects tie women's equality to city design through the call for *parité* democracy.

Hundreds of new design projects, books, and articles have appeared since 1984. Feminist work on built space as a dimension of material life has enlivened architecture, urban planning, geography, economics, and politics. In revising *Redesigning the American Dream,* I have tried to remain close to my original essay, with all of its historical research. In the text, I've added current demographic and economic data, and discussed recent work to extend the argument. The bibliography and notes have been expanded so readers can locate comprehensive new material in areas where I could not expand the book. I was delighted to find that many of the projects I discussed as innovative approaches to neighborhood involvement have survived. Americans still need to critique the current housing practices of major developers and the Federal government, while having confidence in their best non-profit endeavors. Much is left to accomplish.

DOLORES HAYDEN
August 15, 2001

Acknowlegments

ACKNOWLEDGMENTS FOR THE 1984 EDITION

Financial support for this essay came from a Rockefeller Humanities Fellowship, a Guggenheim Fellowship, and a National Endowment for the Arts fellowship. Special intellectual and institutional support for my investigations on women and the city came from Harvey Perloff and Martin Wachs at UCLA. The two designers who first sparked my interest in housing were Shadrach Woods, my teacher at the Harvard GSD, and John Habraken, the head of the architecture department at MIT when I was an assistant professor there. During the last decade many conversations with colleagues have contributed to this project. The people I especially wish to thank for perceptive, detailed comments on the manuscript are Jeremy Brecher, Robert Healy, Temma Kaplan, Susan Krieger, Jacqueline Leavitt, Ann R. Markusen, Peter Marris, Kitty Sklar, Susana Torre, Martin Wachs, Peter and Phyllis Willmott, and Gwendolyn Wright. I am also grateful to Janet Abu-Lughod, Laura Balbo, Thomas Bender, Eugenie Birch, Manuel Castells, Francesco dal Co, Phil Donahue, Margaret Fitzsimmons, John Friedmann, Sherna Gluck, Patrick H. Hare, Mui Ho, Kevin Lynch, Margarita McCoy, Jean Baker Miller, S.M. Miller, Martin Pawley, Jan Peterson, Mary Rowe, Arie Schachar, Donna Shalala, David Thompson, and Gerda Wekerle, who contributed valuable criticisms of earlier articles and ideas. I would also like to thank Martha Nelson and Catharine Stimpson, as the editors of *Signs* who first asked, "What would a non-sexist city be like?" and Carol Houck Smith, my editor at W. W. Norton, who showed me how many choices I had about what to do with the answers to that question.

ACKNOWLEDGMENTS FOR THE REVISED AND EXPANDED EDITION

It was my good fortune to have the help of two wonderful Yale assistants. Gabrielle Brainard accomplished prodigious feats of research on the Internet, in the library, and in new interviews to help me update the text. Miriam

Stewart, an excellent and subtle editor, helped me refine the text and get the revised manuscript across the finish line. Their enthusiasm helped me to see how a new generation will learn about their lives and choices from this book. Peter Marris, my husband, and Laura Hayden Marris, my daughter, have been steadfast supporters. I would also like to thank Nancy Green, senior editor for Norton Professional Books for Architects and Designers, Anne Hellman and Ingsu Liu of Norton, and Ellen Levine and Emily Haynes of Ellen Levine Literary Agency, Inc.

DOLORES HAYDEN
August 15, 2001

CITIES, LIKE DREAMS, ARE MADE OF DESIRES AND
FEARS, EVEN IF THE THREAD OF THEIR DISCOURSE
IS SECRET, THEIR RULES ARE ABSURD, THEIR
PERSPECTIVES DECEITFUL, AND EVERYTHING
CONCEALS SOMETHING ELSE.

—Italo Calvino

SPACE IS POLITICAL AND IDEOLOGICAL. IT IS A
PRODUCT LITERALLY FILLED WITH IDEOLOGIES.

—Henri Lefebvre

REDISCOVER THE CITY THROUGH
WOMEN'S EYES, ABOLISH STEREOTYPES.

—European Charter for Women and the City

Part I

The Evolution of American Housing

TO STUDY THE HISTORY OF THE AMERICAN FAMILY IS TO CONDUCT A RESCUE MISSION INTO THE DREAMLAND OF OUR NATIONAL SELF-CONCEPT. NO SUBJECT IS MORE CLOSELY BOUND UP WITH OUR SENSE OF A DIFFICULT PRESENT—AND OUR NOSTALGIA FOR A HAPPIER PAST.

—*John Demos*

Chapter 1

Housing and American Life

Mired in spring mud, striped with the treads of bulldozers, Vanport City, Oregon, is a new town under construction. Concrete trucks pour foundations and give way to flatbed trucks that deliver cedar siding from the forests of the Northwest. Carpenters, plumbers, and electricians try to stay out of each other's way as they work evenings, Saturdays, and Sundays. Architects from the firm of Wolff and Phillips confer on the site six, ten, a dozen times a day. "All my life I have wanted to build a new town," the project architect confides to a reporter, "but—*not this fast.* We hardly have time to print the working drawings before the buildings are out of the ground."

Near the town site, steel deliveries arrive at several shipyards on the

Columbia River, where production is geared to an even more frenetic pace. The yards are open twenty-four hours a day. Cranes move against the sky, shifting materials. Tired workers pour out of the gates at 8 A.M., 4 P.M., and midnight, each shift replaced by fresh arrivals—women and men in coveralls who carry protective goggles and headgear. The personnel office is recruiting as far away as New York and Los Angeles. They want welders, riveters, and electricians. They offer on-the-job training, housing, child care, and fringe benefits. They also advertise for maintenance workers, nursery school teachers, elementary school teachers, and nurses. In ten months, the personnel office does enough hiring to populate a new town of forty thousand people—white, African-American, Asian-American, and Hispanic workers and their families. This is the first time that an integrated, publicly subsidized new town of this type has ever been built in the United States.

The chief engineer from the Federal Public Housing Authority is checking the last of the construction details as the residents' cars, pickup trucks, and moving vans start to arrive. It has been ten months from schematic designs to occupancy. The project architect is exhausted. Never has he had a more demanding design program to meet, never a more impossible timetable. He has had to rethink many basic questions in very little time and reexamine every idea he has ever had about normal family life, about men, women, and children. The program specified that he design affordable housing for all types and sizes of households, including single people, single-parent families, and nonfamily groups. He also had to make the best use of scarce building materials and energy resources. He was directed to emphasize public transportation by bus. His housing also had to be positioned in relation to several child-care centers and job sites: "On a straight line," said James L. Hymes, the client in charge of child care, because he did not want parents to have to make long journeys to drop off or pick up their children.

"They certainly should become famous for that," the architect asserts, considering the six large child-care centers, open twenty-four hours a day, seven days a week (just like the shipyards), complete with infirmaries for sick children, child-sized bathtubs so that mothers do not need to bathe children at home, cooked food services so that mothers can pick up hot casseroles along with their children, and, most important of all, large windows with views of the river, so that children can watch the launchings at the yards. "There goes mommy's ship!" said one excited five-year-old. It all seems to work very well. And it costs seventy-five cents per day for the first child and fifty cents for each additional child. Kaiser has also built several kindergartens, five grade schools, and seventeen supervised playgrounds to serve nine thousand children.

It is March, 1943. Vanport City, a product of World War II, is nicknamed Kaiserville after the industrialist who owns the shipyards. Everywhere at home and abroad, Americans are singing a song at the top of the wartime hit parade:

> All the day long whether rain or shine,
> She's a part of the assembly line . . .
> She's making history, working for victory,
> Rosie the Riveter!

This amazing American woman has been the client as much as Henry J. Kaiser, who has built this town for Rosie the Riveter and her children. The director of the child-care project, James Hymes, notes that, "In the past, good nursery schools have been a luxury for the wealthy. The Kaiser Child Service Centers are among the first places where working people, people of average means, have been able to afford good nursery education for their children." The range of services offered to mothers by an American employer is unprecedented. So are wartime profits. Henry J. Kaiser and his management team link their economic success to their concern for women's labor power. "The way people live and the way their families are cared for is bound to be reflected in production," says one Kaiser official.[1]

Six years later, another new town for seventy-five thousand people is being built at the same frantic pace near Hempstead, Long Island. In Levittown, nothing is on a straight line. Roads curve to lead the eye around the corner, but every road is lined with identical houses. There is no industry here except the construction industry. Each new Cape Cod house is designed to be a self-contained world, with white picket fence, green lawn, living room with television set built into the wall, kitchen with Bendix washing machine built into the laundry alcove. Every family is expected to consist of male breadwinner, female housewife, and their children. Energy conservation is not a design issue, nor is low maintenance,

1.1 Women working as riveters and welders, 1944.

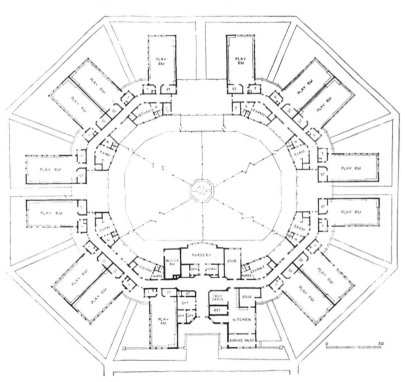

1.2 Wolff and Phillips, architects, plan for one of the day care centers at Vanport City, Oregon, 1944. Wartime services for workers who were also parents were excellent at the Kaiser shipyards.

nor is public transportation, nor is child care. A few parks and public swimming pools are planned to provide recreation.

In March, 1949, the developer is ready to sell his houses. On a Wednesday, the first prospective buyers camp out in front of the sales office that will open the following Monday. It is the end of winter on Long Island, raw, wet, and cold. One of the women on the line of buyers is pregnant. The developer's assistant rushes her to the hospital so she does not have her baby in the street. He returns and sets up a canteen for hot coffee and hot soup. News photographers come by and take pictures. On Monday night, in three and a half hours, the developer sells $11 million worth of identical two-bedroom houses. His company emerges as one of the great business successes of the postwar era. His Cape Cod house becomes the single most powerful symbol of the dream of upward mobility and home ownership for American families. Because of mortgage subsidies and tax deductions for home owners, it is cheaper to buy a house in Levittown than to rent an apartment in New York City.[2]

The promoter of this new town, William J. Levitt, acknowledges that Levittown is not integrated. He explains to a reporter that this is "not a matter of prejudice, but one of business. As a Jew, I have no room in my mind or heart for racial prejudice. But, by various means, I have come to know that if we sell one house to a Negro family, then 90 to 95 percent of our white customers will not buy into the community."[3] In fact, the Federal Housing Administration does not, at this time, approve mortgage funds for integrated communities, or mortgages for female-headed families.[4] The prospective customers do not get a chance to make this choice for themselves.

This second new town—Levittown—becomes known all over the world as a model of American know-how just as the first new town—Vanport City—is being dismantled, some of its housing taken apart piece by piece. Yet both of these ventures had great appeal as solutions to the housing needs of American families, and both made their developers a great deal of money. Vanport City met the needs of a wartime labor force, composed of women and men of many diverse racial and economic groups. The builders of Vanport City responded to the need for affordable housing, on-the-job training, and economic development for workers. They recognized that single parents and two-earner families required exten-

1.3 **Postwar** house with homeowner, wife, and children, Levittown, New York, 1948. This housing represents the haven strategy of building homes as retreats for male workers and as workplaces for their wives. (Bernard Hoffman, LIFE Magazine, © 1950, Time, Inc.)

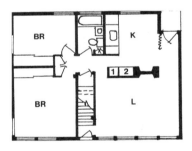

1.4 Plan of a Levitt house, 1952 model. (1) Bendix washing machine (2) water heater.

sive child care in order to give their best energies to production. The site design and landscaping of Vanport City were good, the economic organization was good, and the social services were superb (down to maintenance crews who would fix leaky faucets or repair broken windows), but the housing lacked charm. It looked like a "housing project," and the residents were renters, not owners. Yet it was the most ambitious attempt ever made in the United States to shape space for employed women and their families. The U.S. government supplied $26 million to build the housing. Kaiser made only a $2 profit on it, but he made a fortune on the ships the war workers built for him.[5]

Levittown provided for rather different needs than the ones met by Vanport City. Levitt's client was the returning veteran, the beribboned male war hero who wanted his wife to stay home. Women in Levittown were expected to be too busy tending their children to care about a paying job. The Cape Cod houses recalled traditional American colonial housing (although they were very awkwardly proportioned). They emphasized privacy. Large-scale plans for public space and social services were sacrificed to private yards. Although the houses were small, a husband could convert his attic and then build an addition quite easily, since the houses covered only 15 percent of the lots. Levitt liked to think of the husband as a weekend do-it-yourself builder and gardener: "No man who owns his house and lot can be a Communist. He has too much to do."[6] Levitt aimed to shape private space for white working-class males and their dependents. The pressures of war and the communal style of military barracks made suburban privacy attractive to many veterans, especially those with new cars to go with their new houses. Levitt made his fortune on the potato farms that he subdivided with the help of federal financing from the Federal Housing Administration (FHA) and VA mortgages and federal highway programs to get people to remote suburbs. And as the landscaping matured, Levittown began to look better than the acres of little boxes some visitors perceived at the start.

Ironically, although Kaiser's highly praised wartime town lost the public relations battle to Levitt's postwar suburb, Kaiser himself was not a loser in this contest. He understood changing federal subsidy programs for housing, and after receiving wartime Lanham Act funds for Vanport City, which enabled him to expand his shipyards with new workers, Kaiser entered the post–World War II housing arena with new developments suited to the FHA and VA subsidies. On the West Coast, he built thousands of single-family houses in subdivisions much like Levitt's.[7] "Vets! No down!" read his signs. The losers were not the housing developers but the skilled women workers who lost their wartime jobs to returning white male veterans. Most wartime employers discontinued their day-care programs immediately. The riveters became supermarket check-out clerks, maids, and cafeteria workers. Rosie the Riveter found no postwar

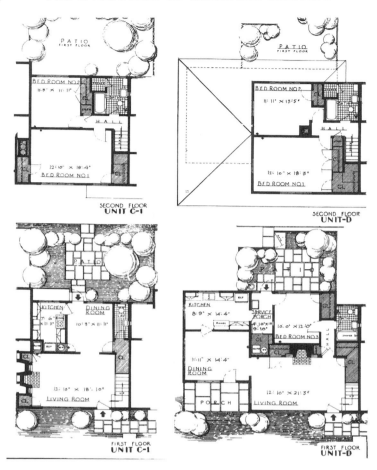

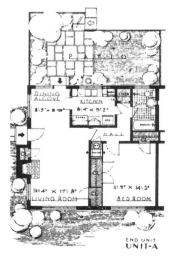

1.5 Clarence Stein, Robert Alexander, et al., Baldwin Hills Village, Los Angeles, 1938–1942. Baldwin Hills represents the neighborhood strategy. The one-bedroom (A), two-bedroom (C-1), and three-bedroom (D) houses were subsidized, rental units organized around shared open spaces.

housing subsidies designed to help her find a new job, a new home, or a mortgage with easy terms.

In the same era a third new town was launched, Baldwin Hills Village in Los Angeles, California. It did not make anyone a fortune, neither an industrialist like Kaiser nor a developer like Levitt. Funded by the FHA and the Reconstruction Finance Corporation, its designers had sophisticated professional ambitions: to reinterpret the tradition of common land at the heart of New England's Puritan communities; to adapt the best low-cost European public housing designs to American lifestyles; and to keep the car in its proper place for the sake of air quality, children's safety, and open-space design.

Unlike the other two projects, the construction of the Baldwin Hills Village dragged on in the early 1940s. City engineers made complaints about the designers' refusal to cut roads through the site. The building department did not like the great variety of apartment and townhouse layouts. The plans had to be redrawn no fewer than ten times. Budget cuts removed three child-care centers and a shopping center. Land acquisition problems canceled the second phase of the project. Clarence Stein, the overall designer, discovered that his proposal for community kitchens had not been funded.[8]

Yet when the project finally opened as subsidized rental housing, several of the collaborating local architects moved to Baldwin Hills Village. As a statement of support for their project, they left elegant private homes in other parts of Los Angeles to be part of the new experiment and to make sure it worked. They felt extremely pleased that they had created low-rise, medium-density housing with generous floor plans, sunlight, and lush landscaping. The cost was almost as low as that of other local public housing "projects."[9] The residents enjoyed a belt of three parks running through the center of the site, as well as smaller landscaped courtyards, tot lots, and private fenced-in outdoor space for each family. There were common laundries and drying yards, common garages, and a community center with a swimming pool.

Baldwin Hills Village was integrated at the start. Within ten years many white tenants left, drawn to new opportunities for home ownership. Renter households were surrounded by home-owners living on suburban plots. Eventually a group turned the

Village into condominiums, prohibited children under eighteen, tore out the tot lots, and installed a miniature golf course on the central green. In the 1980s, the children for whom the village was designed were gone, and many of the elderly residents were too afraid of crime to use its three magnificent parks. Yet, the Baldwin Hills Village revived. Vanport City became a ghost town. Because most Lanham Act housing was designed to be temporary, part of Vanport City was dismantled after World War II. The rest was destroyed in a flood, and today the site of what was once the fifth largest city in the Northwest is a park.[10]

Baldwin Hills Village and Vanport City whisper the stories of planned settlements based on complex visions of the American dream. Both sites raise broad issues in housing and urban design: the relationship of housing to jobs and social services; the need to design for diverse household types; the rights of female workers to housing and jobs; the need for both spatial privacy and spatial community; the need for the regulation of automobiles; the problem of affordability; and the question of homeownership or tenancy as it concerns the stability of residential neighborhoods. Baldwin Hills Village and Vanport City represent earlier struggles to come to terms with the social and economic programming of affordable housing. These projects, now largely forgotten, remind us that the need for affordable housing for all Americans is not a new problem, nor are the design issues and political questions that housing raises novel. What is new is a critique based on gender that suggests how gender is connected to class and race.

Very little of today's housing follows the Vanport City model of the home as a support for women in the industrial labor force or emulates the Baldwin Hills Village model of the home as a part of a well-thought-out neighborhood. Most American housing is based on federal government policy reflected in Levitt's design of the home as a haven for the white male worker's family. In the late 1940s, American builders mass-produced the home as haven and transformed our urban regions to fit this model, with its particular social, economic, and environmental shortcomings. During the last six decades, government subsidized programs have concentrated the bulk of capital resources for housing on the single-family detached house. About 80 percent of the total housing stock in the United States in the year 1999 was built after 1940. With just over

100 million occupied housing units, nearly two-thirds are single-family detached homes. These houses encode Victorian stereotypes about "a woman's place," while single-family neighborhoods sustain the separation of the household from the world of jobs and public life. Together, houses and neighborhoods form an architecture of gender unsuited to twenty-first-century life.

Single-family houses have been getting larger and larger in each decade since World War II. Yet households have been getting smaller. Married-couple families with children under 18 constituted less than a quarter of all households in 2000, and most of these were two-earner families. About a third of all households consisted of one person living alone.[11] As a result of these demographic changes, many individuals and families are now experiencing serious difficulties. Whether they plan to rent or own, many cannot locate well-designed, solidly built housing that is affordable.[12]

The symptoms of this housing crisis begin with young couples. Even if they are both employed, often they cannot qualify for a mortgage. In 2000, the average price of existing single-family homes reached $177,000.[13] To lower their housing costs, they must commute long distances to remote suburbs where land is cheaper. At the same time, the elderly who live on fixed incomes—even those who own their houses outright—often find they cannot meet the property taxes, heating bills, and the demands for physical maintenance of single-family homes. The frail elderly often cannot drive, a necessity in most suburban locations.[14] Single-parent families often lack the support system required if the parent is holding a paid job. Infant care, day care, after-school care, public transportation so that older children can move about independently, closeness to stores and health services, are almost always lacking in neighborhoods where the housing was originally designed for households with a full-time housewife caring for husband and children.[15] Two-earner couples experience many of the same strains.

Single people, male or female, old or young, straight or gay, often find that the housing options available to them lack flexibility, variety, and complexity. Coming home to an empty house or apartment every night can be dreary, but sharing traditional housing designed for the closeness of one family can be frustrating in its lack of privacy. More subtle options are hard to locate, and harder to finance.[16]

Couples undergoing divorce or separation experience additional frustration. If two incomes are needed to support one mortgage, neither partner may be able to afford to buy the other's share of a jointly-owned house. At the same time, it may not be feasible to relinquish one low-interest mortgage in favor of two expensive rentals. Furthermore, some landlords discourage families with children.[17] As families struggle to cope with these dilemmas, rigid zoning laws and financing arrangements that make "granny flats" or "daughter-in-law apartments" illegal only compound the problem.[18] It becomes clear that neighborhoods need a variety of housing types at affordable prices so that single-parent families, singles, and the elderly can live in close proximity to traditional families.

Despite fair housing legislation, segregation in neighborhoods of single-family detached houses has never been dealt with adequately. Informal discriminatory practices of realtors, homeowners, and banks resist regulation.[19] In poor inner-city neighborhoods, banks may refuse to grant loans, despite bans on "redlining." Public housing may create racial segregation based on poverty. Gated communities and second homes for the affluent oppose burnt-out tenements and vandalized public-housing projects at the extremes of the American housing spectrum. On the very lowest rung of the economic ladder, an estimated 2.3 to 3.5 million homeless sleep in shelters or on the street.[20] Women, children, and men lie on the heating vents of New York skyscrapers, under the freeway overpasses in Los Angeles, and in the doorways and parks of smaller cities and towns.

The United States has a housing crisis of disturbing complexity, a crisis that, in different ways, affects rich and poor, male and female, young and old, people of color and white Americans. We have not merely a housing shortage, but a broader set of unmet needs caused by the efforts of the entire society to fit itself into a housing pattern that reflects the dreams of the mid-nineteenth century better than the realities of the twenty-first century. Single-family suburban homes have become inseparable from the American dream of economic success and upward mobility. Their presence pervades every aspect of economic, social, and political life in the United States, because the mass-production of these homes, beginning in the late 1940s, transformed the American landscape.

This book is about the search for more satisfactory patterns of housing, work, and family life in the United States, as well as in other countries where the employment of women in the paid labor force has created similar strains. The first part of the book, "The Evolution of American Housing," looks at the history of American shelter since colonial times. It examines both rural farms and urban apartments, and documents the wide variety of housing arrangements available before the 1940s, when the suburban single-family house became the national norm. It then explores the challenges to the suburban dream house posed by environmental groups, women's groups, and civil rights groups, as well as the threat to dream houses created by changing economic conditions.

The second part, "Rethinking Private Life," seeks to identify the deepest needs and desires associated with the ideal of home. What are the most basic human attachments to a home, and how are they expressed in modern, urban societies? Humans need nurturing, aesthetic pleasure, and economic security. Homes can contribute to the satisfaction of these desires, or frustrate them. Three models of housing in industrial societies emerged in the last third of the nineteenth century: the haven strategy, the industrial strategy, and the neighborhood strategy. These models carried different implications for nurturing, aesthetic expression, and economic development. The strengths and weaknesses of these models are examined. American experience is compared with the experience of other nations, such as China, Cuba, Denmark, Sweden, and Russia, to assess the art of creating housing in world terms.

The third part, "Rethinking Public Life," examines the relationship between better housing design and public space. These chapters explore how and where housing meets community development. They deal with rehabilitation of the existing American fabric of homes and neighborhoods, as well as with suggestions for new construction. They include many examples of demonstration projects—good and bad—undertaken by individuals, small groups, local governments, and national governments.

Finding an egalitarian approach to affordable housing must involve individuals, families, neighbors' groups, citizens' groups, local officials, national policymakers, and practitioners in the planning and design professions. It affects employed parents who are concerned about their children and their children's futures as well as single people and the elderly who seek new options. Employed women and their families constitute an absolute majority of American citizens, a majority whose voices must be heard on questions of housing design and policy.

Chapter 2

From Ideal City to Dream House

Open the real estate section of a major Sunday newspaper in any American city and you will still find dream houses as well as dream apartments, dream lofts, and dream condominiums. Developers often claim they are "planned with women in mind." They argue that women like elaborate stairways and formal entrances where they can greet their guests in style. They believe women favor romantic "master" bedrooms, where they can enjoy large closets, expansive dressing rooms, and extensive bathroom areas.[1] They advertise gourmet kitchens, where women can practice cooking as an art or as a science. Dream houses also have special marketing features for men, such as paneled dens, home workshops, and large garages. One can describe suburban houses as filled with gender stereotypes, since houses provide settings for women and girls to be effective social status achievers, desirable sex objects, and skillful domestic servants, and for men and boys to be executive breadwinners, successful home handymen, and adept car mechanics. There is also a larger meaning to the architecture of gender—entire metropolitan regions have been arranged to separate suburbs of private single-family houses from public urban spaces.

Couples may accept or resist the real estate developers' definitions of their gender roles, but most of all, couples are likely to justify the dream house as a place where they can give their children "all the things we didn't have." While "all the things we didn't have" may include a large backyard, a gas-fired barbecue, swings and slides, shiny bicycles, a big family room, and spacious individual bedrooms, this phrase usually means something more than material acquisitions. It may mean a chance to surmount one's class and ethnic background. In this sense, single-family, suburban houses represent Americanization for a nation of immigrants, and they imply a complete social planning strategy. "The things we didn't have" is also a euphemism for a private life without urban problems such as unemployment, poverty, hunger, racial prejudice, pollution, or violent crime. As a solution to these problems, this housing type offers short-term incentives to a particular kind of economic consumption. It has encouraged Americans to turn their backs on their cities and to pretend that urban problems do not exist.

The dream house is a uniquely American form. For the first time in history, a civilization has created a utopian ideal based on the house rather than the city or the nation. For hundreds of years, when individuals thought about putting an end to social problems, they designed model towns to express these desires, not model homes. The ideal of a good town was once more important to American life than the ideal of a good house. To analyze how Americans gave up the model town in favor of the individual dream house is to understand the fears, hopes, and miscalculations that have generated the current housing crisis.

THE CITY ON A HILL

In the seventeenth and eighteenth centuries, farmers, laborers, shopkeepers, landowners, soldiers, and housewives all came to the

North American continent seeking a better way of life. The Puritans believed they were creating a "city upon a hill," a model for the rest of the world. The Quakers called their settlement a "city of brotherly love." The public spaces they established, such as the town commons of the Puritan villages in New England or the ordered squares of William Penn's Philadelphia, gave form to their collective ideals. Despite a strict, hierarchical organization of society, which they took for granted, these settlers sought a balance between personal space and social space. Their plans expressed a desire for more personal autonomy in terms of land ownership than English society had permitted, and for more lenient treatment of debtors and the poor. Their plans also expressed the settlers' mutual economic and social dependence.[2] While settlers usually tended separate fields at the edge of the settlements, they chose to live side by side. It would have been inconceivable to these first settlers to strive for the good life in America by building model houses rather than working for a model community.

The town commons or village greens created by the New England covenant communities remain some of the most memorable American public spaces. Originally town commons were used for cattle grazing. They formed a verdant heart for every settlement, bordered by the meeting house, the minister's house, and the houses of other settlers.[3] Because they represent American citizens' earliest covenants to provide and maintain public space, the village greens are an important part of our political heritage as well as our landscape heritage. They are our first and best planning tradition.

EACH FARMER ON HIS OWN FARM

By the end of the eighteenth century the New England pattern of town building was challenged by an alternate approach. Thomas Jefferson, the first mainstream American political theorist to attempt a schematic spatial representation of a national ideal of democracy, favored the model family farm over the model village. The Declaration of Independence and the National Survey that Jefferson produced are the crucial statements of the rights of all men to life, liberty, and the pursuit of happiness in a landscape divided into small farms, where every man can own the means of agricultural production. As Jefferson's survey grid appeared on the

American landscape west of the Alleghenies in the late 1780s, this powerful theoretical statement of agrarian life became the framework for a national ideal of land ownership. However, most of the early land sales resulted in the acquisition of large areas by speculators, not by small farmers.

Throughout the nineteenth and early twentieth centuries, the ideal of the model town was still debated, but the spatially and socially coherent settlements of the earliest colonists started to give way to distance between city and country, and between capital and labor. Communitarian socialists—including the Owenites, Associationists, Shakers, and Amana Inspirationists—did continue to argue that the good life could only be achieved through collective economic effort and the shared spaces of cooperatively owned housing in model towns.[4] From Maine to California, they built hundreds of experimental socialist towns. Although tens of thousands of Americans joined their communities, more rural Americans lived on the Jeffersonian grid.

THE AMERICAN WOMAN'S HOME

When the national economy shifted its emphasis from agriculture to industry, housing patterns changed. Between 1840 and 1920, millions of poor farmers and immigrants arrived in New York, Boston, Chicago, and other cities, eager to take any jobs they could find. They had few trade unions. Men, women, and children labored in factories under conditions that included unsafe machinery, foul air, corrosive wastes, and poor sanitation. When a man was crippled for life by a machine, or a woman's jaw rotted from phosphorous in a match factory, or a child lost several fingers in a press, the factory simply replaced the worker. There were no disability benefits, death benefits, or social security schemes, only charity or the workhouse. While these facts are often recounted, few historians convey the desperation and rage such conditions generated.

The urban living conditions of this era were as bad as the working conditions. Tenement apartments often lacked windows, heating, running water, indoor plumbing, and proper sewers. In nineteenth-century cities, one urban family in five took in boarders, despite the crowding. The homeless slept in doorways or alleys.

2.1 Street scene with market and tenements: a Jewish quarter of the lower East Side, New York City, photographed by Jacob Riis, 1900. (Library of Congress)

2.2 Tenement interior, Jersey Street, New York City, photographed by Jacob Riis about 1890. The mother holds her swaddled baby and looks resigned to her squalid home. (Library of Congress)

Food sold in slum neighborhoods was often adulterated or spoiled—water in the milk, powder in the flour, maggots in the meat. Tuberculosis, cholera, diphtheria, and influenza claimed as many lives as did industrial hazards. There were no public housing schemes or medical services, merely a few charitable associations struggling to cope with the needs of millions.

The dangers and discomforts of this urban setting eventually encouraged newly affluent urban businessmen to remove their families from urban centers. There were new forms of transportation, and businessmen began to commute by railroad and then by streetcar from the outskirts of the city to their downtown offices, stores, or factories. The earliest American suburban homes were designed by Catharine Beecher and Andrew Jackson Downing, and promoted by small builders and the editors of women's magazines. Both Downing and Beecher started to popularize such suburban prototypes in the 1840s. These houses were designed to recall the values of the Puritan convenant community but to suit families whose lives centered around the profitable dealings of the new cities.

Downing's contribution was picturesque landscaping for the suburban retreat. Beecher named her 1869 prototype "The American Woman's Home," and her house was a space for woman's domestic labor in service of men and children. Essentially Beecher attempted to update Jefferson's ideal of equal male access to the means of agricultural production. She wanted to give women control over the domestic space of the household to match male involvement in agriculture or industry. She ignored race and attempted to play off gender against class as a way of mitigating urban economic and spatial conflict. She stated that all women, rich or poor, could find a common identity in housework. She acknowledged conflict between men and women within the American family but was over-optimistic about her power to resolve it. Her suburban house was designed to put the American woman, newly described as a "minister of home" and a "true professional," in charge of a well-organized private domestic workplace in a democratic society where public life was run by men.

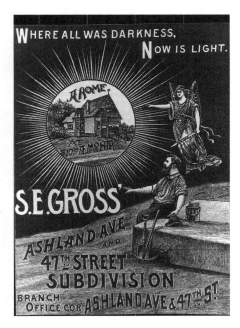

2.3 "The Workingman's Reward, a Home at $10 a Month," as pointed out by an angel with a sword of justice and built by S. E. Gross, Chicago, 1891.

According to Beecher, a woman, nurturing her spouse and children, could create a "model family commonwealth" in her suburban home.[5] Beecher believed that women's exclusion from the paid labor force would mute class conflict, and that women's consumption of commodities would stimulate the economy. She argued that in this home a woman could perfect her capacity for self-sacrifice and thus gain rewards in heaven for what she gave up on earth. Her calculations about the model home did not include the social costs to women or the economic costs to the city.

Whether or not heaven could provide an ideal city for women at some future time, as Beecher claimed, her strategy required more patience than many women possessed, and more wages than most skilled workers earned. Beecher's model houses were built for a small proportion of affluent citizens. Millions of workers, concentrated in the vast slums, could only dream about the small, clean, middle-class suburbs of houses surrounded by grass and trees and advertised by one builder as "the workingman's reward." At the end of the nineteenth century, two-thirds of American urban residents were still tenants, most of them in the tenements.

"THE CITY OF THE FAITHFULEST FRIENDS"

Some of the greatest American writers, activists, and designers hoped for changes in the industrial city rather than an escape to model houses. Against the background of Jefferson's idealized family farm and Beecher's pious suburban house, several remarkable alternative visions of urban public space appeared. Between the late 1840s and the 1870s, the activists of the abolitionist movement and the women's movement gathered the strength to make demands for political and spatial rights that were to inspire generations of reformers. They saw the ideal city as the spatial expression of these rights.

One of the clearest statements of this urban vision came from Walt Whitman. Whitman, an editor, printer, and building contractor who became a great poet, defined the ideal American city in 1856 in his "Song of the Broad-Axe." The great city, for Whitman, was not "the place of the tallest and costliest buildings or shops selling goods from the rest of the earth." "A great city," he proclaimed, "is that which has the greatest men and women. . . ." A great city is "where the slave ceases and the master of slaves ceases." It is:

> Where the citizen is always the head and ideal, . . .
> Where children are taught to be laws to themselves,
>   and to depend upon themselves,
> Where women walk in public processions in the streets
>   the same as the men,
> Where they enter the public assembly and take places
>   the same as the men;
> Where the city of the faithfulest friends stands. . .
> There the great city stands.[6]

The "city of the faithfulest friends" was a city of equal political participation, without regard to gender, race, class, or sexual preference, a city offering all adults access to public space and to public office. It was an urban place diametrically opposed to the sentimental, gender-stereotyped private domestic spaces that Jefferson and Beecher promoted.

Whitman wanted the new American city to reflect "Shapes of Democracy total, result of centuries." He believed that in the great city, where "fierce men and women pour forth," the public domain, accessible to all, would inspire a new, uniquely American architecture. "The shapes arise!" he exulted.[7]

While Whitman always admired happily married couples and parents with their children, there were three other constituencies he was particularly eager to describe. He instructed his readers, in "Poem of Remembrance for a Girl or Boy of These States," to foresee the end of slavery, to "Anticipate when the thirty or fifty millions are to become the hundred or two hundred millions, of equal freeman and freewoman, amicably joined." With regard to female citizens he said: "Anticipate the best women; / I say an unnumbered new race of hardy and well-defined women are to spread through all These States; / I say a girl fit for These States must be free, capable, dauntless, just the same as a boy."[8] When "In the New Garden, in All the Parts," Whitman imagined himself walking through modern cities, he was most interested in finding this type: "with determined will, I seek—the woman of the future, / You, born years, centuries after me, I seek."[9] In addition, as a single man who was given to wandering the streets, Whitman celebrated a public domain open to "the dear love of comrades":

> I dream'd in a dream I saw a city invincible to the
> attacks of the whole of the rest of the earth,
> I dream'd that was the new city of Friends,
> Nothing was greater there than the quality of robust
> love, it led the rest,
> It was seen every hour in the actions of the men of
> that city,
> And in all their looks and words.[10]

Although Whitman's aesthetic of urban space provided him with a "continued exaltation and absolute fulfillment," not every aspect of the American city could satisfy his critical sense of the dangers of bigotry, commercialism, and exploitation.[11] At the very time when he was writing, many men were ridiculing women's desire for access to public space, racial segregation was practiced everywhere, and gay liberation was not even discussed, while the Jeffersonian family farm was still much romanticized.

EVOLUTION OF THE PUBLIC LANDSCAPE

Whitman's wish to create a democratic public life in the American city was matched by the zeal of Frederick Law Olmsted, founder of the profession of landscape architecture. On February 25, 1870, Olmsted traveled to Boston to address the American Social Science Association on the subject of "Public Parks and the Improvement of Towns." Already well known for his work in creating Central Park in New York City, Olmsted gave a bold lecture contending that the American city should be replanned to foster friendly associations among its citizens, rich and poor, female and male, young and old, whether socialites from the salons or immigrants from the steerage.[12] The impetus for this urban spatial ideal was not democracy as an abstraction but specific demands for the equality of women and the assimilation of immigrants, mid-nineteenth-century political events that challenged all earlier definitions of public and private life.

In his address, Olmsted defined a backward society as a nonurban society where the "men counted their women with their horses." Olmsted argued that in a modern society, women would seek their liberation in the city: "We all recognize that the tastes and dispositions of women are more and more potent in shaping the course of civilized progress, and we may see that women are even more susceptible to . . . townward drift than men." Like Whitman, he valued the traditional family but also recognized the independent needs of women and children. Olmsted confessed himself "impatient of the common cant which assumes that the strong tendency of women to town life, even though it involves great privations and dangers, is a purely senseless, giddy, vain, frivolous, and degrading one." Instead, he claimed that the city would attract single, employed women because of its social life. It would attract married women because publicly owned urban infrastructure and socialized labor would relieve them from the isolation and drudgery of the private, patriarchal household. He speculated about the possibility of providing municipal hot-air heat to every home and suggested that public laundries, bakeries, and kitchens would promote "the economy which comes by systematizing and concentrating, by the application of a large apparatus, processes which are otherwise conducted in a desultory way, wasteful of human strength."[13]

It is extremely revealing that Olmsted made little distinction between public sidewalks, public central heating for every home, and public kitchens. He and other social science idealists saw the era of industrial capitalism, when public space and urban infrastructure were created, as a time of urban evolution toward a more equal way of life. He believed that model suburbs with common land, such as Riverside, Illinois, could be linked to the city and could also contribute to such goals, although he abhorred suburban sprawl. Olmsted adopted his belief in evolution as a disciple of Charles Fourier, but many other socialists and feminists, including Edward Bellamy, August Bebel, Charlotte Perkins Gilman, Karl Marx, and Friedrich Engels, substituted other theories of human evolution and came to similar conclusions. All these American and European theorists saw the industrial capitalist city as the product of an economic system that would give way to a completely industrialized, urban, socialist society utilizing modern technology and socialized labor to handle not only industrial production but also housework and social services.

In this light, it is important to see that Olmsted's view of the public landscape as an expression of human social evolution was linked to housing and social service programs. These programs were the cooperative residential neighborhoods advocated by Melusina Fay Peirce beginning in 1869, the municipal housekeeping campaigns launched in the temperance movement by Frances Willard beginning in the 1870s, and the Social Settlement houses developed by Jane Addams in the late 1880s. Olmsted's public parks, Peirce's model neighborhoods, and Addams's settlement houses suggest an ideal city with landscape architecture, housing, and services intertwined. These activists did not divide private life from public life, domestic programs from public programs, economic initiatives from social initiatives, factual knowledge from ethical stances about that knowledge. Their confident wholeness of purpose was their great strength. The understanding that existed between environmentalists, reformers in the women's movement, and social scientists contributed to the appeal this urban vision had for great numbers of American women and men.

THE HOMELIKE WORLD

Peirce and her followers concerned themselves with developing a women's perspective on the relationship between housing and household work.[14] For six decades, these women, the material feminists, defined their movement with one powerful idea: women must create new kinds of homes with socialized housework and child care before they could become truly equal members of society. They raised fundamental questions about what was called "woman's sphere" and "woman's work." They challenged two characteristics of industrial capitalism: the physical separation of household space from public space, and the economic separation of the domestic economy from the political economy. They experimented with new forms of neighborhood organizations, including housewives' cooperatives, as well as new building types, including the kitchenless house, the day-care center, the public kitchen, and the community dining club. By redefining housework and the

2.4 "The Age of Iron," by Currier and Ives, 1868, a satire about the impossibly extravagant demands of women's rights advocates ridicules women who forget their place. Women prepare to go out into urban space while men remain indoors sewing, washing, and minding the baby. Both class and gender are depicted: the coachwomen and the laundryman are working class, while the woman with the bustle and the man with the waistcoat seem to be their employers, and the main tension is in the glance he gives her departing back. This was not a response to female demands for male sharing of domestic work, but a joke about the silly things that would happen if women entered public life. (Library of Congress)

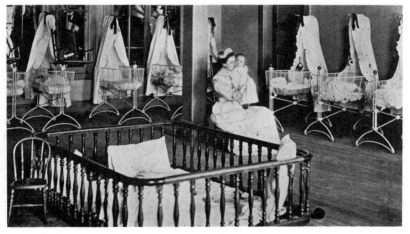

2.5 Nursery and day care center. The Children's Building, World's Columbian Exposition, Chicago, 1893.

housing needs of women and their families, they pushed architects and urban planners to consider housing design as the spatial context for family life. The material feminists thought that domestic space in apartment hotels and new cooperative suburbs promoted domestic evolution in the same way that Olmsted believed public space in parks and parkways promoted urban evolution.

During this period, Frances Willard, Jane Addams, and other leaders of the temperance and settlement movements were demanding women's active presence in urban public space and developing a theory of municipal housekeeping as their contribution to the "city of the faithfulest friends." They believed they were bringing domestic virtues to public life, and they justified women's urban activism as an extension of their work in the home.[15] This activism began in the winter of 1873, a depression year, when temperance women of southern Ohio launched the passionate speeches and startling public marches that Willard later compared to a prairie fire, "like the fires we used to kindle on the Western prairies, a match and a wisp of grass were all that was needed, and behold the spectacle of a prairie on fire . . . no more to be captured than a hurricane."[16] The "Crusades," or the "Women's Whiskey Wars," as popular journalism referred to them, eventually mobilized tens of thousands of American women to demonstrate in the streets of their towns and cities. Women claimed public space and political power in new ways while closing down saloons. This militance flared among women who had never prayed aloud in public, never presided at public meetings, and, of course, were not allowed to vote.[17] Often satirized as prim, severe, anti-booze eccentrics, women in the temperance movement were political activists with a complex purpose and a logical spatial target who used the rhetoric of domesticity in new ways.

The year after the Crusades began, Frances Willard founded the Women's Christian Temperance Union, a national organization based on the crusading spirit of the Whiskey Wars.[18] With the WCTU, Willard attacked the separation of private life and public life on behalf of women. The WCTU ultimately became the most powerful women's organization in the United States, dedicated to temperance, women's suffrage, and urban reform, with two hundred thousand members here and two million affiliates worldwide. Willard defined women's urban work as an essential extension of the "home protection" demanded in the earlier temperance crusades. Her slogan "municipal housekeeping" joined women's presence in urban space and women's traditional work in a metaphor of political cleanup. Willard's acid comment, "men have made a dead failure of municipal government, just as they would of housekeeping," led to her argument that good government was only good housekeeping on a large scale.[19] Her municipal housekeeping campaigns attacked the corruption and filth of the American city in an era when many justified urban horrors as the "survival of the fittest." When WCTU women came out of their homes and into the city, they aimed at regulating industry, ending political corruption, improving housing, education, and health. They helped organize trade unions for women workers. "Make the whole world homelike," said Willard. "Do everything."[20]

In this political effort, settlement workers such as Jane Addams and members of trade unions, suffrage groups, and women's clubs joined WCTU women. Over several decades, the settlement workers built complex urban institutions to bring together individuals of different economic and ethnic backgrounds. They wanted to reform the American economy and restore a sense of community to the American city. As a public place in the heart of the slums, Jane Addams's Hull-House inspired over a hundred similar settlement house projects. Its activities spanned a broad range of interests. Reformers stressed that they could extend the spirit of home to all new immigrants by "settling" in poor neighborhoods. At Hull-House, groups of city gardeners cultivated vacant lots. The residents built the first urban playground in Chicago. They created a child-care center for children of employed mothers. They ran education classes on all kinds of subjects for children and adults, from symphonies to shoemaking. *Hull-House Maps and Papers*, a survey of the physical and economic conditions of the slums of Chicago published in 1895, was a major research effort on the need for urban physical planning and social services.[21] Various residents collaborated on this book. Ultimately they held many influential policymaking positions in city, state, and national government to implement its conclusions. Like Olmsted, the social settlement planners stressed equal access to public space as a healing and strengthening force in a democratic American society. This approach to urban physical and social planning was certainly nourished right in the Hull-House dining room. When settlement residents such as Florence Kelley and Mary Simkovitch called the first national urban planning conference in 1909, their leadership had long been acknowledged.

The settlement workers and the temperance workers formed the coalitions that led to the reforms of the Progressive movement and changed the standards of American urban politics. Unfortunately, as these women gained a popular audience, their organizations were pushed aside by ministers, politicians, planners, and social workers, men who began to take over leadership. Women had created a direct political challenge to their seclusion in the home by demanding a homelike city. Yet many men preferred to promote better government by *men* as defenders of women and children in the home rather than to accept direct female power. The Progressive era thus was a time when women's activism and rage forced change but did not control the shape of change. The right to vote, won in 1920, implied that women would have the political power to make the "homelike world" a reality, but the same period unleashed the Red Scare, and Red-baiting of politically active women.

"GOOD HOMES MAKE CONTENTED WORKERS"

In the early twentieth century, many battles for parks, housing, and better planning were lost, and the distinctive parts of the urban spatial ideal developed by Whitman, Olmsted, Peirce, Willard, and Addams were fragmented and misunderstood. The dense urban centers of industrial capitalism were succeeded by the suburbanized cities of modem capitalism.[22] This change occurred over several decades. Conservative Americans had called on the social Darwinist argument of the "survival of the fittest" to excuse the sordid living and working conditions of the nineteenth-century city slums, but social reformers in the 1880s and 1890s eventually began to express aspirations for a nation of healthy Americans. Workers' anger also hastened change. Between the 1880s and 1920s, reformers began to fear that the American city would be torn apart by angry, propertyless people. The Haymarket Riots of 1886, the Pullman Strike of 1893, the New York garment strike of 1909, the Paterson mill strike of 1911, and the Lawrence strike of 1912 publicized workers' grievances and employers' lack of concern. In 1919, at the conclusion of World War I, four million people were on strike and the future of the American city seemed very uncertain. Workers were angry and veterans were upset that African-Americans and women had taken over the jobs of white males during the war.[23]

Between the 1890s and the 1920s, the National Civic Federation had brought together manufacturers and some labor leaders to discuss industrial policies and long-term planning. By 1919, many manufacturers began to concede that improved wages and housing were essential underpinnings for social order. Urban planners and housing reformers such as Lawrence Veiller and John Nolan had long been campaigning for dwellings to help foster "a conservative point of view in the working man." In the post–World War I era, many union leaders and corporate leaders finally agreed on this tactic. Trade unionists, who had concentrated their organizing on skilled male workers, wanted what they called a "family wage." This meant a wage for male workers high enough to assure that wives and children would not work in industry, a tactic that would, at the same time, lower the threat of wage competition by decreasing the available labor force. Industrialists, who had concentrated their money-making around production rather than consumption, wanted to expand their domestic markets for manufactured goods. They saw the better-paid workers' families as potential consumers of furniture, appliances, and automobiles. Both union leaders and manufacturers agreed that a more spacious, mass-produced form of housing was essential to enable workers and their families to consume. A growing number of employers decided to miniaturize and mass-produce the Victorian patriarchal, suburban businessman's dwelling for the majority of white, male, skilled workers.

As one corporate official described his attitude toward workers: "Get them to invest their savings in homes and own them. Then they will not leave and they will not strike. It ties them down so they have a stake in our prosperity." Or as a housing expert put it, "Happy workers invariably mean bigger profits, while unhappy workers are never a good investment." He advocated long home mortgages, because making the payments would require steady employment: "Good homes make contented workers." Or as another sloganeer put it, showing the capitalist and the worker shaking hands: "After work, the happy home."[24] One political ana-

lyst has argued that the promotion of suburban homeownership
effectively split the territorial base of the Socialist party, because it
was aimed at native-born skilled workers, who moved out of the
tenements, leaving the more recent immigrants in the inner city.[25]

What did this strategy mean for the wives of working men?
Garbed in rhetoric about a woman's place in the home, it reinforced the pressures on women to get out of the wartime labor
force in 1919 in order to give their jobs to veterans. As men were
to become homeowners responsible for regular mortgage payments, their wives were to become "home managers" taking care
of the spouses and children. The male worker would return from
his day in the factory to a private domestic world. In his house, he
would find a retreat from the tense world of work, and his physical
and emotional maintenance would be the duty of his wife. Thus
the private suburban house was a stage set for the effective gender
division of labor. It made gender appear a more important self-def-
inition than class, race, or ethnicity. It made consumption seem to
be as crucial as production.

SELLING MRS. CONSUMER

Corporations moving from World War I defense industries into
peacetime production of domestic appliances and automobiles also
found private homes a key to success. Herbert Hoover, as
Secretary of Commerce, served as president of Better Homes in
America, an organization founded in 1922, designed to boost home
ownership and consumption. There were several thousand local
chapters composed of manufacturers, realtors, builders, and
bankers. The rapid development of the advertising industry in the
1920s was also influential because advertisers promoted the private suburban dwelling as a setting for other purchases.[26] The
occupants of the suburban dwelling needed more than the house
itself. They also had to have a car, a stove, a refrigerator, a vacuum
cleaner, a washer, and carpets. Christine Frederick explained it all
in 1929 in *Selling Mrs. Consumer*, a book dedicated to Hoover that
promoted homeownership and easier consumer credit. Frederick
advised advertising executives and marketing managers about
manipulating American women. She was particularly insistent that
young married couples furnishing their first homes should be seen

2.6. Selling Mrs. Consumer: the groom offers his bride the Domestic Sewing Machine, a ritual gesture equating consumption with love, 1882.

2.7 The realtor offers the housewife a Kitchen Aid dishwasher, *House and Home,* October 1956. This ritual gesture resembles the previous one, but the advertisement suggests that this brand of appliance helps builders sell more homes by persuading "Mrs. Consumer."

as prime consumers: "There is a direct and vital business interest in the subject of young love and marriage."[27]

By 1931, Hoover was President, and his Commission on Home Building and Home Ownership established the construction of private, single-family homes as a national strategy to promote long-term economic growth and recovery from the depression.[28] Eulogizing the rural ideal of "Home Sweet Home," Hoover noted Americans "never sing songs about a pile of rent receipts." The FHA was established in 1934 and began to offer mortgage insurance to projects that met their standards. Elementary schools taught students to make models of ideal houses. General Electric ran a dream house design competition for "Mr. and Mrs. Bliss" in 1935. Also, a personal income tax deduction for mortgage interest was available.[29] Still, this was brave talk with little action. Housing construction had peaked in the mid-1920s, and homeownership for the majority of urban workers remained a distant goal during the foreclosures of the Depression years and the housing shortages of the war years.

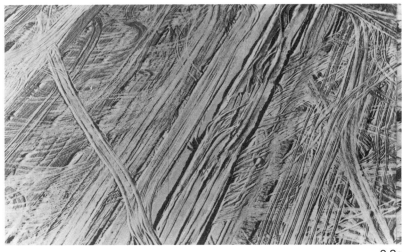

2.8a

2.8b

2.8 William Garnett, four views of a California tract under construction: after bulldozing (2-8a); after house and garage foundations were poured (2-8b); during framing (opposite 2-8c); and as salable space (opposite 2-8d). (Copyright, William Garnett, 1955)

"I'LL BUY THAT DREAM"

After World War II, the strategy of homeownership for white male workers articulated more than twenty years earlier became reality. As in the years following World War I, many defense corporations

Thank You!

1. 14802
2. Albany, NY
3. SUNY University st
4. 50 W University
5. Virginia Rasmussen

Date	Amount	Guests
		680139

Thank You

GUESTCHECK™

525

Total

Tax

www.nationalchecking.com

2.8c

2.8d

wanted to give women's jobs to veterans and convert some defense industries to production of consumer goods. This time, national mortgage insurance programs were in place, the American banking system was ready, highway systems were organized, and the speculative builders took over.

Veterans, with their World War II savings, were encouraged by a national policy promoting homeownership in suburban areas to participate in the transformation of the American city and the American economy. The central city was abandoned by many younger workers and their families in favor of the suburban ring. Young people left their parents and kin in the ethnic neighborhoods of the old cities. Whistling the hit tune, "I'll Buy That Dream," they bought new cars and went to live in new tract houses with nothing down and low monthly payments. Just as the native-born workers had left the more recent immigrants behind in the suburbanization of the 1920s, so the white workers left African-American and Hispanic workers behind in the inner cities in the 1950s.[30] By the late 1970s, three-quarters of all AFL-CIO members were purchasing their homes on long mortgages.[31] Most of these families, headed by working men, identified themselves as "middle class."

The United States housing stock increased from 34.9 million occupied units in 1940 to 105.5 million occupied units in 2000, as tracts of small houses, usually without day-care centers or community facilities, spread over the countryside.[32] At the same time, alternative forms of housing were discouraged. Advocates of multifamily public housing were Red-baited in the 1940s and 1950s. Single-room occupancy hotels (SRO's) were demolished as part of urban renewal. Single-family housing starts by month and year became an important indicator of economic growth. As Hoover had predicted, housing Americans was a big, big business. American banking, real estate, manufacturing, and transportation interests were intimately involved.

For both the huge real estate development firms that emerged in the late 1940s to dominate the housing market, as well as the small builders who erected a few houses at a time, the heart of the housing business was the single-family detached house. In the years between 1945 and 2001, while suburban sprawl became a common phrase in Americans' vocabularies, the construction industry was confident enough to announce that what was good for housing was good for the country.[33] In 2000, Americans enjoyed the largest amount of private housing space per person ever created in the history of civilization. Over a quarter of U.S. households had seven or more rooms in their homes.[34]

The dream house replaced the ideal city as the spatial representation of American hopes for the good life. It not only triumphed over the model town, the dream house also prevailed over two other models of housing, one based on efficient collective consumption of scarce resources, the other based on the model neighborhood. Yet the dream house had its critics, and by the late 1970s their accounting of its environmental, social, and economic costs could not be ignored.

Chapter 3

Awakening from the Dream

WHAT IS THE USE OF A HOUSE IF YOU HAVEN'T GOT A TOLERABLE PLANET TO PUT IT ON?

—Henry David Thoreau

SHE FELT BOUGHT AND PAID FOR, AND IT WAS ALL OF A PIECE; THE HOUSE, THE FURNITURE, SHE, ALL WERE HIS, IT SAID SO ON SOME PIECE OF PAPER.

—Marilyn French

The personal happiness of many Americans has been undermined by poorly designed housing and public space, yet few of us employ the language of real estate development, architecture, or urban planning to trace the contours of loneliness, boredom, weariness, discrimination, or financial worry in our lives. It is much more common to complain about time or money than to fume about urban design. In part this is because we think of our miseries as being caused by personal problems rather than social problems. Americans often say, "There aren't enough hours in the day," rather than, "I'm frantic because the distance between my home and my workplace is too great." Americans also say, "I cannot afford the down payment to live in Newton," or in Marin County, or in

Beverly Hills, rather than, "I'm furious because only the affluent can live in a safe and pleasant neighborhood." Both private and public investment establish the physical settings Americans inhabit. Whether they are harmonious or discordant, residential neighborhoods reverberate with meaning, and disappointments about them affect women and men of all ages, income levels, and ethnic backgrounds.

The dwelling can be read as an image of the body, the household, and the household's relation to society. It is a physical space designed to mediate between nature and culture, between the landscape and the larger built environment. In this sense the dwelling is the basis of both architectural design (as archetypal shelter) and physical planning (as the replicable unit used to form neighborhoods, cities, and regions). Because the form of housing carries so many aesthetic, social, and economic messages, a serious misfit between a society and its housing stock can create profound unrest and disorientation. The squalid tenements of the nineteenth and early twentieth centuries reflected class oppression that at times became a threat to the urban social order. A century later, debates about suburban houses underscore complex conflicts of class, gender, and race that characterize our society.

OUTGROWING OUR PRESCRIPTIVE ARCHITECTURE

The United States is a society of diverse cultures and household types, yet since the 1940s, most American space has been shaped around a simplistic prescription for satisfaction. Cities and housing have been designed to satisfy a nation of white, young, nuclear families, with father as breadwinner, mother as housewife, and children reared to emulate these same limited roles. While prescriptive literature in the form of sermons, housekeeping guides, and etiquette manuals has always been available to define the ideal middle-class Christian family, our post–World War II cities mark the triumph of a prescriptive architecture of gender on a national scale. A nation of homes tied to the mid-nineteenth-century ideal of separate spheres for women and men was something fanatical Victorian moralists only dreamed about, a utopia of male-female segregation they never expected the twentieth century to build. While maxims about true womanhood and manly dominance were the staple of Christian, bourgeois Victorian culture in the United States, England, and many other countries, only in the United States in the twentieth century were so many material resources committed to reinforcing these ideas by spatial design.

In 2002, only a tiny percentage of American families include a male breadwinner, a nonemployed housewife, and children under eighteen. The valiant World War II heroes and their blushing brides have now retired. About a quarter of all households are married couples with children under eighteen, but the father is the sole breadwinner in only 29.2 percent of those families. The predominant family type is the two-earner family. The fastest growing family type is the single-parent family, and five out of six single parent households are headed by women. Over a quarter of all households consist of one person living alone, be they young singles or the elderly.[1]

The veteran, his young wife, and their prospective children appeared as the model family of 1945. Millions of them confronted a serious housing shortage. In the aftermath of war, employing veterans and removing women from the paid labor force was a national priority. So was building more housing, but the two ideals were conflated. Developers argued that a particular kind of house would help the veteran change from an aggressive air ace to a commuting salesman who loved to mow the lawn. That house would also help a woman change from Rosie the Riveter to a stay-at-home mom. Better Homes in America, Inc. had tried to situate the post–World War I family in segregated suburban residential communities, and this attempt, thwarted by the Great Depression, only intensified commitment to the same prescription for family bliss after World War II. The problem was that the spatial rules could have been written by Catharine Beecher in 1870. By 1920 they were anachronistic; by 1950, preposterous.

The outdated ideal of Victorian family life had a function. Exaggerated, socially created male and female roles defined not only the labor market but also the parameters of urban planning. Postwar propaganda told women that their place was in the home, as nurturers; men were told that their place was in the public realm, as earners and decision makers. Residential suburbs were

3.1 Prospective buyers standing in line to view a furnished model home by Kaiser, California, 1950s. Spending Sunday afternoons visiting model homes became a new family pastime.

separated from the centers of cities. Definition of roles by gender was pervasive and acceptable. Segregation by age, race, and class could not be so easily advertised. In the richest nation in the world, economic deprivation, ethnic differences, age segregation, and racial segregation were less visible than a spatial prescription for suburban bliss that emphasized gender stereotypes as the most salient features of every citizen's experience.

CREATING THE CRITIQUE

The dream houses were utopian. No one counted how much they might cost. Dream houses got out of control economically, environmentally, and socially because they carried unacknowledged costs: they wasted available land; they required large amounts of energy consumption; and they demanded a great deal of unpaid female labor.

The earliest critics of the dream house came from the professions of architecture and urban planning. They were angry because basic building activity had bypassed them. Developers received funding from federal housing agencies, bought farmland in a remote part of a metropolitan area—preferably a place without a planning board—and started raising houses instead of potatoes, as they said in Long Island. Many architects were appalled by the designs the builders threw up. Bill Levitt, for example, was considered one of the best developers of solidly constructed houses. He became a popular hero for the speed with which he built homes for veterans, but he simply built one design over and over again in his first development. Praised for his skill in reorganizing the logistics of traditional home construction, he responded to aesthetic critiques by developing three or four "models" that could be alternated on every street, a practice still followed by many builders today. Levitt's peace offering was to sponsor interior design contests and invite well-known designers and architects to be the judges of the interior schemes created by Levittown residents—whether modern, early American, or country French.[2]

The predictable banality of it all was enforced by the federal agency responsible for funding. FHA design guidelines actually penalized any builder who hired a sophisticated architect by lowering the mortgagable values of houses that did not conform to their norms of design.[3] Flat roofs were particularly suspect at the FHA. (Curiously, Nazi policy had also decreed that only peaked-roof houses suited the Aryan race.)[4] But flat roofs had characterized many of the best multi-family housing designs in the twentieth century, including those of Irving Gill, Henry Wright, Clarence Stein, and Rudolph Schindler, who had worked on low-cost housing but managed to make it harmonious.

ARCHITECTS AND URBAN PLANNERS

Architects grumbled, but their social and aesthetic critiques failed to address the basic gender division of labor. While they proposed the advantages of hiring skilled designers or of providing more community facilities and more shared spaces, they did not attack the Victorian programming at the heart of dream-house culture.

Some American architects working with material feminists had led the world in the development of innovative, multifamily housing prototypes between 1870 and 1940, but the practitioners of the 1950s often contented themselves with commissions for individual houses.[5] The Case Study House program in Los Angeles was one example. In truth, most architects loved to design single-family houses, one at a time, and this predilection shaped the profession's acquiescence.[6]

Urban planners, like architects, were early critics of the dream-house strategy, but their concerns, while tied to larger issues of private and public space, still lacked a thorough social foundation. Planners perceived that hasty, uncontrolled suburban developments for veterans' families would produce houses without adequate schools, parks, or other community facilities. They saw that suburban residents would then be taxed to pay for these improvements, while the speculative developers used their profits to build yet more bad subdivisions. They predicted that new suburbs would drain the social and economic activities of the center city, and that urban blight and suburban sprawl would work together to wear away the best pedestrian districts of inner-city areas.[7] Some of them recognized the racism of all-white tracts and worried about the consequences of "white flight" from inner cities.

While planners decried haste, shoddy building, and greed, while they deplored racial segregation and lack of public transportation, few spoke about the outworn gender stereotypes embodied in the basic definition of the household. Indeed, planners themselves relied on the Victorian template of patriarchal family life when they exhorted Americans to pay more attention to community facilities to strengthen that same idealized family. Even Lewis Mumford, the most trenchant of all urban critics, rhapsodized: "Who can doubt that Victorian domesticity, among the upper half of the middle classes, was encouraged by all the comforts and conveniences, the sense of internal space and peace, that brought the Victorian father back nightly to his snug household." He ardently supported providing "a young couple with a dwelling house and a garden" to continue this model, while adding that the city planner must also "invent public ways of performing economically what the old, three-generation bourgeois family once privately encompassed"—care for the elderly.[8]

Planners also used the same outworn family model to study residential choices and to measure needs for new services. The "head of household" and his "journey to work" framed their locational concerns, instead of detailed analysis of the different needs and experiences of men, women, and children.[9] Even when caucuses of Marxist planners responded to the extreme urban fiscal crises of the late 1970s, they also based their statements about housing reform on an unexamined acceptance of the dream house and the gender division of labor underlying it. Chester Hartman and Michael E. Stone proposed a socialist banking policy to keep traditional workers' housing afloat.[10]

In the late 1960s and early 1970s, the activists of two major social movements generated enough anger about housing patterns to spur broader cultural critiques. Ecologists and feminists took up where the designers and planners left off. The former stressed the dire consequences of environmental decline, while the latter emphasized the crippling effects of stereotyped roles for women and men. Both movements turned from critique to active protest. They organized the disaffected to rally against some of the excesses of the post-World War II American lifestyle. Both stressed democracy and emphasized that personal life represented political choices. Neither put architecture in the foreground, but they generated enough debate to illuminate conceptual shortcomings of both architecture and urban planning.

ENVIRONMENTALISTS

Environmentalists and energy planners pointed out that American dream houses and their dispersed settlement pattern used more nonrenewable resources than any society had ever consumed before, because builders had assumed that energy would always be cheaper than materials or labor. In 1999, Americans, as about seven percent of the world's population, accounted for about a fourth of the world's annual nonrenewable resource consumption.[11] A child born to a dream-house family in the United States consumes many times more resources over its lifetime than a child in a developing nation.

Environmental activists showed that the imbalance was partly the result of deliberate but uninformed choices in housing design.

3.2 "Win a houseful of beautiful furniture!" Utopia as single-family bliss and over-consumption.

When developers of the 1950s constructed millions of dream houses lined up on suburban tracts, they broke with traditional regional responses to climate (typical of the adobes of the Southwest or the saltbox houses of New England) in favor of using standardized plans and materials. Huge picture windows created patterns of heat gain or heat loss that had to be compensated for by year round air-conditioning or intensive heating, depending on whether the standardized house was in Arizona or Massachusetts. Traditional siting also broke down. Bulldozers leveled hills and trees that might have provided shade; the same house was built facing north, south, east, and west because the builders did not care about the position of the sun as much as the profitability of the tract.

The dream houses, because of their isolation from community facilities and from each other, also required numerous purchases of appliances such as stoves, clothes washers, and refrigerators. These appliances were often designed to increase rather than minimize the use of energy: in some cases the same manufacturers sold both consumer appliances and municipal generating equipment, as a reinforcement of corporate interests.[12] In addition to the wasteful use of energy, some appliances and all plumbing fixtures intensified the use of water. Toilets, garbage disposals, clothes washers, and dishwashers created an enormous volume of water usage in arid regions as well as in more temperate climates, expanding the American practice of using water as a medium of carrying waste away, rather than reserving water for needed human use and recycling garbage and human waste as compost.

As the suburbs grew, the infrastructure of roads expanded, and expanded again. The journey to work for Americans averaged 11.6 miles one way in 1995. The number of Americans driving to work, and the number driving alone, has grown steadily since 1960. In the 1990 Census, 86.5 percent of employed persons drove to work and 73.2 percent drove alone.[13] To get to distant houses, thousands of miles of roads and freeways were needed. But very few people wanted their dream house next to a busy freeway or shrouded in smog. To provide gas and electricity for these same houses, pipelines, storage tanks, and generating plants were needed, but no one wanted to be near them either.

Ultimately American corporations had to resort to some desperate strategies to assure continued energy consumption. Oil leases in foreign countries brought the accompanying threat of foreign wars. Nuclear power plants were even riskier strategies because of their long-term vulnerability to accidents and because of the lack of safe disposal procedures for nuclear waste materials. In the late 1970s, *The Ladies' Home Journal* carried a pro-nuclear advertisement showing housewives holding up a variety of home appliances and thanking the utility for creating nuclear power to keep their appliances going. The phrase "dream house" began to acquire ironic overtones. Even those families who would have accepted nearby gas or electrical installations refused to be near a nuclear plant.

The political movement launched by environmentalists had one great success by 1982. Steady, sustained political pressure on both utilities and government regulatory agencies had made it clear that nuclear power plants were financially unprofitable to design, build, and operate. This citizen resistance to poor energy planning marked a significant achievement for Americans concerned about the safety of their neighborhoods and the social responsibility of major corporations. Victories were won in the face of massive expenditures by utilities for political contributions and extensive lobbying efforts by utility executives. The environmentalists' common sense dominated the debates; revelations about nuclear power plants built on earthquake faults or built from upside-down blueprints did the rest.

When it came to renewable energy sources, the environmentalists produced only partial reforms. Conservation education often stressed saving more than sharing. Retrofitting of existing buildings might involve elaborate technical skills, but economic and

3.3 Sketch of "The Integral Urban House" established by environmental activists with composting toilet, greenhouse, fish pond, and solar energy, Berkeley, California. (From *The Integral Urban House: Self-Reliant Living in the City* by Helga Olkowski, Bill Olkowski, Tom Javits, and the Farallones Institute Staff. Copyright © 1979 by Sierra Club Books. Reprinted by permission.)

social reprogramming, essential to the better use of space, was often ignored. Ecologists Helga and William Olkowski criticized the ecological and economic parasitism of the suburban dwelling: "The typical home now largely wastes the solar income it daily receives and the mineral resources that pass through it. It takes from the forest for its structure, furnishings, reading materials, and fuel as well. The typical home also takes from the often fragile ecosystems of estuary, swamp, desert and prairie for its food and fiber. It also uses the waterways and mineral riches for its power and the products of the marketplace." After listing the resources consumed, they went on, "The house shelters its occupants, but to the larger community it gives 'wastes.' These latter emerge unappreciated and consequently unsorted: the metals with the glass, organic, paper, and plastic all jumbled together; the toxic mixed with the benign. Because the home is such a total parasite, as are its neighboring urban habitats, it is not surprising that the occupants experience themselves as victims or, at best, ineffectual ciphers in a large, impersonal, centralized system." But the Olkowskis' powerful experiment, the Integral Urban House, a collective project established by six adults, did not stress rethinking family life so much as the introduction of urban agriculture and ecosystems analysis.[14] Other designers of solar homes who received wide publicity had far less to offer; some designs were based on new environmental gadgets for the old dream house but retained the model family in 4,000 square feet of space.

In the same way, discussion of new solar technologies, such as photovoltaic cells, often stopped at a certain level of technological innovation. Big corporations (utilities and defense contractors) received most of the government research and development money to study the profitable future production of these technologies. Neighborhood applications and small-town applications were seldom given the same level of support.[15] Here a mix of economic, social, and technical reforms could have resulted in more innovative programming. Using photovoltaic cells to cover the roof of every existing house in the year 2001 would turn the United States into a nation of 64.5 million private power plants. Between the giant corporations and the tiny houses, environmental alternatives require new social, economic, and architectural innovations as well as new, energy-saving inventions. As environmentalists continue to develop a very effective accounting of the wasteful, destructive patterns of present resource use, reconceptualization of the private home will lead to more concern for neighborhood. Neighborhood scale may be the most productive issue for green architecture in the decades ahead.

FEMINISTS

The problems of domestic life documented by the women's movement also revolve around the hidden costs of building millions of homes on the Victorian model. The connections between home ownership, family structure, and women's status are complex. During the last half-century, while the majority of white male workers have achieved the dream houses in suburbia where their fantasies of proprietorship, authority, and consumption could be acted out, the majority of their spouses have entered the world of paid employment. In 2000, handicapped by the least suitable housing imaginable, six out of ten mothers of children under three were in the paid labor force. Employed women often find themselves with two jobs: one at home, one at work. Pulled between unpaid work and paid work, women race from office or factory to home and back again. They know they have no time for themselves. They have to spend an inordinate amount of time struggling to get husbands or children to do a little more housework instead of leaving it all for Mom.[16]

While this pattern creates logistical problems for the employed mother, those who stay home also have serious difficulties. Michele Rosaldo, a cultural anthropologist, has argued that women's status is lowest in societies where women are most separated from public life.[17] And in the United States, the suburban home is the single most important way of separating women, and thus lowering an individual woman's status. But as geographer Bonnie Loyd points out, much of women's work in the household is status-producing work for the family, connected with the maintenance of the house.[18] So by glorifying her home through executing household tasks, a woman can guarantee her family's social status at the expense of her own. As Loyd notes, such activity often creates psychological conflict. This conflict increases when women who try to create interiors as a focus for entertaining come up against levels of consumption that are new to them because of upward mobility. Terrified housewives who know little about designer furniture or antiques, cabinet work or colors, may consult women's magazines, home and lifestyle magazines, decorators, and department stores. Loyd quotes one psychiatrist who remarked in the 1950s of his female patients: "There is no time at which a woman is more apt to go to pieces than when she is engaged in decorating her home."[19]

Feminists of the 1960s, beginning with Betty Friedan, examined the relationship between women, advertisers, and mass-produced goods. Advertisers presented the home as a box to be filled with commodities. Carpets, curtains, upholstered goods—all came together in the domestic spaces to form Early American, Mediterranean, French Provincial, or some other ersatz decor. Women also criticized kitchens full of single-purpose appliances requiring frequent attention. These machines were lined up in one room, the kitchen, which was often designed to be isolated from the rest of family life. As one appliance manufacturer put it in *Good Housekeeping* in 1965: "This kitchen has almost everything. Tappan built-in electric range and oven, Tappan dish-washer and Tappan disposal, Tappan refrigerator. Only one thing's really missing. You." [20]

One of the most effective feminist explorations of housewives' frustrations was "Womanhouse," an exhibit created in 1971. Twenty-six artists transformed an abandoned Los Angeles mansion into a series of new environments. At the top of the staircase, a mannequin in a wedding dress posed, suggesting the young bride's fascination with the dream house. At the bottom of the stairs, her muddy train and two disembodied feet vanished into the wall. In the linen closet, another mannequin was trapped among the sheets and towels. In the kitchen, everything was painted pink, that stereotypically feminine color: the sink, the refrigerator, the potato peeler, the pots and pans, the walls. Inside the kitchen drawers, newspaper linings revealed stories about women in public life. The bathtub contained colored sand, in the shape of a woman's body. As visitors to the exhibit touched the sand, the figure receded. After two weeks the woman disappeared. There were also rooms dedicated to a woman's enjoyment of her dream house as a place for privacy, fantasy, and playfulness. One room had huge toys. In

3.4 Housewife posed with the products of a week's work, Rye, New York. Photograph by Nina Leen, LIFE Magazine, © 1947 Time, Inc.)

another, a crocheted spider web suggested a place to spin out ideas.

The exhibition included some performances, and in one favorite theater piece, the artist simply walked to an ironing board and ironed sheets for thirty minutes. While the women decided it was hilarious, men were perplexed. "Womanhouse" addressed the ways that Americans have mystified the necessary work done in the house by isolating the housewife who cooks, cleans, and irons. The artists illuminated some of women's positive feelings and attachments to domestic spaces as private places, while criticizing the loneliness and isolation many housewives encounter. Most effectively, they turned domestic space into public space temporarily by the appropriation of a residential structure for the exhibit. Thousands of visitors toured the house.

Just as the artists of "Womanhouse" protested the single-family home as an enclosure for women's lives, the poets Adrienne Rich and Bernice Johnson Reagon cried out for change. Rich's "A Primary Ground" told of the suffocation of traditional family life:

> Sensuality desiccates in words—
> risks of the portage, risks of the glacier
> never taken
> Protection is the genius of your house
> the pressure of the steam iron
> flattens the linen cloth again
> chestnuts pureed with care are dutifully eaten
> in every room the furniture reflects you
> larger than life, or dwindling

Rich underlined the waste of female talent in this old pattern of domesticity:

> your wife's twin sister, speechless
> is dying in the house
> You and your wife take turns
> carrying up the trays,
> understanding her case, trying to make her understand.[21]

The image of "understanding her case" resonated through Rich's writings, as well as the demand for new forms of habitation.

In "The Fourth Month of the Landscape Architect," Rich fused images of pregnancy and a demand for the creation of a new kind of social space, as a female designer reviews the historical experience of women in her spatial imagination:

> I start to imagine
> plans for a house, a park
> . . .
> A city waits at the back of my skull
> eating its heart out to be born:
> how design the first
> city of the moon? how shall I see it
> for all of us who are done
> with enclosed spaces, purdah, the salon,
>   the sweatshop loft,
> the ingenuity of the cloister?[22]

To read Rich's poems was to be exhorted to transcend the architecture of gender that diminished so many lives, yet it was only an
exhortation and not a plan.

Writer, composer, and scholar Bernice Johnson Reagon, in "My
Black Mothers and Sisters," told feminists what the leaders of that
struggle would need to be like:

> She could make space where there was none
> And she could organize the space she had
> My mama
> My grandmama
> Ms. Daniels
> dreamers who believed in being materialists—
> . . .
> We must apply energy to the development of our
>   potential
> as parents
> as creative producers
> as the new way-makers.
> There must not be a woman's place for us
> We must be everywhere our people are
> or might be . . .[23]

To seize and hold more space, to redesign space, to deliver the
goods of survival was an adequate definition of the task in its material and cultural dimensions.

While these women developed a critique of the suburban house
and created a new consciousness that inspired some housewives to
leave the seclusion of their homes, the critique did not go far
enough. Gender was the culprit; material culture was satirized and
criticized, but the architecture of gender was not reworked. The
material feminists' idea that the gender division of labor was reinforced by spatial design was a lost intellectual tradition for most feminist activists of the 1970s, just as it was for architects and planners.

Indeed, some feminists often agitated for something very like
the single-family house but they proposed to put it under women's
control. Articles and manifestos on the housing needs of single-
parent mothers stressed their desire not to be stigmatized by special housing "projects." They wanted their children to feel that
their homes were "just like everyone else's."[24] Emergency shelters
for battered women and their children—which integrated housing,

child care, and social service arrangements—were usually seen as temporary solutions to women's housing needs, and the stated goal of such groups was to return the woman and her children to "normal" housing as soon as possible. Not surprisingly, this "normal" housing created problems when women left the community of the shelter to return to the dream-house world.[25]

Campaigns on behalf of employed women that stressed gaining economic justice through increased access to homeownership also accepted the dream-house design. At HUD, Donna Shalala's "Women and Mortgage Credit" program in the 1970s promoted female ownership with the slogan, "If a woman's place is in the home, it might as well be her own."[26] While this pragmatic program met with quick success, HUD's sponsorship of in-depth research by architects and urban planners revealed that long-term problems with the nature of housing design would demand far more complex policy initiatives. Neither a single-family house filled with solar gadgets nor homeownership for single mothers could address the largest political and spatial issues inherent in the culture.

Renters and Owners

Despite all the social and environmental drawbacks of the single-family suburban house, it offers a level of amenity that many renters are unable to find. When Americans discuss the good life, they still speak about their hopes or their fears in terms of buying houses. Homeownership has symbolized a family's social status ever since developers promoted it as an alternative to wasting money on rent. In the twentieth century, the homeowner became an owner-speculator, an identity advertised by one Florida developer with the slogan, "To her, it's a nest; to him, a nest egg."[27] Anthropologist Constance Perrin has explored why Americans struggle to "climb the ladder of life from renter to owner."[28] After years of mortgage payments to the bank, some older homeowners have needed a speculative profit from the sale of the house to provide adequate retirement income. "For years your house has made you happy. Now it's going to make you rich," claimed Jon Douglas, a California real estate agent seeking couples to list their homes for sale with him.[29]

Homeownership has been closely associated with a federal tax subsidy (mortgage interest is deductible from income for tax purposes) not available to renters. Homeownership has created a sense of progress through life for the two-thirds of American families who have managed to attain it. The process of entering the market is a rite of passage for thirty-year-olds equipped with the savings, marriage, and children to make this choice seem logical. Ownership and intense participation in the culture of home characterize the middle years of life. For the retirees who sell their houses, detachment from gender roles may come with age. Of course, if a family could never afford a house, or faced foreclosure, they would tell a different story.

One-third of American households are not homeowners. They have never had the chance to participate in these rituals. The roots of this problem lie in the history of three groups of Americans that were excluded from homeownership in the late 1940s. First, white women of all classes were expected to gain access to housing through their fathers or husbands, and not to achieve homeownership in their own right. Second, the white elderly working class and lower-middle class, who were no longer wage earners in the prime of life, were left behind in the old inner-city neighborhoods. Third, people of color of all classes were excluded from suburban tracts by racial covenants. The FHA actually had agents whose job it was to keep them out, and they pressured any builder or lender who did not agree.[30] These families were expected to become tenants in old slums in the central cities or owners in other neighborhoods vacated by the "white flight" to the suburbs. The majority of housing units in these segregated neighborhoods were difficult to finance since banks usually refused to give home mortgages in "redlined" areas. Women of color became the domestic servants in white women's suburban houses to earn the money to keep their own families together. Elderly people of color, also left in the declining older cities, often remained in three-generation households, sometimes caring for their grandchildren while their daughters worked outside the home.

Homeownership did develop among approximately 40 percent of African-American and Latino male workers and their families in the late 1960s and 1970s, encouraged by the Fair Housing Act of 1968 (Title VIII of the Civil Rights Act of 1968). The Act outlawed segregation and made blockbusting less possible. Redlining of ghetto areas continued, however, and kept many families from buying. Eventually the Equal Credit Opportunity Act of 1974 also made homeownership possible for a small number of women, forbidding discrimination by mortgage lenders on the basis of sex. This meant that mortgage bankers could not apply the so-called rule of thumb (perhaps better described as the rule of uterus) to discount the income of any women of child-bearing age by at least 50 percent when determining mortgage eligibility. Still, very few employed women of any age had the income to qualify as sole owners, so this law helped two-earner couples more than female heads of households. By 2000, the homeownership rate was 49.1 percent for female-headed households, 47.2 percent for African-American households, and 46.3 percent for Hispanic households, compared to 73.8 percent for white, non-Hispanic households. (Homeownership statistics that combine gender and race are not included in these Census tables.)[31]

STICKER SHOCK

As these groups moved into potential homeownership in 2000, they encountered increasingly inflated prices. Between 1970 and 2000, average prices for existing houses across the nation jumped from $28,700 to $177,000.[32] Demand grew when thirty million baby-boom children of the post–World War II era came of home-buying age in the 1970s; an equivalent or greater number reached their thirties in the 1980s.[33] As the price of houses turned into a

3.5 Mobile homes on a sales lot in Connecticut, 1982.

$43,475?

"You mean, you don't _want_ your own adult children living in your community?"

3.6a

3.6b

3.6 When average house prices in the United States reached the $80,000 range, mobile-home lobbyists began arguing that only their product was cheap enough to "save the American dream." These two ads, aimed at urban planners to make them change zoning so that mobile homes could be legal in districts forbidding their use, were published in _Planning_, December 1982 and January 1983. "$43,475?" suggests that an "all new, 3BR" is still available, provided that planners "allow it to be." "You mean you do not _want_ your own adult children living in your community?" tries to persuade readers that only mobile homes can save the three-generation family.

steadily rising line on real estate agents' graphs, millions of these young Americans, most of them the product of the veterans' suburban tracts, wanted homes. At the bottom of the housing market, makers of mobile homes saw their chance. Changing the name of their product to "manufactured housing," they argued that they could make houses cheaply enough to "save the American dream."

Between 1980 and 2000, all across the nation, a rising percentage of household income was spent on housing. Americans' indebtedness for residential mortgages expanded from $1.1 trillion in 1980 to $5.1 trillion in 1999. Consumer debt, including car loans and credit cards went from $349 billion in 1980 to $1.4 trillion in 1999.[34] While robust sales give satisfaction to developers and auto manufacturers, thoughtful economists find these figures troubling. Others are upbeat. In August 2001, when census data showed that Americans had longer commutes and bigger mortgages, Robert Lang of the Fannie Mae Foundation said, "It's the American Dream updated."[35]

The inadequacies of dream-house architecture can no longer be ignored. To renew democratic, self-sufficient traditions and survive as an urbanized, modern society, Americans must search for an adequate way to organize and pay for the spaces we live in, a way more compatible with the human life cycle. As a rich nation, we need to examine these issues in world perspective if we care about our international influence as a democracy. As a nation that has pioneered self-awareness and personal growth, we must also examine these housing issues from the perspective of our psychological needs as women and men. It is not enough to critique the 1950s dream house with nostalgia about the end of an era, or to despair that America's resources stretched just so far and no farther. We need to reconstruct the social, economic, and spatial bases of our beliefs about individual happiness, solid family life, and decent neighborhoods.

Part II

Rethinking
Private Life

THERE IS NO PRIVATE LIFE
WHICH IS NOT DETERMINED
BY A WIDER PUBLIC LIFE.
—*George Eliot*

Chapter 4

Nurturing: Home, Mom, and Apple Pie

Home is where the heart is. Home, sweet home. Whoever speaks of housing must also speak of home. The word embraces both physical space and the nurturing that takes place within it. Few of us can separate the ideal of home from thoughts of mom and apple pie, mother love and home cooking. Rethinking home life involves rethinking the spatial, technological, cultural, social, and economic dimensions of sheltering, nurturing, and feeding people. These activities, often discussed by men as if they had existed unchanged from the beginning of time, unsmirched by capitalist development, technological manipulation, or social pressures, require expert analysis. Sociologist Arlie Hochschild's *The Second Shift* and economist Nancy Folbre's *The Invisible Heart* break

81

new ground in analyzing the complexities of domestic work.[1] Yet among feminist activists, mother love and home cooking have long been celebrated targets. It is understood that "Home, sweet home has never meant housework, sweet housework," as Charlotte Perkins Gilman put it in the 1890s. It has also been clear that mothering is political. Lily Braun, the German socialist feminist, wrote: "After the birth of my son, the problems of women's liberation were no longer mere theories. They cut into my own flesh."[2] That was 1901. The United States has been slower than the rest of the world to reach a more egalitarian political position on domestic life. Most industrialized nations have developed complex legislation to support women workers with paid maternity leave and quality child care. The U.S. has not.

Nurturing men and children has traditionally been women's work. A brief accounting reveals the many separate tasks involved. Home cooking requires meals prepared to suit the personal likes and dislikes of family members. It is also one of the most satisfying and creative aesthetic activities for many women and men. Housecleaning requires sweeping, vacuuming, washing, polishing, and tidying the living space. Laundry requires sorting, washing, drying, folding or ironing, and putting away clean clothes and linens. Health care begins at home, where home remedies and prescribed medicines are distributed. Mental health also begins at home, when homemakers provide emotional support so that all family members make successful connections and adjustments to the larger society. This is crucial not only for the education of young, but also for adults, who must sustain the pressures of earning a living, and for the elderly, who need emotional support in their frail years.

Equally important are those ties to kin and community that maintain the social status and ethnic identity of the household. Maintenance of these ties often includes cultural rituals—the preparation of Thanksgiving dinners, Seders, Cinco de Mayo celebrations—with all the food, clothing, and special objects associated with each event. Recreation is another home task: arranging for children's play, team sports, birthday parties, and family vacations. In urban societies, recreation also means arranging family experiences of nature, such as visits to parks or camping trips.

Economist Heidi Hartmann has estimated that a good home life for a family of four requires about sixty hours of nurturing work per

4.1 Doris Lee, "Thanksgiving," 1935. (Collection of The Art Institute of Chicago)

week.[3] That work may have been more physically arduous in the past, but never more complex. Beyond the house and the immediate neighborhood, home life includes the management of extensive relationships with stores, banks, and other commercial service facilities, and with public institutions such as schools, hospitals, clinics, and government offices. Part of homemaking involves seeing that each family member's myriad personal needs are fully met. The new dress must be the right size. The new fourth grade teacher must understand a child's history of learning difficulties. Sometimes relationships with stores or institutions turn into adversarial ones. If the new car is a lemon, if the grade school isn't teaching reading fast enough, if the hospital offers an incorrect diagnosis, if the social security benefit check is late, then the stressful nature of the homemaker's brokering work between home, market, and state is exacerbated.

Italian social theorist Laura Balbo has written brilliantly about the key roles women play in sustaining these three sectors of modern society. Not only do homemakers make the bridge between commercial services, government bureaucracies, and the family, they are also low-paid providers of service performing heroic feats of overtime in the commercial or state sectors.[4] Much women's nurturing work requires a high level of skill, understanding, judgment, and patience. Yet when this work is conducted in the private home, women's time and skills often go unrecognized. Traditionally, marriage has been a homemaker's labor agreement—and a rather vague one at that—to provide personal service and nurturing to a man and children in exchange for financial support. Homemakers, as the one group of workers for whom no legal limits on hours, pension benefits, health insurance, or paid vacations have ever applied, have often found that the only time their work of cooking, cleaning, and nurturing compelled attention was when it was *not* done.

While "man's home is his castle," a woman often lacks any private space in her home. Society defines the ideal home as a warm, supportive place for men and children, but for homemakers it has always been a workplace, where a "woman's work is never done." While women may have gourmet kitchens, sewing rooms, and so-called master bedrooms to inhabit, even in these spaces the homemaker's role is to service, not to claim autonomy and privacy. There has been little nurturing for homemakers themselves unless they break down. In crises, women have looked to other women for emotional support. This may be the informal help acknowledged by homemaker and author Erma Bombeck, who dedicated one of her books to the other homemakers in her car pool: the women who, "when I was drowning in a car pool threw me a line. . . . always a funny one."[5] Women's support may also come from mothers, sisters, female friends, and female kin, who traditionally rally in crises. It may come from the range of services provided by the feminist movement, such as discussion groups, crisis centers, health centers, and hostels. Or it may come from husbands and children who finally notice when their wives and mothers break down.

American urban design, social policy planning, and housing design have seldom taken the complexity of homemaking into account. To rethink private life, it is essential to be explicit about the range of needs that homes and homemakers fulfill. Home life is the source of great cultural richness and diversity in an immigrant nation. Home life is also the key to social services—education, health, mental health. And home life is the key to successful urban design, in the patterning of residential space, commercial space, and institutional space, so that the linkages between home, market, and state can be sustained without undue hardship.

Yet in the last half-century, the cultural strength of home has been debated. The success of the family in providing socialization for children has been challenged. The failure of many residential neighborhoods has been noted.[6] A conservative movement for "family values" has been mounted, without much interest in defining this term. In light of the extensive literature on such topics as divorce and family violence, it is surprising to see how few alternative models of home life are discussed in a serious, sustained way. Many critics fail to distinguish between the traditional male-headed family and other models of family life. Others welcome new models but fail to record the struggles to transform the male-headed family that feminists have waged for at least two hundred years.[7] Innovative, egalitarian housing strategies that lead to new forms of housing cannot be developed without a reformulation of the traditional family and its gender division of work. Americans interested in debating these issues can consider the history of three alternative models of home.

THREE MODELS OF HOME

In the years between 1870 and 1930, home life provoked a phenomenal amount of political debate. Because this topic linked the Woman Question to the Labor Question, it attracted the attention of housewives, feminist activists, domestic servants, inventors, economists, architects, urban planners, utopian novelists, visionaries, and efficiency experts. Housework, factory work, and home were all susceptible to restructuring in the industrial city. Women and men of all political persuasions generally agreed that burdensome household work, as it had been carried out in the pre-industrial houses of the first half of the nineteenth century, left most women little time to be good wives and mothers. Industrial development was transforming all other work and workplaces, and it was expected that domestic work and residential environments would be transformed as well. Activists raised fundamental questions about the relationships between women and men, households and servants. They explored the economic and social definitions of "woman's work." They also raised basic questions about household space, public space, and the relationship between economic policies and family life concretized in domestic architecture and residential neighborhoods.

Many proposed solutions drew, in one way or another, on the possibilities suggested by new aspects of urban and industrial life: new forms of specialization and division of labor, new technologies, new concentrations of dwelling units in urban apartment houses or suburban neighborhoods. But domestic theorists also had to deal with a number of unwelcome consequences of these new developments: hierarchy in the workplace, replacement of handcraft skills by mechanization, erosion of privacy in crowded urban dwellings, and development of conspicuous domestic consumption in bourgeois neighborhoods. Although life in the isolated household was burdensome, inefficient, and stifling, many reformers feared that the socialization of domestic work would deprive industrial society of its last vestige of uncapitalized, uncompetitive, skilled work. That is, they worried about mother love and home cooking.

For the most part, the major domestic strategies of the time have been ignored or misunderstood by both historians and political theorists. William O'Neill, in his popular book *Everyone Was Brave*, scathingly condemned the leaders of the American nineteenth-century woman's movement as "weak and evasive" activists, completely unable to tackle the difficult ideological problem of the family. He called them frustrated women who never understood that a revolution in domestic life was needed to achieve feminist aims.[8] Betty Friedan, in her 1981 book *The Second Stage*, reiterated O'Neill's views approvingly, as support for her mistaken belief that twentieth-century feminists were the first to introduce serious concern for domestic life into political organizing.[9] Some contemporary writers still dismiss any serious theoretical concern with housework as a waste of time; they look to wage work to liberate women, much as Bebel did in 1883 and Lenin in 1919.[10]

Almost all American women involved in politics between 1870 and 1930 saw domestic work and family life as important theoretical and practical issues. The material feminists argued that no adequate theory of political economy could develop without full consideration of domestic work.[11] They debated both businessmen and Marxists with an eloquence that has rarely been equaled. The years between 1870 and 1930 produced three major strategies for domestic reform: Catharine Beecher's capitalist haven strategy, a Marxist industrial strategy, and the material feminists' neighborhood strategy. Finding a new approach requires that all of these strategies, and the experiences of trying to implement them, are clearly understood.

THE HAVEN STRATEGY

The leading exponent of the home as haven, Catharine Beecher, explained the technological and architectural basis of a refined suburban home beginning in the 1840s. As discussed in chapter 2, she proposed to increase the effectiveness of the isolated housewife and to glorify woman's traditional sphere of work. Beecher devoted her energy to better design. The housewife would be equipped with an efficient kitchen, adequate running water, and effective home heating and ventilation. She would have a better stove. In *The American Woman's Home,* Beecher suggested that the housewife devote more of her labor to becoming an emotional support for her husband and an inspiring mother for her children. Self-sacrifice would be her leading virtue. The home, a spiritual and physical shelter from the competition and exploitation of industrial capitalist society, and a training ground for the young, would become a haven in a heartless world. Beecher believed this division of labor between men and women would blunt the negative effects of industrial society on male workers. She argued that both rich and poor women, removed from competition with men in paid work, would find gender a more engrossing identification than class.

For Beecher, it was extremely important that the housewife do nurturing work with her own two hands. As she performed many different tasks each day, she was to be a sacred figure, above and beyond the cash nexus. Her personal services as wife and mother were beyond price. The biological mother was presented as the only focus for her children's needs. The virtuous wife was present-

4.2 The haven strategy was expressed in *The American Woman's Home*, 1869, frontispiece. Women are the key figures caring for men and children.

ed as the only one who could meet her husband's needs as well. The spatial envelope for all of this exclusive nurturing was a little cottage in a garden. Nature surrounding the home reinforced belief in a woman's natural, biologically determined role within it. Beecher also showed how domesticity could be adapted to a tenement apartment or a single teacher's residence.

THE INDUSTRIAL STRATEGY

The German Marxist, August Bebel, in his classic book *Women Under Socialism* (1883), wanted to move most traditional household work into the factory, abolishing women's domestic sphere entirely. Bebel argued: "The small private kitchen is, just like the workshop of the small master mechanic, a transition stage, an arrangement by

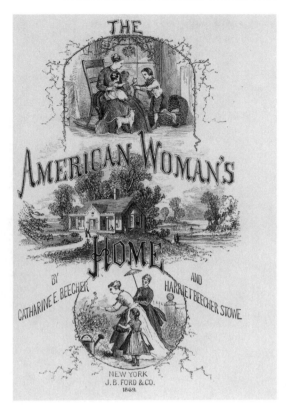

4.3 Title page, *The American Woman's Home.* The man who pays for all of this is shown as a very tiny figure admiring the facade.

which time, power and material are senselessly squandered and wasted. . . . in the future the domestic kitchen is rendered wholly superfluous by all the central institutions for the preparation of food."[12] He also predicted that just as factory kitchens would prepare dinners, and large state bakeries would bake pies, so mechanical laundries would wash clothes and cities would provide central heating. Children would be trained in public institutions from their earliest years. Women would take up industrial employment outside the household, and the household would lose control of many private activities. The effects of industrialization would be general, and women would share in the gains and losses with men, although their new factory work would probably be occupationally segregated labor in the laundry or the pie factory. A life of dedication to greater industrial production and the socialist state would reward personal sacrifice in the Marxist version of the industrial strategy.

4.4 The industrial strategy, as promoted by Bebel, is here illustrated by a view of women as paid workers making frozen dinners on an assembly line, 1945.

In Bebel's version of home life, both nature and biology disappear in favor of industrial efficiency. Bebel believed that nurturing work should be done by women, but he tended to see women as interchangeable service workers. The demand that women nurture with a personal touch, so central to Beecher, was replaced by a sense that any day-care worker could offer a substitute for mother love and any canteen worker could serve up a substitute for home cooking. The spatial container for this interchangeable, industrial nurturing was to be the apartment house composed of industrial components and equipped with large mess halls, recreation clubs, child-care centers, and kitchenless apartments. Of course, service workers would need to be constantly on duty to keep these residential complexes running, but Bebel did not consider this service as labor of any particular value or skill. He underestimated the importance of the socialized home as workplace, even as he recognized the private home as workshop.

The Neighborhood Strategy

Midway between the haven strategy and the industrial strategy, there was a third strategy. The material feminists led by Melusina Fay Peirce wanted to socialize housework under women's control through neighborhood networks. In contrast to the advocates of the haven approach, who praised woman's traditional skills but denied women money, or the advocates of the industrial approach, who denied women's traditional skills but gave women wages, the material feminists argued that women should be paid for what they were already doing. As Jane Cunningham Croly put it in Stanton and Anthony's newspaper, *The Revolution:* "I demand for the wife who acts as cook, as nursery-maid, or seamstress, or all three, fair wages, or her rightful share in the net income. I demand that the bearing and rearing of children, the most exacting of employments, shall be the best paid work in the world."[13]

Material feminists agreed that women were already doing half the necessary labor in industrial society and should receive half the wages. They believed that women would have to reorganize their labor to gain these demands. The first reason for organizing was to present a united front; the second was to utilize the possibility of new technologies and the specialization and division of labor, in order to perfect their skills and to shorten their hours. Peirce argued that "it is just as necessary, and just as honorable for a wife to earn money as it is for her husband," but she criticized the traditional arrangement of domestic work as forcing the housewife to become a "jack-of-all-trades."[14]

Peirce's proposed alternative was the producers' cooperative. She envisioned former housewives and former servants doing cooking, baking, laundry, and sewing in one well-equipped neighborhood workplace. Women would send the freshly baked pies,

4.5 The neighborhood strategy inspired this sketch by Thomas Nast, 1870, of a harried, servantless housewife confronting her labors. Some housewives felt the only solution was cooperation by neighbors working together and sharing tasks.

the clean laundry, and the mended garments back to their own husbands (or their former male employers) for cash on delivery. Peirce planned to overcome the isolation and economic dependency inherent in the haven approach, and the alienation inherent in the industrial approach. While revering woman's traditional nurturing skills and neighborhood networks as the material basis of women's sphere, Peirce proposed to transform these skills and networks into a new kind of economic power for women by elevating nurturing to the scale of several dozen united households.

Peirce also overcame another great flaw in the haven approach. In the early 1870s, there were very few appliances, aside from

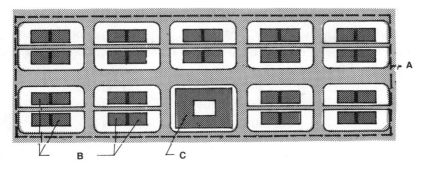

4.6 The neighborhood strategy, as introduced in Melusina Peirce's proposal for cooperative housekeeping: A, district of 36 families; B, kitchenless houses; C, work center for housewives' producers' cooperative, 1868–69.

Beecher's own inventions and architectural refinements, to help the housewife who worked alone. Almost all of the major advances, such as clothes-washing machines, dishwashers, refrigerators, and new kinds of stoves, were being developed for commercial laundries, breweries, hotels, hospitals, and apartment houses. They were designed to serve fifty to five hundred people, not one family. Peirce proposed, like Bebel, to use this technology, but to use it at the neighborhood scale, in a community workplace.

Peirce understood economic activity as both industrial production and human reproduction. She argued that her cooperative housekeeping strategies would lead to complete economic equality for women, because men could sustain farming and manufacturing while women ran the new, expanding areas of retail activity and service industries, in addition to their old standby, household production.[15] Thus she retained a gender division of labor but planned to revise national measures of productive economic activity. In this part of her analysis, Peirce anticipated Richard Ely, Helen Campbell, and Ellen Swallow Richards, who attempted, beginning in the 1880s and 1890s, to introduce home economics (or domestic economy) into academic debates and public policy as the "economics of consumption" on an equal plane with the economics of production.[16] All of the material feminists knew what many later Marxist and neoclassical economists alike have tended to forget: it is not the wage that defines work, it is the labor.

When Catharine Beecher, August Bebel, and Melusina Peirce framed their views of what the industrial revolution should mean to domestic life, they set up models of women's work and family life marked by all the hopes and fears of the mid-nineteenth century. They accepted gender stereotypes so strong that not one of these three models incorporated any substantial male responsibility for housework and child care. Yet Beecher's and Bebel's models of home continued to shape home life and public policy for over a century. The haven strategy and the industrial strategy became the ruling paradigms for domestic life in capitalist and in state socialist societies where the paid employment of women was a fact, not a hope or a fear.[17] Neither model of home life incorporated any substantial critique of male exclusion from the domestic scene. Both models disconnected household space from other parts of the industrial city and its economy. Attempts to repair their conceptual difficulties accelerated in the years after World War I, but neither model has undergone the total revision that would enable planners of housing, jobs, and services to create the spatial settings for modern societies where the paid employment of women is essential.

As a result, women have become disadvantaged workers in both capitalist and state socialist societies. If we look at the evolution of these two models, we see that there have been many ingenious modifications and ideological surprises as capitalists attempted to industrialize the haven strategy or state socialists attempted to domesticate the industrial strategy. The neighborhood strategy of Peirce met a rather different fate. Its adherents advanced their cause effectively in the United States and Europe, creating many interesting small experiments. As a result, they extended their argument for justice and women's liberation, but never had to provide a framework for government policy.

The evolution of all three models of home in different societies during the twentieth century reveals a great deal about capitalism and the role of the state in advanced capitalist societies, socialism and the role of the state in state socialist societies, and feminism and the persistence of male economic control of female labor. It is a story far too complex to be told in full here, yet a brief review may provoke readers of many different political persuasions. While the story does not deal at all with the fate of home life in economically developing nations, it may be read as a cautionary tale for any nation just beginning to make policies about housing and the employment of women. In the American context, the history of the three models of home may suggest ways to salvage the housing stock we now have while leaving the Victorian conventions of gender behind.

MODIFYING BEECHER'S HAVEN STRATEGY

MINIATURIZED TECHNOLOGY AND
HOUSEHOLD ENGINEERING

The first to modify the house as haven were manufacturers who introduced industrially produced appliances and products into the home. These were profitable extensions of the market economy, presented as aids to the hardworking homemaker. What is astonishing is that these inventions eroded the autonomy of women at least as much as they contributed to saving women's labor. Eventually the haven strategy produced not a skilled housewife happy at home, supported by her husband's "family" wage, but a harried woman constantly struggling to keep up standards.

The years since 1900 have seen the production of privately owned clothes washers, clothes dryers, refrigerators, gas and electric stoves, freezers, dishwashers, toasters, blenders, electric ovens, food processors, vacuum cleaners, and electric brooms.[18] Many of these appliances were the result of an extended campaign to miniaturize earlier hotel technology in the post–World War I era, and their potential for lightening household labor was tremendous. Unfortunately manufacturers began their sales of all such appliances and home improvements by advertising in women's magazines with themes of fear and guilt.[19] "For the health of your family . . . keep your foods sweet and pure, free from odors, impurities, and contamination," read the copy for McCray Sanitary Refrigerators. "Don't apologize for your toilet! Modernize it," said Pfau Manufacturing Company. Women were also told that liberation could be bought: "Electricity has brought to women a new freedom [represented by the figure of Liberty, wearing a crown and classical drapery] . . . the easy scientific method of cleaning with the Western Electric Vacuum cleaner."[20] The "laboratory-clean home" was what the housewife had to achieve.

In the first three decades of the twentieth century, industrial engineers and home economists joined forces to show housewives how to apply Frederick Taylor's factory-oriented, time-and-motion studies to their tasks at home. Since there had been no division and specialization of labor in the home, the industrial paraphernalia of task analysis with stopwatches made housewives into split personalities. They were the "managers" supervising their own speedup. As Christine Frederick put it, "Today, the woman in the home is called upon to be an executive as well as a manual laborer."[21] Or as one woman complained, "The role of the housewife is, therefore, analogous to that of the president of a corporation who would not only determine policies and make overall plans but also spend the major part of his time and energy in such activities as sweeping the plant and oiling the machines."[22]

Household engineers made women feel guilty for not doing tasks fast enough. Advertisers made both men and women feel guilty through emotional blackmail. Men were told that if they loved their wives, they owed it to them to buy particular appliances. Women were told that if they bought certain items, men would love them more. "Man seeks no club, when the home has a Hub," wrote one stove manufacturer. The American response to such ad campaigns was extensive purchasing, but researchers who have studied time budgets find that conflicts within the home continued and the work of the "haven" housewives was still "never done." Jo Ann Vanek reported in her 1974 survey in *Scientific American* that household standards had risen but women's time had not been saved.[23] To take just one example, Vanek showed that the full-time urban or rural housewife spent more hours doing laundry in the 1970s than in the 1920s, despite all the new washing machines, dryers, bleaches, and detergents. Why? Her family had more clothes and wanted them cleaner. The classic "ring around the collar" commercials of the 1960s dramatized the issue. A husband and his five-year-old son jeered at a woman for using a detergent that could not remove the stains on their shirt collars. Her response—to buy a new product—exemplified the ways that conflict within a family was exploited. Manufacturers often present ownership of multiple appliances as an integral part of a rising standard of living. This is misleading: many appliances require more labor than they save.

The popularity of gourmet cooking, the expansion of houses, and the increasing complexity of home furnishings have also contributed to an increasing demand for female labor hours in the home. Another development launched in the 1920s, which continued into the twenty-first century, was the creation of a culture of mothering that demanded intense attention to children at every stage of their development. Although the numbers of children were shrinking, mothers were expected to spend more time with each one. When American manufacturers introduced television, many households used it as a baby-sitting machine. However, television created as many problems as it solved, since children listened to endless commercials for candy and toys. Some inventions are better eliminated from home life.

COMMERCIAL SERVICES

When increasing numbers of American housewives and mothers entered the paid labor force in the 1960s and 1970s, and commercial services became a fast-growing sector of the economy, there was a second major modification of the haven strategy. In 1978, it was estimated that Americans spent a third of their food budgets in restaurants and fast-food establishments. From 1970, when Americans spent $6 billion on fast food, until 2000, when they spent over $110 billion (an almost twenty-fold increase), fast-food logo buildings have lined the highways.[24] The proportion of restaurant food eaten by two-earner couples was, as might be expected, higher than for one-earner couples with a full-time housewife. A McDonald's slogan, "A Mom making time," captured the mood of some customers. "It's nice to feel so good about a meal," sang Colonel Sanders' chorus. "We're cooking dinner in your neighborhood," ran the folksy copy line for a California chain of fast-food restaurants. Happy family life and the consumption of industrially produced meals have collided, just as political liberation for women and the purchase of electrical appliances meshed as themes in the 1920s.

Harland Sanders, the goateed Kentucky colonel dressed in a white suit with a black string tie, smiles at motorists from the street corners and roadsides of America. A man who started his career in 1929, running a small cafe behind a gas station in Corbin, Kentucky, he became the king of the take-out chicken business in the late 1950s. By 2000, Colonel Sanders' Kentucky Fried Chicken franchised 10,800 businesses doing $8.9 billion worth of fast food annually, worldwide.[25] When fast food came of age as one of many commercial services supported by working women and their families, Sanders became a hero as an entrepreneur. When Sanders died in 1980, his body lay in the rotunda of the state capitol in Frankfort. In Louisville, his hometown, the flags on city buildings were flown at half-staff. But was Sanders a hero to women? His franchises employed thousands of non-union women at low wages to prepare and serve his industrial food products. These commercial services and products filled in for home cooking, but they drained a woman's salary. One woman's precarious haven was sustained by the products of another woman's small wages in this fast-growing sector of the market economy. Those theorists who argued that such commercial services "liberated" women considered only the consumer and not the producer. Of course, the quality and price of commercial fast food varies greatly, as do the costs and conditions of production. In 2000, upscale businesses run by professional cooks, with catchy names like "A Moveable Feast" and "Perfect Parties," offer a range of carefully prepared soups, main courses, and desserts to affluent households whose members have no time to create elegant dinners.

Almost as common as the fast-food place on the corner is the commercial child-care facility. Profit-making child care is also big business. Most are independent operations run by licensed day-care providers. The fastest growing group are more carefully calculated to run as franchises, such as the Kinder Care chain, with 1,240 centers in thirty-nine states and the United Kingdom. Their education director in 1980 was an ex–Air Force colonel who designed a program for children in the chain's standardized plastic schoolhouses.[26] At the high end, expensive day-care services may provide developmental child care for the children of affluent families. At the low end, many in-home, "family" day-care centers exist.

Other types of profitable, personalized commercial services now offered to the home-as-haven include private cooks, nurses, maids, baby-sitters (long employed by the affluent), and Internet grocery-shopping services. One, called nyerrands.com, advertised in 2001, "Give us your to do list." Their fees are $30 per hour for waiting around for home deliveries, 20 percent of the bill for drugstore or grocery errands, and 25 percent of the bill for category-killer discount stores like Costco. Should you require "life management" assistance such as cleaning your closets or organizing your refrigerator, services in most big cities will provide a price quote on demand. The bargain end of the spectrum on personal service is the maid franchise operation. Such services pay workers extremely low wages. When author Barbara Ehrenreich went on assignment as a maid, she received $6.65 an hour, while customers were charged $25 an hour.[27]

EMPLOYER BENEFITS AND STATE SERVICES

American employers may provide services to workers who are mothers when there are bonanza profits to be made; the state intervenes to provide services to employed women when there are wartime labor shortages. These crisis times reveal just how much can be gained by supporting women's economic activities. As discussed in chapter 1, Kaiser Shipyards in Vanport City, Oregon was an impressive demonstration of how employers could make a difference for women. In less than one year, Kaiser management created a dazzling array of inducements for mothers with children to take on jobs as welders, riveters, and heavy construction workers. Almost sixty years later, American women workers still lack national legislation requiring that all employers treat women as valued workers and offer similar programs.

In 1993, the United States enacted the Family and Medical Leave Act. It requires employers with over fifty workers to provide up to twelve weeks of unpaid leave for "certain family and medical reasons," including childbirth, adoption, and the need to care for a spouse, child, or parent who is seriously ill, as well as a serious health condition of the worker. An international study of 152 countries in 1998 showed that 80 percent offered *paid* maternity leave.

A European official commented sadly on the U.S., "it's a do-it-yourself maternity plan."[28] Since employers provide no pay, only affluent workers would be able to take time off. Mother and fathers who want a year off to bond with a new baby and create a secure attachment are out of luck.

The child-care situation is no better. A national day-care bill was passed by both houses of Congress in 1971, only to be vetoed by Richard Nixon, who argued that he was defending the American family. The need for developmental child care has been fought by conservatives, who fail to appreciate that while 65 percent of the mothers of children under six are in the paid labor force, only a small percent of the children of employed mothers enjoy quality child care.[29] Most parents have to struggle to find anything. Latch-key children are on the rise. When the topic turns to welfare mothers, the lack of day care becomes a clear example of inept policy. Welfare reformers in the Clinton era told women they must get off welfare and find paid employment. Often there was no public day care and no adequate provision for commercial child-care expenses, which might take a third or half of a woman's pay.

Experiments in flex-time, or flexible work schedules, have been heavily publicized as employers' initiatives to help employed parents at little cost to themselves. So have experiments in telecommuting, or work at home on the Internet. Such arrangements do not eliminate the double day, they merely make it less logistically stressful. Flexible work schedules are worth campaigning for, but trade unions and women's groups recognize they are only a small part of a broader solution to women's double workload.

Swedish Parent Insurance

It is instructive to mention Swedish benefits, which guarantee women and men workers more rights to economic support for parenting. Gender equality was not the only motivation for their legislation. Politicians agreed that more Swedish women in the paid labor force were preferable to large numbers of guest workers (migrant laborers) for political reasons. So, during the 1960s and 1970s, elaborate maternity insurance, child-care provisions, and incentives to employers evolved in order to avoid bringing guest workers from Southern Europe into the country in large numbers. Eventually, by 1999, 70 percent of Swedish women had joined the paid labor force; Swedish Parent Insurance was a monument to their economic importance to the nation, and to their role as mothers.

Swedish Parent Insurance, established in 1974, provides for economic benefits and leaves from paid work for either new mothers or new fathers. As Sheila Kamerman, a specialist in the comparative analysis of social welfare programs, has described it, "this is a universal, fully paid, wage-related, taxable cash benefit." It now covers the year after childbirth. Either parent can remain home to care for the infant. Kamerman explains how it might work: "A woman might use the benefit to cover four months of full time leave and stay home. Then each might, in turn, work two months at halftime, followed by two months at three-quarter time (a six-hour day). Employers are required to accept part-time employment as part of this benefit, for childcare purposes." When only 10 percent of the eligible men used this benefit in 1976, the Swedish government appointed a Father's Commission to recommend changes. New legislation added thirty days of leave for fathers only. Men had to use it during the child's first year, or lose it. Men also got an additional benefit which provided ten days leave at the time of birth, and eighteen days of paid leave per child for either parent to care for sick children at home. In some parts of Sweden, Kamerman notes that workers will also come to the house to care for a sick child so that both parents may go to work, and another Swedish program has offered state subsidies for employers who hire women in fields dominated by men, or hire men in fields dominated by women. Sweden has recognized that there may be economic disruption caused by giving equal work to women and men, where jobs previously were segregated. This legislation makes it possible for employers to recoup some of the cost of this social change.[30] This is the kind of economic equity that can improve the lives of both women and men.

Male Participation

One last attempt to modify the round of tasks for the housewife in the U.S. has been the call for male participation. Training boys for housework and child care, and insisting that adult men take part, educates them and improves their skills. Imaginative projects along these lines include grade-school courses for boys on how to take care of babies and YWHA play groups for fathers and children.[31] Both traditional consciousness-raising and these new courses reveal to men and boys the skills needed for nurturing, the time involved, and the role that space plays in isolating the nurturer. They find that kitchens are often designed for one worker, not two; that supermarkets are designed for the longest possible trip, not the shortest; and that men's rooms, like women's rooms, need a safe place where a diaper can be changed. Men who do housework and parenting then begin to see the patterns of private and public life in the divided American city.

In the United States, we have had active struggle for male participation in housework since the 1970s. Yet sociological studies suggest that American men do only 10 percent to 15 percent of household work (a smaller percentage than children contribute) and women still bear the brunt of 70 percent, even when both members of a couple are in the paid labor force. Sociologist Arlie Hochschild reported in *The Second Shift* that employed women averaged 15 hours more of housework and child care per week than men, a finding consistent from the 1980s through the 1990s. Indeed, economist Heidi Hartmann suggests that men actually demand eight hours more service per week than they contribute.[32] Other studies have found that the work week of American and Canadian women is 21 hours longer than that of men.[33]

A closer look at male behavior in different classes reveals common gender stereotypes underlying the struggle over housework within the family. Men pretend to be incompetent or they call the jobs trivial.[34] They may also have very heavy overtime (whether at executive or blue-collar jobs) and argue that their time is always worth more than a woman's time. Men may also find that even if they do participate, a couple with young children still can't manage alone if both partners are employed full-time. An even more insurmountable problem to male participation is the absence of men in many households.[35] Men's reluctance to take part in nurturing the next generation is only part of the problem. In many cases the ideal of male involvement has blinded many angry women to the severe logistical problems presented by the house itself. Women's hope

for male cooperation, some time in the distant future, obscures the
need for sweeping spatial and economic reforms.

MODIFYING BEBEL'S INDUSTRIAL STRATEGY

In the same way that Beecher's haven strategy of keeping domestic work out of the market economy was slowly eroded, so Bebel's
ideal strategy for the state socialist world has also been betrayed by
the retention of a second shift of private life and home cooking.
Bebel argued that only a comprehensive program of industrial
development for all women, including the design of new services
and new housing forms, could improve women's position.[36] This
has never been realized. Domestic drudgery accompanied industrial work for women; it did not wither away under the "dictator-
ship of the proletariat," just as the state did not.

Between the 1950s and the 1990s, one might have expected
more comprehensive planning of services in state socialist countries such as Cuba, China, and the former Soviet Union, where the
state owned the factories, ran the shops, ran the day care, ran the
transit, and owned the housing. At the state's discretion, day care
and other services could be located in the factory or in the residential neighborhood. Indeed, day care, other social services, and
even the factory itself could be placed in the residential neighborhood. Despite this potential ability to meet employed women's
needs, such decisions were not usually made in ways that
increased women's autonomy.

THE HOUSE FOR THE NEW WAY OF LIFE

The first opportunity for fulfilling Bebel's ideal occurred in the
Soviet Union, after the October Revolution of 1917. Lenin and
Alexandra Kollontai led Bolshevik support for housing and services for employed women. They argued for the transformation of the
home by the state and experimented with these ideas as the basis
for national housing policy. Lenin, in *The Great Initiative*, wrote
about the need for housing with collective services in order to
involve women in industrial production: "Are we devoting enough

attention to the germs of communism that already exist in this area [of the liberation of women]? No and again no. Public dining halls, creches, kindergartens—these are exemplary instances of these germs, these are those simple, everyday means, free of all bombast, grandiloquence and pompous solemnity, which, however, are *truly* such that they can *liberate women,* truly such that they can decrease and do away with her inequality vis-a-vis man in regard to her role in social production and public life." Lenin conceded that, "these means are not new, they have (like all the material pre-requisites of socialism) been created by large-scale capitalism, but under capitalism they have firstly remained a rarity, secondly—and particularly important—they were either hucksterish enterprises, with all the bad sides of speculation, of profit-making, of deception, of falsification or else they were a 'trapeze act' of bourgeois chari-ty, rightly hated and disclaimed by the best workers."[37] Following Lenin's encouragement, the new regime developed a program of building multifamily housing with collective services, beginning with competitions by architects to generate new designs for the "House for the New Way of Life."

While the competition had a strong intellectual impact on design-ers of mass housing all over the world, ultimately, few of the projects were built as intended. The USSR lacked the technology and the funds to follow through on its commitment to urban housing under Lenin. Under Stalin, the commitment itself dissolved. Stalin's ascen-dancy in the 1930s ended the official policy of women's liberation. Divorce and abortion were made difficult; "Soviet motherhood" was exalted, and experiments in collective living and new kinds of hous-ing ended. Only the most minimal support for women's paid labor-force participation was provided: day care in large, bureaucratic cen-ters stressing obedience, discipline, and propaganda.

SOVIET MOTHERHOOD

As a result, women in the USSR were encouraged to join the paid labor force without recognition of their first job in the home. In 1980, Anatole Kopp, a specialist in Soviet housing, concluded that "Soviet society today has but little connection with the fraternal, egalitarian, and self-managing society dreamed of by a few during the short period of cultural explosion which followed the Revolution." Workers lived in small private apartments in dreary, mass housing projects, where miles and miles of identical buildings had been constructed with industrialized building systems. Individual units were cramped and inconvenient. Appliances were minimal. Laundry was done in the sink; cooking on a two-burner countertop unit without oven. Refrigerators were rare status symbols for the favored elite. "Soviet architecture today well reflects daily life in the USSR. . . . It reflects the real condition of women in the Soviet Union—a far cry from the idyllic pictures once painted by Alexandra Kollontai."[38]

Research on the time budgets of women and men in the former Soviet Union showed the extent of inequality: 90 percent of all Soviet women between the ages of twenty and forty-nine were in the paid labor force. While women's housework time decreased somewhat between 1923 and 1966, men's time spent in housework did not increase. As a result, women's total work week was still seventeen hours longer than men's.[39] Moscow was one of the few cities in the world to provide enough day care for the children of all employed mothers, but while this allowed women to function as full-time paid workers (51 percent of the Soviet Union's labor force), their housing was not designed to include either Bebel's industrialized housekeeping services or American kitchen appliances.[40] So, one could compare women's work in the United States and the former Soviet Union. The USSR emphasized state subsidized day care and women's involvement in industrial production. The U.S. emphasized commercial day care and women's consumption of appliances and commercial services. In both cultures, the majority of married women had two jobs, worked 17–21 hours per week more than men, and earned about 60 to 75 percent of what men earned. The "new way of life" in the USSR was as elusive as the "new woman" in the U.S.

HOUSEWIVES' FACTORIES IN CUBA AND CHINA

The situation for employed women has been quite similar in other state socialist countries whose economic development was influenced by the Soviet Union. Given that standing in long lines to

purchase scarce food supplies and consumer goods has long been
a problem for housewives in state socialist societies, Cuba developed the Plan Jaba or Shopping Bag Plan in the early 1970s to permit employed women to go to the head of lines in crowded stores.
However pragmatic the Plan Jaba was, as a solution to the woman's
double day as paid worker and mother, and as a solution to the
hours of queuing, one could hardly call it a major theoretical innovation. The publicity given to it as a fine example of socialist liberation for women was overdone. In much the same vein, Cuba also
offered employed women special access to rationed goods and factory laundry services.[41] Such services cannot correct more basic
problems. The location of factories in neighborhoods was not a
service to women but a disservice when the well-located factories
offered only low-paid work for women. In Cuba, a textile factory
staffed primarily by low-paid women was located in the Alamar
housing project outside Havana; a shoe factory staffed by low-paid
women was placed in the José Martí neighborhood in Santiago. In
addition, the large and well-designed day-care centers in housing
projects employed only women as day-care workers, at low
salaries, because child care was considered a woman's job.

Chinese examples of residential quarter planning for employed
women are similar. During the Great Leap Forward, so-called
housewives' factories were located in residential neighborhoods.
The female workers received low wages and worked in relatively
primitive industrial conditions. All this was justified for some time
as a transitional stage of national economic development.
However, in 1980, the Chinese planned an entire new town, which
included new housewives' factories, to accompany a large new
steel plant for male workers who would earn much higher wages.[42]
Chinese residential neighborhoods, like the Cuban ones, have also
employed women as day-care workers and community-health
workers at very low wages. So, while the socialization of traditional women's work proceeded at a rapid rate to support women's
involvement in industrial production, both the industrial workers
and the service workers remained in female ghettos, and female
responsibility for nurturing work remained the norm.

During the last three decades, women in state socialist countries
have raised the issue of male participation, as have their counter-
parts in the United States. Cuban women developed a strong cri-

Finished! Now to cook, wash, and iron!

4.7 Unfulfilled promises of the industrial strategy are satirized in this cartoon from Cuba showing a woman who has cut mounds of sugar cane: "Finished!" she says, "Now to cook, wash, and iron."

tique of what they call the "second shift," or their responsibility for housework once the paid shift is over. A cartoon shows an agricultural worker with a mound of sugar cane she has just cut, saying "Finished! Now to cook, wash, and iron!" As a result of such campaigns, the Cuban Family Code of 1974 was written. In principle, it aimed at having men share what was formerly "women's work." In practice, the law depended upon private struggle between husband and wife for day-to-day enforcement. Men feigned incompetence, especially in the areas of cooking and cleaning. The gender stereotyping of low-paid jobs for women outside the home, in day-care centers for example, only reinforced the problem at home. Some Cuban men made an effort, but many argued that domestic sharing could wait for the next generation. While Communist Party policy urged male cadres to assume half the domestic chores, Heidi Steffens, a writer for *Cuba Review*, recounted a popular mid-1970s anecdote. A well-known member of the Central Committee of the party took over the job of doing the daily laundry, but he insisted that his wife hang it out and bring it in from the line, since he didn't want the neighbors to see his loss of *machismo*.[43] The power of *machismo* was also evident when men cited pressure to do "women's" work as one of their reasons for emigration.[44]

In China, where there have also been general political policies that housework should be shared, the ambience is even less supportive. Sometimes the elderly—more often a grandmother than a grandfather—will fill in. The history of party pronouncements on housework can be correlated with the need to move women into or out of the paid labor force. When a party directive instructed male members not to let themselves be henpecked into too much domestic activity at the expense of their very important political work, it was clear that full male participation in housework was a distant goal rather than a reality.[45] In state socialist countries, as in capitalist ones, the hope of male participation hides the inadequacy of the basic model concerning work and home. It encourages both women and men to think that the next generation might negotiate a better solution, rather than to consider the overall inadequacies of spatial and economic planning.

MODIFYING PEIRCE'S
NEIGHBORHOOD STRATEGY

While the haven strategy and the industrial strategy suffered slow disintegration into the double day, Melusina Peirce's neighborhood strategy of material feminism never became mainstream. Like Bebel and Beecher, she failed to incorporate male participation in housework and child care, but at least she had a strong economic reason for the exclusion. Peirce wanted to overcome the isolation of housewives, the lack of specialization of tasks, the lack of labor-saving technology, and the lack of financial security for any woman who had spent a lifetime in domestic labor. She saw men as a threat to women's traditional economic activities and wanted women to defend and expand their household activities on their own terms, rather than have them taken over by men's commercial enterprises.

In 1868, Peirce herself organized a bakery, laundry, grocery, and sewing service in Cambridge, Massachusetts.[46] In the next half-century, dozens of other experiments were conducted, including a family dining club in Warren, Ohio from 1903 to 1923, and a Cleaning Club in Northbrook, Illinois in the late 1940s. In Massachusetts, between 1926 and 1931, Ethel Puffer Howes made an even more ambitious experiment, providing models of commu-

Cleaning Club Meets Today

Here is an idea,
originated by four friends,
that could be emulated in
almost any community

By RUTH W. LEE

LAMENTING THE FACT they were so completely tied to their household tasks and to their homes, due to the scarcity of regular help or even sitters, four friends and neighbors in the village of Northbrook, Illinois, jointly hit upon an idea which has solved many of their problems.

It's a Cleaning Club, the members of which combine forces once a week to help each other with household tasks. They meet from about nine-thirty in the morning until five, bring the children with them, and make a social occasion out of any major task which the hostess wants done. In return for their joint efforts, which have included window washing, mending, painting, housecleaning and dressmaking, the hostess cooks and serves lunch, and keeps her eye on all the

children. The dividends have been far greater than merely accomplishing some household task. Not only have the members had the pleasure of being together weekly, and the keen satisfaction of getting things done, but the children have become good friends, have learned to get along well together, and have thrived on their daylong visits to the members' homes. Even the husbands have shared the fun by occasionally joining in for potluck suppers.

At the beginning, the mothers drew lots for the first meeting, which was won by Mrs. L. D. Gordon. Her planned job for the day was having the windows washed. The mothers arrived shortly after the older children had gone off to school. Mrs. Carroll Daley brought three-year-old Susie to play with Mrs. Carl J. Nelson's two-year-old Meredith. Kay, aged six, daughter of Mrs. Peter Brown, had companionship in Jim Gordon, who is the same age. The children were enchanted to play with new toys in a new room, and proved to be on their best behavior. They happily took naps in strange beds and, after the older ones came home from school in the afternoon, all played together outside while the mothers continued their work.

At the second meeting of the club, Mrs. Nelson (Turn to page 93)

4.8 The neighborhood strategy, as developed by members of a housewives' mutual aid Cleaning Club, Northbrook, Illinois, *Parents' Magazine*, January 1945. This was based on bartered labor.

nity-run services: a cooperative dinner kitchen for the home delivery of hot food, a cooperative nursery school, a home helpers' bureau, and a job placement advisory service for Smith graduates. As the head of the Institute for the Coordination of Women's Interests at Smith College, Howes believed that her model institutions could be recreated throughout the nation by housewives who also wished to enter paid employment. Unfortunately, during the Depression, prejudice against women's employment, combined with the Smith College faculty's suspicions that Howes' ideas were unacademic, ended this project after five years of successful operation.

Recruiting adequate capital to initiate change was a consistent problem for all of these neighborhood experiments. Some housewives' experiments failed because husbands found their wives' demands for pay too expensive—they believed that marriage was a labor contract, making housewives' labor free. Other experiments— including some that lasted the longest—relied on ties between neighbors and kin but involved little money changing hands. This tradition of housewives' neighborly sharing of tasks moved too slowly for many nineteenth-century feminists who attempted to push the neighborhood strategy in the direction of more businesslike enterprises run by professional women. They believed that the increasing employment of women outside the home could provide the paid jobs and paying customers necessary to transform traditional domesticity. Yet while more cash was a resource, the neighborhood organization of women suffered as a result.

In the 1890s the idea of neighborhood domestic reform as "good business" became quite popular when the American feminist Charlotte Perkins Gilman proposed the construction of special apartment houses for employed women and their families. In *Women and Economics,* she noted that employed women required day care and cooked-food service to enjoy home life after a day of paid work, and argued that if any astute business woman were to construct an apartment hotel with these facilities for professional women and their families, it would be filled at once. She believed that female entrepreneurs would find this "one of the biggest businesses on earth."[47]

SERVICE HOUSES, COLLECTIVE HOUSES, AND COOPERATIVE QUADRANGLES

Gilman's work was translated into several European languages, and her argument was taken up by many European women and

men looking for a better approach to housing. The builder Otto
Fick constructed the first "service house" in Copenhagen in 1903,
a small apartment house occupied by tenants who enjoyed food
service, cleaning, and laundry service. The building was explicitly
designed for married women in the paid labor force, but Fick
thought career and motherhood incompatible and prohibited children.[48] A second fault can be seen in Fick's claim that he was the
"inventor of a new mode of living which simultaneously has all the
features of a profitable business venture."[49] His claim depended
upon residents paying the service personnel low wages and making a profit on the market price of shares in the residents' association when they sold out. Nevertheless, Fick achieved a level of
social and technological innovation that Gilman had only proposed, and his project operated until 1942.[50]

Another successful design for live/work housing was developed
in Sweden in the 1930s. In 1935, feminist Alva Myrdal (later
awarded the Nobel Prize for her work on world peace) collaborated with architect Sven Markelius to create housing with work
space, food service, and child care. Their project in the center of
Stockholm included fifty-seven small apartments of very elegant
design. Some of them could also be used as offices or studios. Not
only did Markelius design these, he moved into the building himself and served as an unofficial handyman for thirty years, in order
to make sure everything about the building worked, and to demonstrate his commitment to social housing.[51]

In 1945, *Life* magazine praised this project as a model for
post–World War II reorganization of American housing: the
reporter suggested that Americans should copy its design for
women in the wartime labor force who wished to continue their
careers.[52] The only disadvantage was that most residents did not
wish to leave after their children were grown, and new parents
could not find space in the building. The day-care center ultimately had to take in neighborhood children as well as residents' children to stay in business. The restaurant food became less economically competitive when cheap eating places appeared in large
numbers in the city.

Olle Enkvist, a Stockholm contractor who became involved
with the combination of housing and services, built the collective
houses Marieberg (1944), Nockebyhove (1951), Blackeberg (1952),

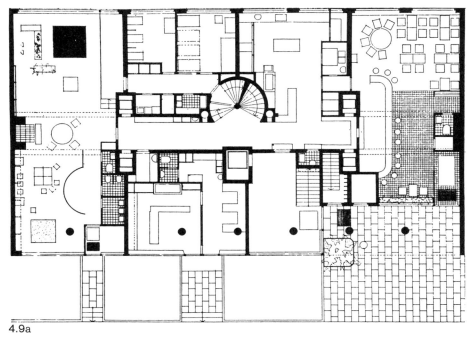

4.9a

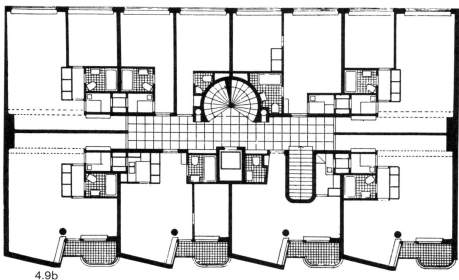

4.9b

4.9 *Life* recommended Sven Markelius's and Alva Myrdal's Collective House, built in Stockholm in 1935, as a model for housing American mothers who wished to keep their jobs after World War II. The first floor plan (4.9a) includes a restaurant and child-care center. Food could be sent up to private apartments in "food lifts." The second-floor plan (4.9b) shows elegantly designed private apartments that could also be used as studios or offices.

and Hasselby (1955–56). All had restaurants and full child care. Unlike Fick, who believed in joint stock ownership by a residents' association, Enkvist owned these buildings as benign landlord. His success was measured in long waiting lists of prospective tenants. After his death there were numerous tenant confrontations with the new management, especially when, in the 1970s, the new management wished to close the collective dining rooms because they didn't generate as much profit as the rental apartments. This probably would have seemed most ironic to Enkvist, who decided against delivery systems for cooked food (such as the elevators Fick had used for food) on the grounds that a large dining room with private family tables was more conducive to social contacts. Hasselby tenants did prove they could cater for themselves without losing money (serving about one hundred people daily for three years), but management found this level of participation cumbersome and decided to eject the tenants. The turmoil of decollectivization then led to the impression that these projects were social or financial failures, although many functioned smoothly for thirty years. Their main failure was that the landlord did not turn a high profit.[53]

In England, Gilman's arguments were taken up by Ebenezer Howard, founder of the Garden Cities movement, who proposed the "cooperative quadrangle" as the basis of new town planning in 1898.[54] Howard's cooperative quadrangles were to be composed of garden apartments served by a collective kitchen, dining room, and open space. They were designed to release women from household drudgery in the private home, and between 1911 and 1930 several of these projects were built for various constituencies, including single female professionals and the elderly, as well as two-earner couples. Howard himself lived in Homesgarth, a cooperative triangle at Letchworth. The quadrangles never became the standard housing available in the Garden Cities, but they did provide some very successful alternative projects within these new towns. In time, their dining rooms also seemed expensive compared to local restaurants. After World War I, Clementina Black of London argued for the postwar adoption of "Domestic Federations" similar to Howard's designs.[55] After World War II, Sir Charles Reilly, member of Parliament and head of the School of Architecture at Liverpool University, also proposed a plan for reconstruction that incorporated many of the features of Howard's cooperative quadrangles.[56] He organized neighborhoods of duplex houses around nurseries, community kitchens, and open spaces.

Apartment Hotels

In the United States, Gilman's ideas were reflected in the apartment hotels built between 1898 and 1930 in major cities. Mary Beard, the well-known historian, lived in one such apartment hotel with her husband and children; they were located on the bus line to the New York Public Library. Knowing that three meals a day would be served to her family, she was able to hop on the bus and tend to her research. Georgia O'Keefe lived in a similar hotel with good light for painting. For less affluent women, Finnish and Jewish workers' housing cooperatives provided child care, bed-sitting rooms for the elderly, and tea rooms adjacent to family apartments.[57] The Workers Cooperative Colony in the Bronx, organized and owned by workers in the needle trades, was an early example of this kind of project in the mid-1920s. Again, the cost of providing services with well-paid unionized service workers made competition with commercial groceries, restaurants, and laundries difficult.

Cash or Community?

All these attempts to define supportive residential communities for employed women and their families ran into two related economic difficulties. First, the economic value of housework was never adequately understood. Second, the economic value of the new services was unclear, in relation both to the old-fashioned system of hiring personal servants and the new commercial services and industrial products developed for haven housewives. Such services, when produced by low-paid female workers, were cheaper, if less intimate and desirable, than community-generated alternatives. Economies of scale worked in favor of the nationally distributed products and services, even if they were impersonal. Once the substitution of cash for personal participation by residents had been arranged, the difference between industrial and neighborhood services might be difficult to discern. So professional women, if they attempted to buy services, had to be very careful to treat the women service workers well. Otherwise, they wound up closer to Colonel Sanders, year by year.

Family Allowances and Wages for Housework

In much the same way, housewives struggling for economic independence through the neighborhood strategy found themselves closer to the haven strategy if they focused on wages and omitted the ideal of reshaping household work in community form. Eleanor Rathbone, an economist, feminist, and Member of Parliament in England, formed a club to lobby for wages for wives as early as 1918.[58] Some Americans also supported this cause in the 1940s.[59] Rathbone started by seeking a decent wage for housework; in the late 1940s, she won for mothers the Family Allowance: a small subsidy for a second child and any additional ones. Inspired by the concept of Family Allowances, and the potential of organizing to increase them, some British feminists revived the idea of larger payments for housework in the early 1970s. Led by Selma James, a group called Wages for Housework demanded that the state pay wages to all women for their housework. To attract supporters, the organizers ran skits about women's work in urban neighborhoods on market days. They passed out free potholders with their slogan to remind women of the campaign for wages every time they picked up a hot pot. They used union techniques of insisting on wages, wages, wages. "Just give us the money. All we want is the money," James incanted at one meeting.

Wages for Housework organized effectively among welfare recipients and single-parent mothers. They created special suborganizations: Lesbians for Wages for Housework, and Black Women for Wages for Housework. The campaign developed successful recruiting tactics, but there was no mass movement. Organizers demonstrated the value of a housewife's day but their emphasis was on cash. Their campaigns had some of the weaknesses of American welfare-rights organizing of the 1960s. Wages for

Housework did not confront the isolated home as haven, the setting for housework. They accepted females as domestic workers and identified the welfare state (rather than employers or husbands) as the primary target of their activities. Furthermore, they included sexual services as "all in a day's work" for the housewife. This made it easy to organize angry women who felt sexually exploited, but the model of wife as paid maid and prostitute made it difficult to articulate a more sophisticated position on male-female relationships.

4.10 The neighborhood strategy, as developed by advocates of cash for housework: "Should Housewives Be Paid a Salary?" The article on the economics of the neighborhood strategy was inspired by Eleanor Rathbone's successful "family allowance" campaigns in England, and published in *American Home*, February 1947.

Wages for Housework never lacked vitality, even if it lacked sub-
tlety. A china bank in the shape of a rolling pin, made in the 1940s,
carried the message of the earlier British feminists, "If women
were paid for all they do, there'd be a lot of wages due."[60] But just
as Rathbone had found a wage for haven housewives politically
impossible in the 1940s, so it was in the 1970s. Even if they had
won, financial recognition from the state for the work of homemaking would not have been enough to transform the haven
housewife's situation.

Trade-A-Maid

Gary Trudeau's *Doonesbury* cartoon on "Trade-A-Maid" schemes,
in which American haven housewives swap chores, points out this
problem as well. As Nichole, the "Alternate Life Stylist" explains it,
"Housewife A and her best friend, Housewife B, spend weekdays
cleaning each other's home. Their respective husbands pay for
their services, just as they would for those of a first-class maid.[61]
The employed wives then become eligible for Social Security and
for tax deductions on cleaning equipment. They receive cash but
neither husband suffers loss of family income since the swap
means both wives are paid equally. However, they still work in isolation, since receiving a wage for housework (whether paid by individual husbands or by the state) does not transform the home as
haven, nor does it utilize the full range of technologies available in
twentieth-century society. "It's illegal, though, right?" worries the
interviewer. "Not yet," says Nichole.

NICHE

Another American proposal captures the essence of the neighborhood strategy and avoids the question of industrial technologies by
stressing the value of women offering social services to each other in
the neighborhood. In 1977, Nona Glazer, Lindka Mjaka, Joan Acker,
and Christine Bose suggested institutionalizing housewives' cooperative services by establishing government funding for Neighbors in
Community Helping Environments (NICHE).[62] In *Women in a Full
Employment Economy,* they explained how to start Neighborhood
Service Houses, where women would supervise children's play, care

for sick children, facilitate repair service to homes, encourage bar-
tering, distribute hot meals, and work with battered women, abused
children, and rape victims. In return for providing these family and
community services, women would receive at least a minimum
wage. This proposal recognized that women's cooperation to socialize homemaking tasks could transform women's experience.
NICHE also saw economic recognition of domestic labor as essential, but it did not involve proposals for male participation. Since
NICHE was relying on the state to provide the wages, they had
selected almost as difficult a program as the Wages for Housework
campaigns. In a Democratic administration concerned about full
employment the proposal looked possible; when Republicans took
office and slashed social services, the proposal looked even more rel-
evant, but funding appeared impossible.

COMPLEXITY

All of these campaigns to transform models of home life underscore the need for complex social, economic, and environmental
innovations. Successful solutions would reward housework and
parenting as essential to society, incorporate male responsibility
for nurturing, build on existing networks of neighbors, kin, and
friends, and incorporate new technologies, in order to promote
equality for women within a more caring society. Yet before any
specific policy changes can be proposed, it is essential to recognize
the consistent economic and spatial failures that marred previous
attempts. Beecher's and Bebel's models were too simplistic. If
Beecher's glorification of the homemaker attempted to recover a
pre-industrial past, Bebel's rejection of the homemaker embraced
the fantasy of a totally industrial future. As public policy, these
strategies led to ironies compounded upon ironies; after a century,
women had gotten the worst of both worlds, having been economically disadvantaged by the double day and spatially manipulated
by the refusal of designers and planners to treat the home as a
workplace.

Yet the most humiliating aspect of women's experience as nurturers was not their economic or spatial frustration, but the sup-
pression of the neighborhood approach to home life, in order that

the haven and industrial strategies could be presented as modern. The advocates of neighborhood networks were attacked as socialist sympathizers in the United States in the 1920s, and as bourgeois deviationists who should be expelled from the Communist Party in Germany and the USSR. Women have had warmed-over Beecher presented to them as women's liberation through Western Electric vacuum cleaners and Colonel Sanders; warmed-over Bebel presented as women's liberation through the Plan Jaba and the housewives' factories. Full recognition of what women actually contribute to society in the current century is essential to recover nurturing from the domain of corporate or bureaucratic planning. No one has put the problem of nurturing more succinctly than Melusina Peirce: "Two things women must do somehow, as the conditions not only of the future happiness, progress, and elevation of their sex, but of its bare respectability and morality. 1st. They *must* earn their own living. 2nd. They *must* be organized among themselves."[63] If this is still the best advice to women about how to deal with their traditional work, two huge areas of concern remain, architecture and economics. The three models of home life that have characterized nurturing have also had strong implications for housing design and for economic productivity, as house forms and systems of national accounting have reflected underlying ideas about the nature of home.

Chapter 5

Economics: Getting and Spending

Definitions of essential work and national economic development are still poorly formulated in urbanized societies, and this confusion works to the disadvantage of both women and men. Women suffer the double day, occupational segregation, and unequal pay; men suffer from too much pressure to be breadwinners and from too little family time. Getting and spending money takes up a major part of most adults' lives, yet it often seems an illogical process. Home life is the least understood part of economic activity, although Americans know housing is extremely expensive. To probe more deeply into the question of what the United States can or cannot afford in housing, it is crucial to establish some basic definitions of economic activity—what it is, what it is not, and how it relates to both housework and housing construction. Without such a framework, it is impossible to calculate the costs of any new housing arrangements to the society, to the household, or to the individual.

PAID AND UNPAID WORK

Both neoclassical economists and Marxist economists have overemphasized wage work and rejected household work in their overall definitions of economic productivity, economic growth, and national product. These faulty definitions can be traced to the nineteenth-century doctrine of separate spheres for men and women. At the same time, neoclassical economists and state socialists have taken very different views of housing construction as an economic activity. In the United States, it is viewed as a key sector of production, crucial to stimulating the entire economy, sustaining banks and the real estate industry, creating jobs, and maximizing consumption of cars, appliances, and furnishings. In state socialist countries such as the former USSR, China, and Cuba, an opposite view has prevailed. Housing construction has been seen as resource consumption, and every effort has been made to minimize the use of scarce resources by limiting space in housing units as well as limiting time and money spent on decorative effects and consumer goods. Both calculations of housing construction miss the essential nature of home as a domestic workplace. Whether resource consumption is maximized or minimized, the single most important component in the reproduction of life is a parent's labor.

In 1979, the United Nations released a report that shattered economists' conventional views of labor and economic development: women, the report showed, were performing two-thirds of the world's work hours, counting both paid and unpaid labor. They received only ten percent of the world's wages. And they owned only one percent of the world's property. A similar U.N. report from 1995 stated, "There is an unwitting conspiracy on a global scale to undervalue women's work and contributions to society. If women's work were accurately reflected in national statistics, it would shatter the myth that men are the main breadwinners of the world."[1] Among American political leaders, one of the first to

anticipate these numbers was Cl
tor from Illinois. In 1977, he wro
required American officials to c
statement of the effects of all
women.[2] While both Percy's am
have called attention to women's
world economy, the debates launcl
led to consistent national policies f
izer of the National Congress of Ne
ation of working-class women based
"Why don't we have a Percy Amendi
well as for foreign aid?"[3]

Taking into account both paid and
United States average many more hours of work per week than
men. Economist Ann Markusen states: "Human energy is largely
spent in one of two activities, the production of commodities for
market exchange and the reproduction of labor power." She
explains that production of commodities takes place in "plants,
shops, or offices, where employers hire workers." The reproduction of labor power takes place through government social services, such as schools and hospitals, and through the household.
While cooks, nurses, and other public sector workers involved in
the reproduction of labor power receive wages for their work, just
as commodities production workers do, housewives and mothers
do not. Marriage, according to Markusen, "is an implicit rather
than explicit contract for the exchange and organizational control
of labor power in the household." Women work there, but no
wages change hands. In 2001, Ann Crittenden estimated the cash
value of a full-time housewife's nonmarket labor at over $100,000
per year.[4]

Heidi Hartmann, an economist with a special interest in
women's labor, has argued that we should define the current U.S.
economic situation as a capitalist mode of production harnessed to
a precapitalist, patriarchal structuring of reproduction.[5] Crucial
here are the "family wage" and the family home, both controlled by
men. A man must earn enough to acquire the physical plant, raw
materials, and the labor power necessary for survival—that is, his
home, his groceries, and his wife's unpaid labor time. Most costly
of these is the home, the "plant" where her unpaid labor is used.

a labor contract) represents a very large claim
nergy, when a woman also enters the wage labor
a disadvantaged worker. While men, even childless,
, now expect to receive "family wages," many employ-
e expected to pay women, married or single, with or with-
children, even less than the cost of reproduction of their own
abor power. Most mid-twentieth-century wages for women barely
met subsistence. In 1979, female college graduates averaged less
than male high-school dropouts.[6] By the year 2000, college-edu-
cated women had gained some ground.

Women's earnings have always reflected the ways the "labor of
love" in the home turns into low-paying jobs outside the home.
In 2000, American women earned three-quarters of men's earnings for full-time, year-round work. Why does this wage gap
endure? Occupational segregation historically has relegated
women to specific areas. Jobs requiring traditional "womanly"
skills of homemaking have been rated as unskilled or low-skilled
work. In 1975, a day-care worker was rated in the national
Dictionary of Occupational Titles as less skilled than an attendant
at a dog pound; a nursery school teacher as less skilled than an
attendant at a parking lot. In 1999, a day-care worker still earned
less than an animal caretaker, a manicurist, or a motion picture
projectionist.[7] These stereotypes were reinforced by women's
spatial disadvantages because of the location of their homes.
Home was often the given, with paid work arranged around it.
Women put up with low-paying jobs to gain more flexible schedules or better commuting patterns in order to continue their nonmarket labor of love. Women's cheap, non-union, paid labor has
been much sought after by employers in marginally profitable
industries and in periods of boom, because employers do not
have to commit themselves.[8] Industries can bring in women and
use their labor to maximize the possibilities of expansion when
the economy looks strong, and minimize the disruption of firing
when the economy is weak.

Entrepreneurs have made spectacular profits throughout the
history of American economic development by drawing on women
as a reserve army of labor. Young women staffed the cotton mills of
Waltham and Lowell, which marked the birth of the American corporation in the early nineteenth century. As larger enterprises

began to separate production from administration in the late nineteenth century, central city corporate headquarters developed. The new clerical staff was female. When service industries became important in the twentieth century, again the new workers were predominantly female. As conglomerates and multinational corporations moved their capital from union to nonunion areas in the late twentieth century, they preferred regions of the United States or developing countries where they could count on nonunion, female labor. Robert Goodman, in *The Last Entrepreneurs*, gives numerous examples of local economic development planners who try to attract new industries to their areas by advertising that large numbers of dexterous but docile female workers are available to employers. Or, as one hiring supervisor in a Silicon Valley shop said, "Just three things I look for in hiring: small, foreign, and female. . . . These little foreign gals are grateful to be hired—very, very grateful—no matter what."[9]

GNP AS MEASUREMENT

Men could not be persuaded to sacrifice their days as tireless breadwinners, nor could women be manipulated in and out of the national labor market, unless woman's place was explicitly in the home. American policies on "family wages" for men, homeownership for men, and wage labor as a measure of economic productivity were all developed within the crucial years following 1919. As we have seen, both production and reproduction were restructured around the concept of the single-family detached house. In 1920, the National Bureau of Economic Research (NBER) was chartered in the United States, and its staff began to develop estimates of National Income and National Product. These economists decided to exclude all household work for which no wage was paid. During earlier debates on these issues, in the 1880s and 1890s, distinguished economists such as Richard T. Ely in the United States and Alfred Marshall in England had argued that household production was essential to all national economic calculations.[10] By the 1920s, the NBER economists claimed that a mother's love had no price and should not be counted, a view later reiterated in Paul Samuelson's popular economics textbooks.[11]

As economist William Gauger contended in 1973, "Let's face it. If household work had traditionally been a man's job, it would always have been included in GNP." Gauger pointed out that even the founders of the NBER conceded that there might be two problems resulting from their 1920 decision. First, they noted, "comparisons are thrown askew between communities or classes that differ widely in the proportion of women who work at home and women who work for wages." Second, and most important, they recognized that if more housewives did enter the paid labor force in succeeding decades, and if they produced fewer goods at home—homegrown vegetables, home-cooked foods, and home-made clothes—the amount of useful goods not paid for with money would shrink.[12] Therefore, while national income would appear to grow, the official figures might actually hide a decline in quantity of goods and services produced. The figures might also hide a decline in quality, as homemade bread (not counted) was replaced with Wonderbread (fully counted).

The statistical evidence of steadily increasing female participation in the paid labor force from 1800 to 1920 was available to the men who made this decision. So was the knowledge that women had just achieved the right to vote and were demanding more power in public affairs and more access to jobs previously controlled by men. However, these economists were working in the aftermath of World War I, when many women workers were being laid off. These were the years when manufacturers were hoping to find that "Good homes make contented workers," the years when Mr. Homeowner was supposed to get together with Mrs. Consumer. These economists put female labor force data and female political participation aside, along with all their reservations about bad methodology, and banked on mother love as "priceless" and on "family wages" for men. They could not have made a more serious error.

Between 1920 and 1980, female participation in the paid labor force doubled. GNP became a systematic overestimate of economic growth. Throughout the last half-century, the greatest visible economic gains have occurred in the expansion of consumer goods and services, exactly those that replace women's unpaid labor in the home and are the most impossible to calculate under the present system. Thus, no one has known the real state of the American economy for decades. Some women find it difficult to convince members of their households that the nurturing they do is valuable. At the same time, the struggles of some men to persuade their wives to obtain paid work are also ineffectual because of the mystique of "priceless" love and the reality of low wages for women. Economist Nancy Folbre, in *The Invisible Heart: Economics and Family Values*, has explored the erosion of both unpaid and paid nurturing work in the context of the market. "The quantity and quality of care work can depend heavily on cultural values of love, obligation, and reciprocity—values that are seldom adequately rewarded in the marketplace."[13]

The category of "housewife" as unpaid worker also leads to great confusion about national measurement of unemployment. If women are fired from paid work and discouraged from seeking new employment, they may be listed as housewives rather than as unemployed persons.[14] The phenomenon of the "displaced homemaker" has also shown that the housewife who is divorced or widowed may wind up desperate after a lifetime of unpaid labor. She needs an unemployment benefit but cannot get it.[15] Similarly, housewives are not eligible for Social Security in their own right and for the health and disability benefits given to paid workers. In this respect, it may be noted that the Social Security system, as originally established in the 1930s, was not designed to suit either employed women or the two-earner family.[16] For decades it has provided different types of benefits to an eligible woman as her husband's widow and as an earner in her own right.[17] Only a single woman finds her status the same as a single man. The imbalance between men's and women's benefits should be corrected. Had housewives been contributing to the system from the start, and been receiving more equitable benefits, both the system and the female elderly would now be in better shape.

ECONOMIC EQUITY FOR WOMEN

Failure to analyze the national economic importance of the labor of women has led to wasteful government spending, as well as an inability to predict economic growth or decline. Among the most unwieldy policy areas are transportation planning and housing economics. Each has been saddled with problems attributable to Victorian definitions of male and female activity patterns.

TRANSPORTATION: WOMEN'S JOURNEYS VERSUS MEN'S

In 1981, economist Ann Markusen noted that urban economists have usually studied the male "head of household" to gain statistics about journey-to-work or choices between "work" and "leisure."[18] Elaborate decisions about the most efficient urban locations for public and private investments made exclusively in terms of the male earner could be quite harmful to women and the efficient performance of their economic tasks. Economists' "journey to work" studies of this kind overlooked women twice. First, they ignored the unpaid work done in and around the home and the transportation patterns necessary to accomplish these tasks. Second, they overlooked the fact that married women are also in paid work and that they travel, not only to a paid job, but also to and from day-care facilities on the way to and from the paid job. In the same year, urban sociologist Gerda Wekerle noted that a study on transportation and day care in Paris concluded that "women are subject to daily harassment in trying to coordinate work hours and commuting schedules with the hours of these facilities."[19] Or, as one American mother put it, "I was driving triangles all the time." If the simple male journey from home to job is planned for, and the complex female journey from home to day care to job is ignored, women's time is squandered.

The field of time-space geography has introduced ways to represent women's and men's options graphically, showing the constraints upon mobility imposed by both time and distance in relation to daily tasks.[20] Time-space geography can illuminate the conflict within the two-earner family and lead to better regional studies as well. Markusen has observed that some patterns of urban and regional migration, such as the rehabilitation of older urban neighborhoods and the growth of small cities can also be predicted much more accurately by a two-earner location theory model. The growing areas may be physically or culturally less attractive, but women find they are better able to interweave housework, day care, and paid work because of manageable distances.[21]

Major decisions have also been made about investments in public transportation based on male patterns of movement. Such planning is wasteful if survey money is spent getting only half the picture asking about men's journey to work and then public transit money is spent on the wrong routes. The tendency of planners to disadvantage women workers is compounded by the fact that at the national level, the federal government has preferred to support the automobile industry through the construction of roads rather than to support public transit. The Interstate Highway Act of 1956 initiated a gigantic public works project, and by 1980, one out of seven American workers earned a living building, selling, repairing, insuring, driving, or servicing vehicles and highways. Almost all of these workers were male, so it can be argued that road culture in the United States represents economic development for male workers as well as convenience for drivers. As transportation planner Martin Wachs noted in 1981, "In some households the automobile is simply the man's domain. In many other households, a car is a shared resource, and quite simply it appears that male members of the household have systematically more control over the use of that resource." At that time, Wachs found that about three-quarters of the miles driven in the U.S. were driven by men, and while men made the majority of their auto trips as drivers, women made the majority as passengers. Wachs noted that when suburban women were drivers, they made over 11 percent of their trips solely to serve another passenger. That is, they were providing the transit service that planners had chosen not to offer.[22]

Transportation planner Sandra Rosenbloom reported major changes in women's travel by 1990. Women aged 16 to 64 were driving 51.5 percent more miles annually than in 1983, while men were driving only 14.5 percent more miles. The one-car family was no longer viable. Women over 65 had increased their mileage just as much as younger women. Rosenbloom argued that the increased involvement of women in the paid labor force was behind these higher numbers, as was the suburbanization of homes and jobs. She also argued that the need for women to care for frail elderly as well as their own families was increasing their miles.[23]

Jane Holtz has described the United States as an "Asphalt Nation," where road building interests are allied with car manufacturers. Still, many American women have found car culture attractive, as planner Edith Perlman reminded us, "Once at the wheel, any boy could pretend he was a man. And any girl could pretend she was a boy." The automobile assisted women in their search for a spacious and private life in suburbia, although Perlman noted that it took women "a generation to discover that space meant loneliness, and privacy, privation." Meanwhile women were finding roles in the driver's seat: "There was superWife, on her way to execute half a dozen household errands. There was superMom, trundling the children to various enrichments. For the less domesticated, there were superBitch and superWhore, all played by Elizabeth Taylor with the top down. Most recently there has been superMs., racing toward a job whose salary maintains her smart little roadster." Still, Perlman maintained that women were losers: the automobile "requires and supports a detached life that isolates families from other families; the act of riding itself, with its grim, face-forward configuration, isolates members of the family even from each other."[24]

While transportation planners have often used women, explicitly or implicitly, to provide services for men and children, they have not always used transport planning to provide services for women. In 1981, Wachs cited a New York State study (excluding New York City) showing that four times as many women as men used transit for the journey to paid work. He also showed that in locations as diverse as Seattle, Washington, Davenport, Iowa, and Hicksville, New York, between two-thirds and four-fifths of all bus trips were made by women.[25] Women's job choices and hours were limited by their reliance on bad public transit. Both sociologist Helena Lopata and Wachs have emphasized the special problems car culture creates for the female elderly.[26] They are even less likely than younger women to have access to cars, and may endure extreme isolation. The even more ominous spatial consequence of female dependence on transit was underlined by Wachs: "most assaults on women which are committed by persons who are not acquainted with the victim do occur in relatively deserted public places, when the victim is travelling or waiting to travel."[27] Across the country, transportation policy will continue to disadvantage female workers and increase women's vulnerability to assault unless women's travel patterns are fully integrated into transport planning.

The difficulty of dislodging old ideas can be illustrated by the experience of Sandra Rosenbloom, a nationally known expert in transportation planning. In 1977, she was asked by the Department of Transportation in Washington to organize a major conference on the effects of transportation policy on American women, to examine the ways in which women's needs were not being met by current programs. Since millions of dollars had already been spent for research on the "head of household's" choices that revolved around men's journeys, Rosenbloom had high hopes for the importance of the conference.

Then Senator William Proxmire, the Wisconsin Democrat, decided that Professor Rosenbloom was an ideal candidate for his Golden Fleece award, given to those projects he considered to be fleecing the public treasury. Proxmire considered it extremely funny that anyone could possibly see differences between men and women in their relationship to buses, subways, and highways.[28] A senior HUD official, Donna Shalala, rushed to Proxmire's office to explain that women actually did use public transit two or three times more often than men. The Golden Fleece was given to someone else. But the problem remains. Many public officials still believe in an ideal of a good city and a good society that has nothing to do with women's active involvement. If they believe that a woman's place is in the home, any urban research or urban program that involves women's labor or women's independent movement in the city seems peculiar and unnecessary.

HOUSING CONSTRUCTION AND JOBS

During most of the twentieth century, the construction of single-family detached houses has provided benefits to banks, developers, and construction workers. Publicly supported housing has had a similar role. Often American trade union leaders have favored public housing as a source of jobs for their members, workers in the construction trades, but they have showed little concern for the prospective residents of the projects, who were often people of color and women. These residents were excluded from most apprentice and training programs in the trades that benefited from constructing the housing. A few examples of tenants and neighborhood residents turning their lives around through construction suggest the potential for counting residents as producers of housing and neighborhoods, not just consumers.

Sweat Equity for Tenents

"There are three utilities in New York—Con Ed, Brooklyn Union Gas, and 519 East 11th Street," boasted one organizer at 519 East 11th Street.[29] At this building, also known as the Solar Tenement, the urban homesteading approach to the problems of inner-city housing was developed in 1974 by Rabbit Nazario, Ruth Garcia, Travers Price, Michael Freedberg, and other architects and community organizers. They were concerned about the abandonment of 30,000 units of deteriorated housing every year by landlords in New York City. They determined to turn the situation around and create a model of cooperative homeownership by tenants whose labor on the rehabilitation of a tenement would be their only capital investment. The project involved training local male residents in construction skills, as well as experimenting with new technologies to create demonstrations of solar and wind energy. In the neighborhood, the residents of 519 also developed a community garden called El Sol Brillante on five vacant lots. When they lacked fertilizer, ingenuity brought them to Ringling Brothers' circus, where they found free elephant manure. On the Lower East Side of New York, they raised a first crop of peanuts and sent some to the White House in the Carter administration as a public relations gesture.

While the phrases "urban homesteading" and "sweat equity" have entered the vocabulary of many planners, and new projects have been developed in Chicago, Hartford, Oakland, Cleveland, Boston, and Springfield, Massachusetts, the sweat equity approach is time consuming. Freedberg noted that dealing with municipal bureaucracies in the cumbersome process of loan packaging and building rehabilitation "remains a deterrent to all but the most determined homesteaders."[30] And while the novelties of wind generation and elephant manure kept up organizers' spirits, constant external obstacles generated internal management problems. So did starting with abandoned buildings that landlords had run down by avoiding maintenance costs and taking tax deprecia-

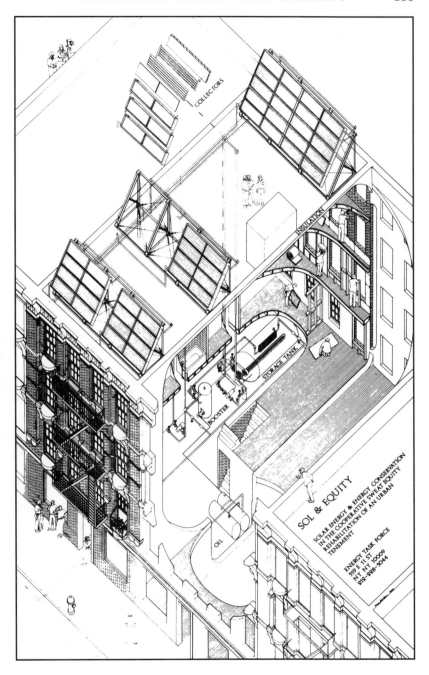

5.1 The Solar Tenement, 519 East 11th Street, New York, New York.

tions. Yet there were eleven new cooperative owners at 519, a neighborhood park, and a number of men with better jobs in the construction trades. Twenty-five years later, in 2001, the Solar Tenement is still a low-income limited equity cooperative. Although they are not using solar technology, the community garden is still in existence.

The Solar Tenement demonstration project was the basis for a new program in New York City, the Tenant Interim Lease (TIL) Program, that has resulted in the rehabilitation of thousands of units. Tenants are trained in building management by the Urban Homesteading Assistance Board, and can then buy their buildings from the city, which also helps pay for physical rehabilitation.[31] Jacqueline Leavitt and Susan Saegert documented successful groups of Harlem tenants in their book, *From Abandonment to Hope*. "That poor black older women and men were in the forefront," they noted, "... is generally ignored in the development of most low-income housing policy."[32]

Jobs on Site in Housing for Single Parents

For women and men to be both paid workers and parents, it is helpful, and perhaps necessary, to overcome the physical separation of paid jobs and parenting in urban and suburban settings. Two projects, one from England and one from Rhode Island, demonstrate how this can be accomplished. Both offer supports for poor women and single parents.

Nina West, a housewife and mother in London, England, was divorced in the early 1960s. She did not know how she could possibly support her young children and take care of them at the same time. She had no alimony or child support, and did not want welfare. She did not know how to find day care, housing, and a job, let alone find all three together. She was a typical single parent, a decade and a half before single parents constituted a substantial proportion of households.

Nina West recognized the economic and social dimensions of her predicament, as well as the personal ones. She tackled the problem of bridging private life and paid employment in her creation of a pioneering housing project. She began with a small building including several apartments and a day-care center serv-

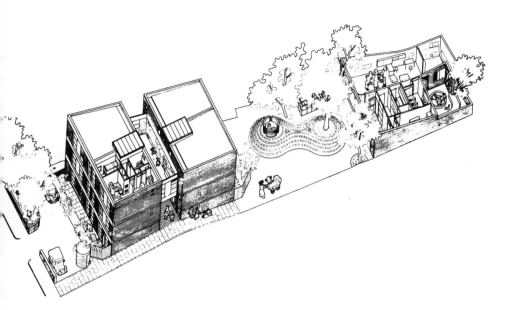

5.2 Nina West Homes, designed by Sylvester Bone for single parents and their children, London, England, 1972, axonometric drawing. The child-care center is at the back of the site on the ground level; the corridor between apartments also serves as a children's play area. Kitchen windows offer easy observation of the corridor, and intercoms link units for easier babysitting.

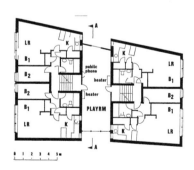

5.3 Nina West Homes, plan of housing units and corridor used as playroom.

5.4 Nina West Homes, plan of child-care center.

ing the entire neighborhood. Single parents (male or female) could occupy the housing, use the child care to free themselves for paid employment, and in some cases, even find suitable employment in the center itself. She had built a bridge between private and public life.

As her first project provided a successful base for single parents, Nina West began to expand her operations. She bought more small buildings in different locations around London and organized them in the same way. She received state support and charitable contributions. Ultimately, she was able to hire an architect, Sylvester Bone, and build a new building with twelve apartments. Fiona House, opened in 1972, offered many design features to help single parents. The interior corridors doubled as playrooms, with carpeted floors and windows from each apartment looking in, so that a parent cooking could watch a child at play. Intercoms linked apartments, enabling parents to baby-sit for each other by turning on the intercom and listening for children crying. By 1980, Nina West had several other projects under construction, and visitors from many parts of the world were studying her operations. When she died in 1988, her programs continued. By 2001, Nina West's twelve housing projects had been taken over by a larger nonprofit housing group, and the four nurseries she started were still running.[33]

West's success represented several significant advances over earlier projects. First, she recognized that single parents were usually very poor. All of her housing units were tiny by American standards—efficiencies or one-bedroom apartments. But they were a realistic response to the poverty of single parents. Second, West argued that the residents would have to find a market for their services in the neighborhood if they intended to establish new jobs on their housing site. This attempt to generate both jobs and housing controlled by women gave West an economic base most housing providers lacked. The collective houses discussed in chapter 4 did have day-care programs, but they never thought of asking residents to work there. West did begin to get extensive state support for her housing services in the 1970s. Although she was able to replicate her original project, it did not offer a permanent community to its residents. It helped them to make an economic transition over one or two years' time, but after that, residents were expected to seek jobs on their own and other housing of a traditional kind.

The Women's Development Corporation

An American experiment took West's approach one step further. In the 1970s, Architects Joan Forrester Sprague, Katrin Adam, and Susan Aitcheson founded a successful summer school for women students in architecture and urban planning from all over the United States. All three felt the need to work closely with low-income urban women, many of them single parents, in order to develop an economic and spatial program that would meet women's needs. They called their project Housing with Economic Development, and their organization the Women's Development Corporation. For six years, they prepared the project while working at other jobs.

They started operations in 1978 in the inner-city area of Elmwood in Providence, Rhode Island. They made connections with numerous church and community organizations, as well as with city, state, and national agencies. They surveyed run-down housing and located ten residential buildings suitable for rehabilitation. They examined commercial spaces and discussed the problems of sustaining local small businesses with economic development experts. They established an informal day-care network so that women could come to meetings, and began training women in self-help.

In a community with 10 percent Hispanic, 25 percent white, 40 percent black, and 25 percent Laotian households, they found that over half the households were headed by single, widowed, or divorced women. Most of these households were living below poverty level. Yet, as Sprague noted, the women had distinctive skills. The Hmong women from Laos could create magnificent handicrafts but had few markets for them. Another local woman ran tours by bus from Providence to New York but did not see herself as a potential travel agent until the organizers suggested this. Others wanted to be trained as building maintenance workers and construction workers.

Slowly the Women's Development Corporation found a constituency in Providence. By 1980, 225 women were registered as participants in the program, many of them single parents in their twenties, with one to eight children. Twelve women became active in the housing program, intending to rehabilitate buildings and make them small limited-equity housing cooperatives owned by residents. The residents would be able to pay the monthly charges because they had established new jobs and new small businesses (through a Small Business Administration training program) to revitalize a nearby commercial street. By 1983, the project was focused on rental housing with a mix of new construction and reha- bilitation, drawing on federal support and local corporate cospon- sorship. Practical success along these lines meant postponing their earlier, more ambitious scheme to generate a mix of traditional and nontraditional jobs, from beauty culture and needlework to con- struction work. However, they built on a broader base of econom- ic activities than Nina West's child-care center, and actively con- tested the gender segregation in the well-paid construction trades by establishing jobs for women as builders and developers. They extended their economic activities into the community, contribut- ing to a larger urban revitalization project by giving attention to a declining commercial street.

The Women's Development Corporation struggled against women's problems in obtaining housing and jobs simultaneously, and emphasized economic self-sufficiency and long-term physical rehabilitation of the neighborhood. They moved from identifying single parents' need for safe and affordable housing to creating a program for social reconstruction as a result of their substantial experience in community organizing and building. They developed a project which could be replicated in rural areas as well as urban areas. As they said, "Many women need reinforcement, support, and a chance to plan positively for their own and their children's futures."[34] Joan Sprague went on to win a national planning award for her 1991 book, *More than Housing: Lifeboats for Women and Children*, dealing with designs for emergency, transitional, and per- manent housing for women and children across the United States.[35]

COUNTING WITH WOMEN IN MIND

These examples of struggles for economic equity and spatial rein- tegration suggest the ways Americans might begin to reevaluate planning and housing budgets. A standard for evaluation must be:

Does a particular economic arrangement reward all the men and women who participate in it? One can also ask: Does a housing program recognize a community's energy resources and job training needs? Does a housing or job program support full economic recognition for traditional homemaking skills, and does it develop new skills and capabilities the society will reward? Most of all, one must ask if a housing or job program diminishes the double day, or if, in its basic definitions of separate spheres of "home" and "work," it denies that many paid workers are parents, and that most parents are paid workers.

When economic equity and spatial reintegration have been accepted as complementary approaches to economic planning, a society can move beyond the conventions of gender embedded in traditional patterns of housing and consumption. Economist Nancy Folbre has established five guiding principles:

1. Reject claims that women should be more altruistic than men, either in the home or in society as a whole.
2. Defend family values against the corrosive effects of self-interest.
3. Confront the difficulties of establishing democratic governance in families, communities, countries, and the world as a whole.
4. Aim for a kinder and wiser form of economic development.
5. Develop and strengthen ways of rewarding the work of care.[36]

To realize such an economic program is a major challenge. However, female workers and their families constitute a majority of American citizens, a large group of people who will find it to their advantage to consider these issues.

Chapter 6

Architecture: Roof, Fire, and Center

The house forms of tribal societies dazzle the world traveler with ingenious responses to the challenge of building for various sites, climates, and household types. Jungle houses on stilts near the upper Amazon, three-story adobe complexes of the pueblos in New Mexico, white-rimmed cave dwellings of the fishermen of Southern Morocco, tall wind-scoop houses of Hyderabad in India, dark, arching Bedouin tents, turf-insulated Mongolian yurts, all are the work of skillful builders. The women and men who constructed them exploited the potential of sun and wind, and made maximum use of reeds, ice, mud, rock, clay, goat hair, or grass. House forms reveal the varied marriage and kinship patterns of pre-industrial societies. The long houses of the Iroquois accommodate many firesides consisting of a woman and her children. The circular dwellings of the Hakka represent an Asian communal tradition. The painted tipis of the Kiowa communicate hierarchies in a nomadic culture. The compounds of the Yoruba enclose the patriarchal lineage. The high thresholds of the Han courtyards keep evil spirits and strangers from joining the extended family. The high-walled houses and carved doors of Muslim Lamu enforce purdah, the traditional seclusion of women. Each of these designs encompasses a web of economic arrangements: through the organization of space they reinforce people's relationships to land, tools, rooms, animals, fire, food, and each other.

Vernacular house forms are economic diagrams of the reproduction of the human race. They are also aesthetic essays on the meaning of life within a particular culture, its joys and travails, its superstitions and stigmas. House forms cannot be separated from their physical and social contexts. One cannot imagine a pueblo in Alaska or an igloo in the Amazon Basin any more than one can conceive of an Iroquois woman living in a house designed for purdah. These climatic and cultural connections are all the stronger because in the pre-industrial world, house and household goods are a unity. The cooking vessels, the rugs, the doors, and the beds—all reflect the inhabitants' fears, desires, rituals, and taboos, entwined with the experiences of heat, cold, hunger, feasting, marriage, birth, and death.

In industrial societies, humans retain a strong desire to own a piece of land, a house, and meaningful household objects in order to communicate, to themselves and to others, just who they are and how they wish to be treated. Unfortunately, ordering the domestic sphere in an urbanized society is no longer always so direct an expression of personality or culture. The processes of making pots, weaving rugs, praying for rain, or dancing for good harvests have given way to the act of purchasing art as a commodity in an art gallery, and the process of building a dwelling has given way to purchasing mass-produced space through a realtor. The design and production of most residential space in the United States is handled by speculative developers, although sometimes developers hire architects to help them make aesthetic decisions. As a result of treating housing space as a commodity, residents' uncertainty about the meaning of roof, fire, and center is profound—as profound as the ambivalence about home, mom, and apple pie. The transition from vernacular house forms to modern housing has left everyone, architects included, confused about styles, periods, places, and cultural symbols. The aesthetic confusion and the familial confusion compound each other, and neither can be unraveled without the other.

THREE MODELS OF HOME TRANSLATED INTO BUILT FORM

When nineteenth-century theorists generated three schematic models of how home life might be developed in industrial society, they also generated three schematic building programs for housing types, strongly related to three architectural styles. The haven strategy produced the program for the detached, single-family suburban house treated as a primitive, sacred hut. The industrial strategy produced the program for high-rise mass housing treated as an efficient machine for collective consumption. The neighborhood strategy produced the program for low-rise, multifamily housing treated as a village with shared commons, courtyards, arcades, and kitchens. The earliest formulations of the haven strategy and the industrial strategy required constant revision in the twentieth century. They evolved as models of family life with many borrowings from each other and from the neighborhood strategy. In the same way, basic programmatic deficiencies in the sacred hut model or the efficient machine model for housing were soon apparent. Architects, urban planners, and builders began to copy each other's materials and details. Primitive hut buildings were realized with machine-aesthetic materials. Mass-consumption buildings were trimmed with primitive half-timbering. The designers of both kinds of projects also borrowed the rhetoric of the neighborhood strategy to declare that they "freed women for modern life" or that they offered "an unsurpassed sense of community," although this rarely meant that they included significant, shared social services or spaces.

A building program is the implicit or explicit statement of spatial requirements to be fulfilled within the constraints of available sites, budgets, and technologies. It can be simple or elaborate, but it will usually define the building type (such as detached one-family house, or thirty-unit apartment house) and the intended activities such as eating, sleeping, or parking the car. A program will also usually specify what kinds of spaces are to be provided for these activities, such as kitchen, dining room, bedroom, or garage; how large these spaces must be; and what sorts of natural or artificial light and mechanical systems are necessary. At the same time that the building program conveys the economic, social, and technical requirements for built space, the architectural style chosen for a building conveys the cultural requirements. The choice of style may be made by the client or by the designer—it can be as enduring as any religious dogma or as fleeting as high fashion.

The one thing that architectural style cannot do is transform the building program. So if the basic social model of home is outdated, or the basic economic model of home is not appropriate, then architectural design cannot save the situation. Architects cannot make outmoded family etiquette modern; they cannot make false economic definitions of market and nonmarket work equitable. Because architectural style and building program represent form and content (or, if you will, cultural superstructure and material base), architectural styles and building programs often conflict in industrial societies. Architectural fashions fail to convince when the program is inappropriate.

Few housing experts acknowledge this. Urban planners and social scientists have tended to divide the content and form of housing by focusing almost exclusively on programmatic analysis and treating aesthetics as irrelevant. Architects and art historians have tended to conflate content and form by focusing on the aesthetic analysis of design and subsuming the program under this formal discussion. Because program and style have often been analyzed as unrelated parts of a shelter planning problem, or as identical aspects of a housing design solution, contemporary practitioners in architecture and urban planning often sound confused.

The architectural historian Kenneth Frampton has written that modern architects, since the Enlightenment, have wavered between rationalism and piety, between the geometric utopias of a designer such as Ledoux and the piety of a Gothic revivalist such as Pugin: "In its efforts to transcend the division of labor and the harsh realities of industrial production and urbanization, bourgeois culture has oscillated between the extremes of totally planned and industrialized utopias on the one hand, and, on the other, a denial of the actual historical reality of machine production."[1] For all their aesthetic differences, Pugin and Ledoux shared a nineteenth-century commitment to separate spheres for men and women, and to a male double standard of female conduct. Ledoux, after all, had temples to both virgins and prostitutes in his ideal city. Such romantic views of gender underlie the designers' predicament: most modern practitioners have been unable to develop more subtle definitions of private and public domains. Thus housing is the great missed opportunity for the design professions in the last century. Under every modern economic and political system, most architects have failed to understand the social programming and the aesthetic complexities essential to the production of space for modern family life. They have, instead, tended to follow Beecher or Bebel, seeing women as pre-industrial hearth tenders, or as industrial wage workers identical to men. As architectural critic Ada Louise Huxtable has put it, "Housing remains architecture's and society's chief unsolved problem."[2]

THE HAVEN STRATEGY: THE SINGLE-FAMILY HOUSE AS PRIMITIVE SACRED HUT

For many Europeans, and for many settlers in North America who came from Europe, the archetypal house is a hut with a peaked roof, a strong door, and small windows to resist snow, wind, and rain. The house may be constructed of wood, if it is near a forest; or stone, if it is near a quarry. One large hearth provides a warm, bright place, the center of nurturing activity. The archetype can be elaborated in its English, French, German, Scandinavian, and American versions. As *ham, domus, bauen,* or log cabin, the image has been analyzed, romanticized, sanctified, psychoanalyzed, celebrated, and copied, a process traced with great wit and insight by geographer Kathleen Ann Mackie. In her intellectual history of the ideal of home, she notes that home distinguishes "familiarity from strangeness, security from insecurity, certainty from doubt, order from chaos, comfort from adventure, settlement from wandering, here from away."[3]

Clare Cooper and Carl Jung see the house as a symbol of self.[4] Lord Raglan, Martin Heidegger, Mircea Eliade, and Francesco Dal Co all contend that building a dwelling involves the construction of a temple and a world view.[5] Joseph Rykwert showed that Adam and Eve's house in paradise provided an archetype for many architects' endeavors.[6] John Brinckerhoff Jackson brought to life the "westward-moving house" as an image of the expansion of the United States.[7] For Adrienne Rich, "protection is the genius of your house," and many of her best poems explore the archetype.[8]

When any culture clings to a rural house type—the sacred hut—rather than devising a successful urban house type, it remains a culture of people trying to be farmers and rejecting city life. Americans have preferred the single-family farm on the Jeffersonian grid to the New England Puritan farm village. Many Americans still earned a living on the family farm before 1950. Their descendants have struggled to keep the sacred hut alive: in mass suburbia, in the affluent classes' search for colonial farmhouses as second homes, and in the hippie fondness for building

6.1 House as primitive shelter: John Curry and wife in front of their sod house, near West Union, Custer County, Nebraska, 1886, the agricultural precedent for the suburban architecture of gender. (Nebraska State Historical Society)

primitive shelters. However pervasive the nostalgic attachment to rural house types, this is not a fully conscious, political choice. The aesthetic disjunction between the pre-industrial ideal of sacred hut and the reality of housing in the United States is very poorly understood, and therefore Americans still crave gratification from single-family dwellings that no architect or builder can possibly provide.

Early settlers lived in wigwams, sod houses, dugouts, log cabins, and a variety of crude structures they generally were eager to replace. *The Bark Covered House* is one American's account of upward mobility achieved in Michigan through clearing the land, building a log cabin, and then building, over time, two more substantial frame dwellings.[9] Settlers did not cherish the memory of the crude shelters, at least not until they were ensconced in something more comfortable. By the early nineteenth century, when the Greek Revival became a popular style for farmhouses as well as public buildings, the builders of New England and the midwest created some of the most austere and beautiful structures in America, with roof lines defining a pediment, and delicate, wooden, geometric ornament displaying their skill and taste. Sketches of such farmhouses often appeared in atlases of various counties, testaments to their owners' success and the builders' sensitivities.

ECLECTIC STYLES

By the 1840s, suburban development around Eastern cities leaned to Gothic Revival, guided by Downing's and Beecher's books, because this style was thought to enhance the sacredness of home. Downing sought spiritual connectedness in picturesque suburban landscaping and provided Gothic cottages to suit any budget; Beecher put three crosses on the roof line of her house, as well as numerous altarlike spaces inside, just so that no one could miss her point about woman's role as "minister" in the "home church of Jesus Christ."[10] In the last third of the nineteenth century, a series of other styles became popular. French Mansard, Italianate, Queen Anne, Romanesque Revival, and even Egyptian Revival competed with Gothic; eventually Colonial Revival created the greatest enthusiasm in the early twentieth century. In this eclectic scene, only the housewife performing the sacred rites of cooking and cleaning remained constant to sanctify the home church.

In the twentieth century, architects began to challenge these eclectic, ornamented styles and attempted to produce modern architecture, but they kept the old rituals intact and, in some cases, even tried to add to them. For many architects, Frank Lloyd Wright, designer of prairie houses and author of manifestos on organic architecture, represents the best of modern design. He explored horizontal lines, flowing spaces, and functional interests such as sliding partitions and single surface workspaces in kitchens (earlier developer by Beecher). Yet Wright's Affleck House of 1938 returns to the forms of the German peasant's cottage of 1750. Wright reproduced the "Lord's Corner," or Herrgottswinkel, almost exactly as the superstitious peasant patriarchs would have built it: a cult corner next to the dining table where the householder sits as head, with his sons and male servants on the high-backed bench next to the wall, and his wife, daughters, and female servants on the backless bench next to the kitchen (nearer to the stove and better able to serve the food).[11] While Wright described the Affleck House as an uncluttered, informal area for modern living, the pre-industrial religious orientation helped the businessman preside at home.

ELECTRIFICATION

In her scathing, witty book, *The Home*, published in 1902, Charlotte Perkins Gilman asked, "By what art, what charm, what miracle has the twentieth century preserved, alive, the prehistoric squaw?"[12] The answer was, by taking attention away from program and focusing on style. Home economists and household engineers soon attempted to provide a more modern answer, to sweep the sacred hut into the twentieth century with the magical power of technology. Cooking with electricity, first illustrated as harnessing the force of lightning bolts in an alchemist's laboratory in the late nineteenth century, was tamed into an aesthetic of single-purpose appliance consumption by the 1930s. The architectural competition for "The House of Modern Living," or the house for Mr. and Mrs. Bliss, sponsored by *Architectural Forum* and General Electric

in the Depression era, celebrated the traditional nuclear family—
the father an engineer, the mother a college graduate in home economics, two children, one boy, and one girl—and showed how
electricity could transform their domestic lives. The winner incorporated thirty-two different electrical appliances in his design,
every one made by General Electric, including radio, electric
iron, mixer, waffle iron, coffee maker, stove, refrigerator, dish-
washer, air-conditioner, sun lamp, razor blade sharpener, and curl-
ing iron.[13] The aesthetic for modern living with electricity was, in
the first-prize winner, streamlined modern with a flat roof, but the
judges had no single strong position about architectural style or
the cultural meanings attached to it. In the second-prize house
the force of modern technology inhabited a Cape Cod colonial
with dormers.

Whatever the facade, electricity gave modern man a way out of
household chores: Mrs. Bliss does all her own housework, the
architectural program stated. "She actually enjoys the work."
While the unfortunate word, "actually," failed to convince, the
competition organizers quickly followed up with a most effective
advertising slogan: "Electricity is her servant." Housewife as home
minister had divine power working for her.

By the time the Levitts grappled with the aesthetics of the
sacred hut in Levittown in the late 1940s, almost all of the serious
aesthetic and spiritual dilemmas about the suburban tract house
had been resolved for them by the formulas of architects, household engineers, and corporate marketing experts. The Levitts had
only to deliver the cultural and architectural package more effectively than the competition, which they did, and then to contend
with the gasps of horror that ensued because of the awesome,
urban scale of their mass production of rural, sacred huts. The les-
sons of GE were not lost on the Levitts; a washing machine was
provided as part of the standard equipment with each identical
house in the first Levittown.[14] True to Downing's view of suburban
landscaping as an essentially religious process, the modified Cape
Cod houses sat on sacred ground fenced with white pickets. An
additional refinement was achieved in a later development, when
Levitt not only supplied television as a standard item, but also built
it into the living-room wall so that it qualified as an integral part of
the house that could be financed on the mortgage.[15] Next to the

hearth, the bright eye of the screen reassured both children and adults that the new physical community of the mass-produced sacred huts was redeemed by the magical electronic community created by national television.

Following Levitt's example, the tracts grew and the tract builders prospered into the twenty-first century. Choice for consumers was a superficial stylistic one of eclectic facades on close-to-identical houses with close-to-identical appliances. Fads came and went. The average size of new houses doubled between 1950 and 1975. Many critics got tired of berating suburbia for its stylistic blandness; it became acceptable to praise it as "popular culture," or at least let it pass as good enough for the blue-collar inhabitant. One professor of architecture surveyed homeowners in two American subdivisions near Buffalo, New York, and reported that they preferred tract houses in nostalgic styles, such as Midwestern farmhouse with porch, English Tudor house with half-timbering, Western Ranch house with fieldstone chimney, Mediterranean house with archways, or colonial American with brick front and end chimneys. This research, funded by the National Endowment for the Arts, was not much more far reaching than most tract developers' marketing surveys, since the researcher concluded that "builders are providing a viable range of home styles."[16]

A more critical assessment of the suburban aesthetic was offered by Tom Wolfe in *From Bauhaus to Our House*, but like many other high-culture critics, he sneered at both the blue-collar residents, for their kitschy taste, and the white-collar architects who had failed to enlighten them about greater aesthetic joys. The architects, he claimed, were fools twice over: once for accepting European definitions of a "non-bourgeois" modern machine aesthetic, and twice for trying to apply it in competition with speculative private-home builders in the United States context. As Wolfe put it, there was no need for anyone to get interested in low-cost housing, especially multifamily housing, since there was no constituency for it: "The workers . . . bought houses with pitched roofs and shingles and clapboard siding, with no structure expressed if there was any way around it, with gaslight-style front-porch lamps and mailboxes set up on lengths of stiffened chain that seemed to defy gravity—the more cute and antiquey touches, the better—and they loaded these houses with 'drapes' such as baffled all description and wall-to-wall carpet you could lose a shoe in, and they put barbecue pits and fish-ponds with concrete cherubs urinating into them on the lawn out back, and they parked the Buick Electras out front and had Evinrude cruisers up on two trailers in the carport just beyond the breeze-way."[17]

This is the image that Bill Owens' documentary photographs in *Suburbia* give us also, but with irony to replace Wolfe's disdain. Owens shows the failure of suburban spaces to reflect cultural diversity—black and Asian families and white ethnic families struggle with the same ersatz "Colonial" styles and furnishings.[18] Owens and Wolfe both observe that American women and men have to assemble their interior home decor from a range of machine-made products. What is most disconcerting is that these are all advertised as luxury goods but designed for rapid obsoles-cence. In earlier times American women made handsome quilts and painted stencil decorations on their walls and floors, but today's American housewife faces synthetic materials, all simulat-ing something more expensive: wallpaper resembling bamboo, linoleum resembling ceramic tile, plastic paneling resembling wood. It is her job to confront the interior of the badly designed suburban home (or urban apartment) and make it homelike. Her husband's job is usually to maintain the exterior of the house and the car under similar stresses, also caused by poor design: shoddy building and unrealistic automotive styling. Only the yard will respond well to care; it often becomes the focus of one or both partners' attention, the essential connection to nature, the green justification for the design failures around it.

Denise Scott Brown and Robert Venturi were kinder to subur-bia in their aesthetic appraisal, *Signs of Life*, a Renwick exhibit. They took gaslights and cherubs, Sears' Chippendale and Caldor's Colonial Revival seriously, and dissected them semiotically as meaningful objects, carrying archetypal messages.[19] Yet, like Wolfe, they missed the point: consumer choices of mass-produced, machine-made goods cannot carry the same aesthetic meanings as the houses and household objects made by the inhabitants of a pre-industrial folk culture who have not experienced the commodifica-tion of land, house, and household goods.

MANUFACTURED HOUSING

If electricity was used to give the sacred hut a new magic and acceptability in the 1920s and 1930s, the current development likely to prolong the program for the single-family dwelling is the industrially produced mobile home, renamed "manufactured housing." These boxes make suburbia look warm, personal, generous, and human in comparison. Mobile homes derive from Conestoga Wagons and gypsy wagons; the idea of living on the road was first popularized with the introduction of the automobile and survives in recreation vehicles (RVs) and the many institutions their owners have founded, from snow-bird parks and CB networks to Good Samaritan Clubs on the road. Yet most mobile homes now move only once. Many manufacturers saw in the mobile home the legal and economic possibilities for cheap shelter, financed on the installment plan like an automobile, and designed to standards lower than local building or zoning codes might have permitted for regular tract housing. The vagaries of the construction trades could be bypassed in the factory; so could some of the rules made by planning boards and mortgage bankers. Choice of styles expanded. The industry grew, until in 1999 an astonishing 20 percent of new single-family dwellings were mobile homes.[20]

Companies offer pop-up roof lines, pop-out bay windows, decorative door treatments, double-wide units made by joining two mobile homes, and similar modifications to make the basic metal box look less like a freight car and more like a sacred hut. Today manufactured housing comes in Colonial, Tudor, Mediterranean, and every other style, just like tract houses. While the walls are thin, a full line of appliances can be installed. Manufactured housing represents a final attempt to miniaturize the Victorian gentleman's suburban villa, with dimensions far more cramped than Levittown. Increasingly, local planning authorities are pressured by some residents to permit more mobile home parks and also to accept mobile homes as second units on existing sites. The elderly may want to live next to their children's houses; the mobile home (in one case soberly renamed "The Elder Cottage") offers a quick way to increase suburban densities at lower cost.[21] But cheap shelter does not have to be shoddy or kitschy: the manufactured box exploits the assembly line to prolong the problems of inadequate architecture and neighborhood planning.

HIGH-PRICED, HIGH-TECH, AND HIGH-CULTURE HUTS

While mobile homes are often purchased by the working class, even the wealthy can make themselves uncomfortable, given the confusion about the aesthetics of housing. Those who buy large tracts of land and enormous houses may suit their personal tastes in ways that mass production cannot. But rather than achieving some elegant personal space, many have paid for the emperor's new clothes. This is not an entirely new phenomenon. Henry James commented on the conspicuous consumption of the owners of "ample villas" in eclectic styles in the New Jersey suburbs in *The American Scene* in 1904: "It would have rested on the cold-blooded critic, doubtless, to explain why the crudity of wealth did strike him with so direct a force . . . nothing but the scale of the houses and their candid look of having cost as much as they knew how. Unmistakably they all proclaimed it—they would have cost still more had the way but been shown them; and, meanwhile, they added as with one voice, they would take a fresh start as soon as ever it should be. 'We are only installments, symbols, stopgaps,' they practically admitted, and with no shade of embarrassment; 'expensive as we are, we have nothing to do with continuity, responsibility, transmission, and don't in the least care what becomes of us after we have served our present purpose.'"[22] James concluded that large new houses for newly rich clients, looming in bright green grassy lots next to the road, symbolized business success at the expense of both privacy and community, "in such conditions there could not be any manners to speak of...the basis of privacy was somehow wanting for them."[23]

Thorstein Veblen also condemned the trappings of eclectic late-nineteenth-century domestic display: "The canon of beauty requires expression of the generic. The 'novelty' due to the demands of conspicuous waste traverses this canon of beauty, in that it results in making the physiognomy of our objects of taste a congeries of idiosyncrasies. . . . It would be extremely difficult to find a modern civilized residence or public building which can claim anything better than relative inoffensiveness in the eyes of anyone who will dissociate the elements of beauty from those of honorific waste."[24] Yet Robert Woods Kennedy, in his influential book of the 1950s, *The House and the Art of Its Design,* recommended that designers promote the "honorific waste" that James and Veblen so deplored. Kennedy argued that, as an architect, it was his job to provide houses that helped his clients to indulge in status-conscious consumption, and he showed how to display the housewife "as a sexual being" as well as how to display the family's possessions "as proper symbols of socio-economic class," claiming that both forms of expression were essential to modern family life.[25] He thereby evaded the problem the architectural profession needs to solve. Then, as now, while architects are not responsible for the overwhelming majority of housing units constructed by builders, they are responsible for accepting or rejecting the basic program for housing presented to them by those clients they do have. And they are responsible for the values they express when speaking about the goals of good design to each other and to their students, as well as to their clients and the general public.

At the start of the twenty-first century, single-family houses designed by many fashionable architects reflect a rather academic approach to the question of how to dwell. Rather than attempting to expand the sacred-hut program or alter the context, many architects have strained to enhance the experience of dwelling with images of the sacred, the arcane, the difficult. Other designers have embraced the engineering tradition. Buckminster Fuller's Dymaxion house of 1927, suspended on a mast off the ground, and his Wichita house of 1944, were for decades the definitive statement of the machine aesthetic applied to the sacred-hut program. In the 1970s Stanley Tigerman updated this fantasy. His futuristic "house that thinks for itself" incorporated home computers and robotized carts to execute many household functions. Here the Victorian dwelling's spatial program was sustained by microchip technology. Shopping, bill-paying, and taxes could be done on the computer; a robot could fetch laundry from a bedroom hamper and take it to a washing machine and dryer; a computer provided children's games to add a second, more engaging baby-sitting machine to the television, one that could accommodate children's participation. Surveillance systems of various kinds were integrated into the computer, so that when anyone intruded into the private haven of this suburban home, the violation was noted and reported to the local police.[26] *The Un-Private House*, a 1999 show at the Museum of Modern Art in New York, curated by Terence Riley, explored the possibilities two decades later. Twenty-six dwellings were included, some science-fiction like, such as "The Digital House" by Gisue and Mojgan Hariri, which featured two home offices and main walls made from liquid-crystal displays (LCDs). The futuristic look of the house concealed its traditional residential program. Only the home offices justified the curious term, "unprivate."[27]

TELECOMMUTING FROM THE HAVEN

Other designers have called residences with home offices "live/work houses," or "flex-houses." The possibilities of the home office were noted in the 1980s in *The Electronic Cottage*, by Joseph Deken.[28] One can see telecommuting as a support for freelancers and for flexible schedules, or as the end of unionization drives and the beginning of cottage industries handling all white-collar work as piecework. Employers are looking for ways to reduce overhead and cut costs. The computer programmer or secretary who winds up with a terminal at home could become more like a pre-industrial weaver on the putting-out system than like a worker of the modern world. The historical isolation of the housewife as an invisible worker in the sacred hut could be the model for the manipulation of more and more paid workers back into the isolation of the private sphere. Already observers have noted that female telecommuters are less likely than male telecommuters to have well-equipped, separate home offices and suitable child-care arrangements. Mom may be telecommuting at night on the kitchen table. Some analysts have suggested that neighborhood workplaces could offer a social setting for telecommuting and the benefits of more flexible hours.[29]

Does the industrial strategy or the neighborhood strategy offer any stronger, more coherent solutions for incorporating digital

technologies? Certainly the industrial strategy has no less complicated a history than the haven strategy in its evolution over the
past century.

THE INDUSTRIAL STRATEGY: MASS HOUSING AS MACHINE

With the Industrial Revolution, many European designers thought
that the peasant farmer's single-family home was outmoded, but
the housing that replaced these rural cottages was frightening. The
sordid tenements spawned by industrial production were about as
far from the sacred properties of roof and hearth as one could get.
Because of their inadequate sanitary design and overcrowding,
they were the first human dwellings that actually killed people
who tried to live in them. To take the place of both huts and tenements, designers proposed to create new multifamily buildings for
sheltering and feeding the workers relocated from country to city.
Perhaps the most extreme example of this aesthetic, and one of the
earliest and most influential, was Jeremy Bentham's Panopticon.
Bentham, associated with the philosophy of Utilitarianism and slogans such as "the greatest good for the greatest number," developed his architectural scheme to show how, at a minimum expense
to the British taxpayers of the 1780s, the urban poor might be kept
from starving. In the Panopticon, Bentham arranged people in
tiers in a multisided building with a single all-seeing person supervising from the center. The building had folding beds ranging in
size from cradles for babies to bunks for adult males—reflecting
the preoccupation with body measurements first developed by
slave-ship owners and ultimately a staple of *existenzminimum*
(minimum existence) housing. The basic design, Bentham thought,
could be used as a poorhouse, an orphanage, a penitentiary, a hospital, a mental asylum, or a school. In other words, the poor, the
deviant, and the wards of society could be housed there. Only
prison officials literally adopted this architectural program, but the
attitude of architectural determinism that Bentham launched
became quite pervasive. Bentham chortled, "Morals reformed—
health preserved—industry invigorated. . . . all by a simple idea in
architecture!"[30] Many architects and politicians took up his belief

in the power of spatial design to change society, ignoring the necessity for more basic economic reforms.

PANOPTICONS, PARALLELOGRAMS, AND PHALANXES

The Panopticon was a poorhouse designed as an architectural machine. The model-housing schemes of Robert Owen and Charles Fourier, called the parallelogram and the phalanstery, were "social palaces" scaled to suit new groups of male and female workers in model settlements. Owen owned a textile factory in New Lanark, Scotland. His community resembled the grand squares of town houses built by the English aristocracy. Fourier was inspired by Versailles and the Palais Royale. Their conceptions relied on the isolated, experimental community as an alternative to the city but were far more generous in the dimensions of private housing space and collective services than Bentham's design—and less rigidly deterministic. Both Owen and Fourier hoped to unite social, economic, and aesthetic improvements in their new communities for one to two thousand people. In the United States, some of the most influential intellectuals of the 1840s, such as Margaret Fuller and Nathaniel Hawthorne, adopted Fourier's ideas as residents of Brook Farm. When they built themselves a phalanstery to house an experimental community of both workers and intellectuals, their friend Thoreau came over from Concord to West Roxbury to have a look at the imported new design for collective housing, child care, and dining. Fresh from the woods around Walden Pond, Thoreau shook his head and muttered, "Huts, huts are safe."[31] Of course, he went to dine with his mother or sister whenever his hut lost its appeal.

SOCIAL HOUSING

Ideas about collective housing tried out in the model communities of the 1840s led to new urban experiments for all classes, including worker's model tenements, apartment hotels, and neighborhood public kitchens. In the 1880s, Bebel drew from this tradition when he predicted a future of industrial equality and collective living, based on mass housing and state control. The continuing construction of urban philanthropic and public housing for workers was given a great push during the reconstruction following World War I. The American housing expert, Catherine Bauer, brilliantly chronicled the experiments in building housing for a social purpose in her excellent *Modern Housing* of 1934, covering Holland, Germany, Belgium, France, and England.[32] Socialist architects such as Ernest May and Bruno Taut were particularly influential in exploring the social and physical issues involved in designing multifamily dwellings.[33] Most unconventional of all were the Bolsheviks in the Soviet Union, who promoted the "House for the New Way of Life," the collective house designed for the family with both adults employed.

In the prospectus for the 1926 Competition for a Communal Dwelling, the Moscow City Society instructed architects to reorganize the traditional home:

> It is the duty of technological innovation, the duty of the architect, to place new demands on housing and to design in so far as possible a house that will transform the so-called family hearth from a boring, confining cell that at present burdens down women in particular into a place of pleasant and carefree relaxation.

> A new life demands new forms.

> The worker does not desire his mother, wife or sister to be a nursery maid, washerwoman or cook with unlimited hours; he does not desire children to rob him and particularly their mother of the possibility of employing their free time for social labor, mental and physical pleasures.[34]

As a result of this competition and others, programs for apartment houses including day-care facilities, dining rooms, and recreation rooms were adopted by numerous well-known Soviet architects.

Many of these projects were designed by individuals intoxicated with the machine aesthetic as a statement about modernity. Some of the Soviet architects subscribed to the spirit of the Italian Futurists, without understanding the antihumanist, antifeminist bias behind their sketches. Filippo Marinetti had exulted in his 1909 manifesto of Futurism: "Time and space died yesterday.

Already we live in the absolute, since we have already created speed, eternal and ever present. . . . We wish to glorify war—the only healthy giver of the world—militarism, patriotism, the destructive arm of the anarchist, the beautiful ideas that kill, the contempt of women. We wish to destroy museums, the libraries, and to fight against moralism, feminism, and all opportunist and utilitarian meanness."[35]

When Soviet architects attempted to join Bebel's program for women's paid work and collective services run by the state with the antihearth, anticulture, pro-industry machine aesthetic of Marinetti, a conflict between the housing program and its architectural expression occurred. Following Bebel, Zetkin, and Kollontai, the architects of the collective dwellings began to strip away traditional patriarchal definitions of family activities and space. But they proposed to replace family houses with minimal one-person spaces, including folding beds, tables, and chairs placed in rooms often calculated by size more than quality. They removed traditional family spaces like the hearth, and social functions like dining, from the private dwelling unit in order to make cooking and eating collective activities. One designer actually drew an assembly line to speed the distribution of food down the center of the collective table. Another development was the use of industrial components such as metal frame windows and metal stairs in housing design, especially in large community spaces. The results were stark. In contrast, the Soviet graphics, paintings, set designs, and costume designs of the same era were often more intriguing than the architecture, largely because the smaller scale of experimentation encouraged humor and seriousness without self-consciousness, qualities the architects and planners often lacked.

Ultimately, very few of these Soviet housing projects were built, and construction problems made some that were realized not merely cold but chilling. There were shortages of building materials and technical problems with detailing. A national housing shortage in the 1920s caused extreme crowding of more than one family in many existing and new units, hardly the social context in which any new program for collective living could be promoted as revolutionary and desirable. Alexandra Kollontai did attempt to evaluate the aesthetic and practical results of the experiments in

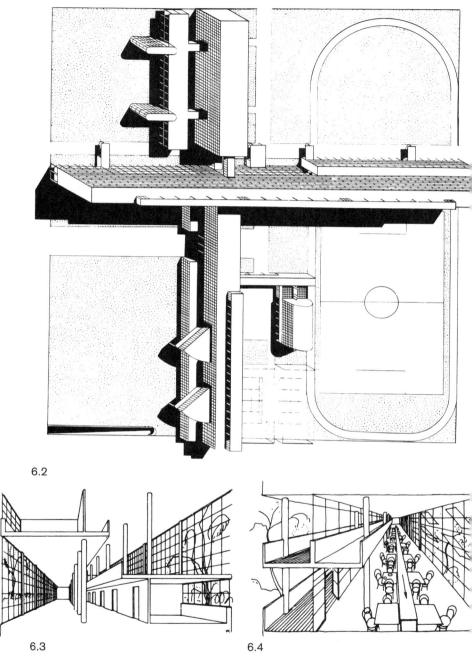

6.2 Home as efficient machine for collective consumption, Barsch and Vladmirov design for a communal house, USSR, 1929. 6.3 Interior view of the communal house. 6.4 Dining room with assembly line for food.

her book *Women's Labor in Economic Development:* "where previously the women were particularly anxious to have a household of their own . . . today, on the contrary, it is the husband who suggests that it would not be a bad idea to take a flat, have dinner at home and the wife always about—while the women, especially the growing numbers of women workers who are being drawn into the Republic's creative activities, will not even hear of a 'household of one's own.' 'Better to separate than to agree to a family life with a household and the petty family worries; now I am free to work for the Revolution, but then—then I would be fettered. No, separation would be preferable.' And the husbands have to make the best of it."[36] There were great attitudinal changes among some Soviet women, but they did not receive adequate material support.

The Soviet housing problem was later complicated by the devastation of World War II, so that as late as 1957, a slogan used to cheer on Soviet builders was "A separate apartment for each family." Historian Anatole Kopp notes that this "allows us to imagine what the real housing situation in the USSR was like."[37] In the post–World War II era, an extreme focus on quantity and a push for prefabricated systems obscured many issues of variety and quality, from the scale of the unit plan to the scale of the site plan.

Of all the housing designers influenced by the Soviet experiments, the most influential was Le Corbusier, who admired their plans more than their politics. He made a lasting impact when he suggested that the choice for the twentieth century was architecture or revolution, and announced, "Revolution can be avoided."[38] Le Corbusier worked in Paris, and his plan for a Contemporary City showed machine-aesthetic housing in an urban context, towers in a park, connected by freeways, an image of the 1920s that remained influential through mid-century. Drawing on the ideas of Charles Fourier, and believing that women would remain in paid work, Le Corbusier also designed the Unité d'Habitation, an apartment building with services. Several of these were built after World War II in various locations. The most famous one in Marseilles included a roof-top day-care center and an internal street of small shops and services within the apartment complex. Sculptural concrete gave these buildings a rough, dynamic quality enhanced by Le Corbusier's lively sense of color. They became powerful aesthetic models for architects interested in high-rise housing in the United States, Western Europe, Eastern Europe, and the Soviet Union for the next two or three decades, although the programs of Fourier and the Soviets underlying this design were not always well understood by those who copied the form.

Unfortunately, as prefabrication techniques improved and government supports for housing increased, it became possible to put up large groups of high rises with crude industrialized building systems. Not 1,620 residents (Fourier's ideal number, retained by Le Corbusier), but 16,000 or 60,000 might be accommodated; not sculptural concrete but factory-made panels, all identical, could be used. While talented designers, such as Shadrach Woods, managed to build successful housing projects that overcame the disadvantages of precast systems and even reflected the cultural identities of different groups of tenants in significant ways, most housing architects failed to cope. The 20,000-person, postwar housing project, divorced from any context of social idealism, was the perfect job for an egomaniac—or a hack. Just as Americans of the 1950s gasped at the urban scale of Levittown's sacred huts, so Europeans gasped at the urban scale of the new industrialized housing estates, "machines for living." Since a home is neither a sacred hut nor a machine, these popular aesthetic responses in both Europe and the United States made sense, but often cultural critics and designers idealized the opposing tradition. Some Americans thought high-rise housing more elegant than eclectic suburbia; some Europeans preferred the variety of the single-family suburban houses to the towers of identical units they deplored. There was never enough effort to explore a middle ground between the supercongestion of one and the isolation of the other, although a few designers did take up this task.

SUPPORT STRUCTURES

The inventive Dutch designer N. J. Habraken attempted to soften and personalize mass housing, beginning with his book *Supports: An Alternative to Mass Housing* in 1964.[39] Habraken rightly criticized the totalitarian, soulless, sameness of mass housing estates produced for the post–World War II reconstruction of Europe. He proposed instead to limit industrialized building systems to the structural frameworks for new housing, and then to establish a more personalized tradition of the insertion of wall panels, doors, windows, and interior partitions and equipment according to the tenants' own purchases from a wide range of available manufactured products. Habraken saw tenant participation in design as desirable, and he believed community-oriented local architects could work with tenants to help them complete their apartments. He allowed for various types of households and for changes in the household over the life cycle by specifying that apartments should expand and contract through attachable capsules and movable exterior and interior walls. Several such projects were built through the energy and dedication of Habraken's disciples, who conducted heroic campaigns to educate public housing agencies, private developers, and tenants about the benefits of such user participation.

In housing, flexibility was not the only issue. Social services and community spaces serving diverse households had to be part of a larger program. In order to keep the efficient collective consumption of space from becoming too privatized, the special social needs of families headed by women, the elderly, and single people had to be highlighted. One of the most innovative support structures in the early 1970s included the provision of services for the larger community as well as for tenants. In Rolf Spille's Steilshoop Project in Hamburg, Germany, a group of parents and single people modified public housing by keeping the structural framework but building interior dwelling units of varying sizes, along with shared dining and child-care spaces, private work spaces, and social services.[40] The project also included a number of former mental patients as residents and served as a half-way house for them. Steilshoop suggested the extent to which residential stereotypes could be broken down. The sick, the aged, the unmarried were integrated into new types of households and housing complexes, rather than segregated in separate housing projects. Every group of six or seven households became a little neighborhood in itself.

In the United States, the technical side of Habraken's approach was adopted, without much understanding of its social and economic bases, by James Wines and the architectural firm SITE.[41] Their "Highrise of Homes" proposal in 1982 showed suburban sacred huts with trees and grass filling the floors of a nine-to-eleven-story support structure. Component catalogs offered choices of doors, windows, and wall treatments, but no social space was emphasized. This drawing layered the sacred huts and the machine for living together quite dramatically, but did not attempt to overcome the programmatic problems of either model, nor did it explain why the speculators' sacred huts were worth the trouble of such intensive engineering efforts.

Cuban designers made another kind of attack on the machine-aesthetic and prefabrication. In the 1970s, they received the industrialized building systems exported to them by the Soviet Union as part of their foreign aid package. The Cubans redesigned these systems; they organized an unusual microbrigade strategy to get more housing built by unskilled workers; and in addition, they had a lively indigenous tradition of graphic design. They simply spent time, money, and energy painting the gray concrete four story walk-ups in every possible wonderful color combination—red and yellow, white and orange, green and blue, until they had produced results not unlike the sculptures of De Stijl or Purism, but with a less academic, more Latin flavor. Lush tropical landscaping was added, greenery and sun took over, and the results were a great improvement on the mass housing designed by Soviet engineers and architects. They reconciled the need for mass production with varied collective—rather than individual—expression.

SOCIAL ENGINEERING

By the mid-twentieth century there also developed a large corps of behavioral experts who professed to be able to help designers of mass housing match tenants' lifestyles with appropriate spatial responses, thus ensuring more pleasant aesthetic and social experiences. Women might have expected sociologists, social geographers, and environmental psychologists to scrutinize their needs more accurately. Some behavioral scientists who began to work on architectural programming and postconstruction evaluation did claim to research "needs." However, the researchers attracted to housing design were often not the most sophisticated social scientists, but those most limited in their political interests and methodological approaches. While some exceptional researchers such as Florence Ladd, Susan Saegert, and Clare Cooper were skillful in illuminating the spatial needs of teenagers, the elderly, and families, others presented tired stereotypes as good practice, "social science," or "self-awareness." The clients likely to employ them were often the largest bureaucracies with the strongest interest in standardizing human behavior—housing agencies at the flexible end of the spectrum, big corporations in the middle, social welfare groups and departments of correction, heirs of the Benthamite tradition, at the rigid end. The result was the programming of space in mass housing to suit highly normative schemes of human values.

The evolution of Parker Morris housing standards, originated in England but disseminated in "Homes For Today and Tomorrow" throughout the rest of the English speaking world, provides a case in point. In the 1970s, first-year design students were still studying these sketches of residential life accompanied by little scenarios of home activities, complete with standard dimensions for housing space. There is nothing wrong with the dimensions, but the scenarios, even in the 1972 edition, are what Octavia Hill, the Victorian housing manager so influenced by Ruskin, might have drawn up in the 1890s had she the option of programming new buildings instead of managing old ones. The characters are respectable, clean, tidy parents, heavy TV-watchers and appliance-users, never rowdy, drunk, lustful, sick, or careless. Most of all, they move through life in a rigidly frozen division of labor. At noon, for instance, "When the children play indoors Mother needs to be able to see them from the kitchen, but they should be away from the kitchen equipment and not under her feet." Or at 7 P.M., "When Father repairs something, he needs to be out of Mother's way in the kitchen and where he will not disturb sleeping children." He washes the car, she gets out of the kitchen occasionally to vacuum the floor and dress the baby. As a supposed concession to changing roles, the designer is now instructed to plan the interior and exterior carefully, "to give working wives a better chance of doing both jobs [housework and paid employment] without too much strain."[42]

The next generation of researchers claimed even more authority to help people verbalize and enjoy their experience of housing. Like their Parker Morris predecessors, they were normative. Their great norm was not respectability but "do your own thing." An example of one very flawed work of this genre is Glenn Robert Lym's *A Psychology of Building: How We Shape and Experience Our Structured Space* (1980). He offered a chapter on "Spatial Orders," and another on "The Spatial Order of the Home" in which he analyzed two couples, their apartments in multifamily housing complexes, and the life choices they were supposed to represent. In each example the man and woman were fighting over territory in a two-bedroom apartment. In each couple, the male attempted to seize the second bedroom and make it into a personal, inviolable work space his wife could not enter. In the first example the male seized the second bedroom for his private study, while his wife did her work on the dining-room table. The male also appropriated the couple's only oriental rug for his study. Lym quoted the wife, who declared: "When my husband is not home, I open the study door, even though I know the cat will go in and pull up on the rug. I just leave it open and that way the study becomes a part of the apartment." Lym decided that this woman had achieved emotional growth because she had developed a personal, door-opening ritual to get a look at the jointly-owned rug and "to make herself feel whole again."[43] The question of where she worked and when was never addressed.

In Lym's second example, the male wanted to use the second bedroom as a work space for ceramics, his hobby, and his wife wanted it to be a clean, unchaotic, dining room, since there was no other place for their dining table. The husband protested: "We should each have a place that is all our own, that we can just do whatever we feel like, make all kinds of mess or noise. I'd have my pots all over. And when I would get done potting, I wouldn't clean up." Lym's analysis was confined to cheering this husband for resisting the role of "son to a manipulatory wife-mother." Lym did not ask who cooked and served the food, nor did he consider the dining room a work space. He also failed to ask how the wife was to get comparable space of her own, since there was no other room available. Lym claimed that the male in this case "evolved a spatial order of the home as a single personal space amid collective space." He praised him and others who "entered into a responsive dialogue with their physical environments" and "used housing to reflect upon and to help come to terms with themselves."[44]

On the subject of male-female territory, Virginia Woolf, in *A Room of One's Own* in 1928, had more perceptive things to say: "I thought how unpleasant it is to be locked out; and I thought how it is worse to be locked in. . . ." Woolf saw "the safety and prosperity of one sex and . . . the poverty and insecurity of the other,"[45] but for many social scientists concerned about housing her essay seems never to have become required reading. Often territorial analysis has failed to deal with gender and aesthetics, at a theoretical as well as an empirical level.[46] New research on spatial cognition in the context of gender socialization will continue to be important.[47]

DYNAMITE

The social scientists claimed to be able to help people adjust to mass housing and the industrial aesthetic. When Le Corbusier said, "Architecture or Revolution. Revolution can be avoided," the social workers and social scientists responded, "We can help manage the architecture." In the United States, Le Corbusier's ideas about the ideal city as a collection of residential towers in a park influenced public housing agencies, who, after the 1949 Housing Act, were empowered to construct for the poor who could not afford suburban tract houses. Subsidies were greatest for the FHA/VA homeowner (suburban mortgage supports, tax deductions, and highways, rather than direct housing construction and public transportation subsidies), while the public housing that was built was often cheap, nasty, and badly thought-out. Pioneers of housing reform such as Edith Elmer Wood and Catherine Bauer, who had drafted, lobbied, and nursed the Wagner Act through Congress in 1937, were dismayed. Bauer herself repudiated "the dreary deadlock of public housing" in the 1950s.[48] Conventional construction was generally used for public housing in the United States, rather than industrialized building systems, but this was a testament to the power of the building trades' unions and of construction materials suppliers more than any resistance to the machine aesthetic of Europe. The buildings were similar in scale and uniformity of units.

Public housing projects in New York, Chicago, Boston, and smaller places were, in the 1950s and early 1960s, usually grim, brick structures badly sited in islands of asphalt, whether three sto-

ries high or thirty. Although the mid-1960s introduced more varied, low-rise designs, on scattered sites, the earlier "projects" continued to house the poorest people with no other housing choices.
Female-headed families predominated. The projects became sites
of crime, none more so than the Pruitt-Igoe complex in Saint
Louis, designed in the mid-1950s by Minoru Yamasaki and demolished as an unlivable place in 1972.

Pruitt-Igoe came to stand for the confrontation between the
public housing bureaucracies and ghetto residents who objected to
the building program as much as to the aesthetic. Ignoring the subtle social and architectural analyses of Pruitt-Igoe by sociologist
Lee Rainwater, architectural critic Charles Jencks pushed aside all
of the complexities of female-headed families and ghetto residents'
lives to identify the dynamiting of Pruitt-Igoe as the start of an era
when architects would stop trying to resolve social issues and
return to an "art for art's sake" approach to design. For Jencks,
mass housing was so identified with the Modern movement in
architecture that when mass housing was challenged as an architectural program, he felt able to denounce any worth in the
machine aesthetic as an architectural style. Thus he wrote that the
end of the modern movement in architecture, as a style, occurred
at exactly the hour when the public housing complex by Yamasaki
was demolished: July 15, 1972, 3:32 P.M., "Boom, boom, boom."[49]

Jencks became famous when he announced the arrival of post-
modern architecture as an aesthetic alternative, with a collection of
examples by practitioners known for their stylistic eclecticism.
Architects long frustrated by the overall conditions of work in the
profession rushed to follow these new aesthetic adventures and
abandon their sense of guilt and frustration about the larger problems of patronage for housing. In the ensuing stampede, many
modest examples of good multifamily housing with careful social
and aesthetic planning, such as the Mackley Houses, built by
Oscar Stonorov in Philadelphia in the 1930s, or some of the projects done by Lynda Simmons of Phipps Houses, a nonprofit housing developer in New York, were overlooked as uninteresting,
"built sociology."

Just as the single-family, sacred hut architects had borrowed
more and more heavily from the machine aesthetic, so Jencks
encouraged machine aesthetic designers to return to the sacred

hut and its archetypal significance. He himself began to work on a single-family house with murals of the four seasons and 52 steps, one for each week of the year, claiming that cosmological symbolism (what he called "programming") reached the heart of architectural meaning.[50] One can contrast Jencks' response to Pruitt-Igoe to that of Jan Wampler, a more socially concerned housing architect and critic, who used the same moment of reconsideration to begin an ambitious design project to modernize a large public housing complex, Columbia Point, in Dorchester, Massachusetts.[51] Wampler tried to reprogram the buildings to suit the African-American and Hispanic single-parent families who lived there. He combined small units to make larger ones, introduced extensive spaces for day care and community facilities, redesigned windows and added landscaping. Unfortunately, just after his project won a major award, Wampler chose an inopportune moment to testify against corruption in public works and public housing in Massachusetts. His design was never implemented, although another architect, Joan Goody, later received a commission to redesign the project, which is now called Harbor Point.

While Wampler reprogrammed his housing to deal with poverty and women's needs, he was much less influential than Jencks, who did try to write about the social and economic puzzles of corporate and government patronage, but was unable to analyze the programmatic faults of either sacred-hut or machine-aesthetic housing. Instead, Jencks developed a series of oppositional categories such as warm/cold and female/male to try to sort out aesthetic issues. He opposed warm, female, organic, complex, and ornamented qualities, against cold, male, synthetic, straightforward, high-tech qualities, but his confusion between program and style was obvious.[52] In his influential 1977 book, *The Language of Post-Modern Architecture,* he could not resist including an interior perspective of "A Brothel for Oil Men in the Desert" (complete with scantily clad prostitutes) as an example of warm, complex, pneumatic architecture, although it distracted from his larger argument. Jencks' "female/male" stylistic dichotomy represented the same old program for gender: earth mother and organization man, prehistoric squaw and racing-car driver, prostitute and petroleum engineer.

Just as the advocates of the haven strategy had secluded women in the home to keep the human race partly protected from the market economy (and then asked women to undertake wage work to help pay for the seclusion), so the advocates of the industrial strategy had demanded the full integration of women into the socialized labor of industrial society (and then asked women to keep the hearth fires burning too). Neither model of home life led to an acceptable building program for housing in the twentieth century. Ingenious schemes for community participation cannot correct the wrong program, any more than new technologies can fix the tracts of sacred huts. Modern family patterns and housing needs are too complex for either caricature. The housing bureaucracy's dynamite did not help, nor did any use of this incident to date the end of an era, when, in fact, hundreds of millions of urban residents all over the world live in high-rise mass housing and will continue to do so. Several million Americans in high-rise public housing may find their future aesthetic satisfaction depends on learning how best to modify these structures in social, economic, and aesthetic terms. If the tracts of suburbia fail to offer solutions, perhaps the history of the neighborhood strategy and its aesthetic offers some clues.

THE NEIGHBORHOOD STRATEGY: THE CLOISTER AND THE VILLAGE

The models for the neighborhood strategy were the cloister and the village. The designers who favored this approach believed that in terms of housing, the whole must be more than the sum of its parts. For private space to become a home, it must be joined to a range of semiprivate, semipublic, and public spaces, and linked to appropriate social and economic institutions assuring the continuity of human activity in these spaces. The neighborhood strategy not only involved thinking about the reorganization of home in industrial society, it also involved defining "home" at every spatial level—from the house, to the neighborhood, the town, the homeland, and the planet. If the haven strategy stressed privacy, and the industrial strategy stressed efficiency, the neighborhood strategy highlighted accountability.

THE ACADEMICAL VILLAGE

Just as Bentham's Panopticon prefigured later interest in the home as machine, so Thomas Jefferson's "academical village" at the University of Virginia prefigured later interest in the home as part of a neighborhood. Although Jefferson had also promoted the isolated family farm, his University of Virginia commission offered him the chance to build housing for students and faculty beginning in 1817. He organized the students' rooms along an arcaded walk punctuated by pavilions serving as faculty residences and lecture halls. The scheme culminated in a domed library. Among the precedents for this project were French hospital designs of the late eighteenth century, but Jefferson also cherished the Carthusian monastery of Pavia, near Milan, as a model of collective living and he visited it before commencing his design work for Charlottesville.

An archetypal expression of the relationship between privacy and community, Pavia consisted of private cells for each monk, connected by a generous arcade to a communal dining room, church, and large estate (where produce was grown to support not only the praying monks but each of the lay brothers and agricultural workers necessary to provide the economic base for the spiritual activity). The cells looked like sacred huts. They were peaked-roof houses with walled gardens, heavy doors, small windows, and well-defined chimneys. The monks devised ingenious, flexible, minimal furnishings for each hut that still look modern. At the same time, the monastery was a collective. A broad arcade gathered the meditating monks into a common dining room. When Jefferson translated the spatial program at Pavia into the University of Virginia, in the early nineteenth century, the monks' huts become the professors' pavilions. There, too, hierarchies of labor were required: just as the monks had lay brothers, the young men had personal servants and the professors had household slaves. Using this monastic model, Jefferson's design of the academical village still stands as an American statement about how to link individuals, households, and work spaces.

Throughout the second half of the nineteenth century, as American women began to experiment with the neighborhood strategy and its implications for housing design, plans for courtyards and arcades appeared. Following the work of Caroline

Howard Gilman, Jane Sophia Appleton, and Amelia Bloomer, Melusina Peirce began to develop a more thorough analysis of the architectural implications of cooperative housekeeping.[53] When she proposed a housewives' producers cooperative in 1868, she also introduced the idea of a model neighborhood of thirty-six houses with a single work center, a building with a central court-yard and arcades. Marie Stevens Howland tried to develop this idea.[54] In the 1890s, Mary Coleman Stuckert of Denver reiterated Peirce's and Howland's ideas when she exhibited a model for an urban row house development with a central open space, central kitchen, and shared child-care facilities. In 1915, Alice Constance Austin tried to develop a new Californian city with the same cen-tralized services.[55] While they built relatively little, the influence of these material feminists on architects and planners in both the United States and Europe was considerable.

QUADRANGLES IN THE GARDEN CITIES

The designers of the Garden Cities movement, including Ebenezer Howard, Raymond Unwin, and M. H. Baillie Scott, translated the material feminists' ideas into built form. Their over-all objectives included ending the split between town and country, easing the conflict between capital and labor through cooperative production, and ending the servant problem and the exploitation of women through cooperative cooking and dining.[56] The physical framework for this activity was the new town of 30,000 people, designed around "cooperative quadrangles," or living groups of about thirty households with a common dining room. Unwin's sketch of the earliest cooperative quadrangle suggests an Oxford or Cambridge college, or a medieval village, which was the inspira-tion many designers, such as M. H. Baillie Scott, also adopted.

The cooperative quadrangle looked like home—albeit an insti-tutional one. The inglenooks, half-timbering, stucco, peaked roofs, massive hearths, numerous chimneys, and the interior detailing with wood and handmade ceramic tile, recalled the Arts and Crafts movement led by Charles Ashbee and William Morris, and their polemics against the machine. The cozy feeling of these cloistered housing quadrangles was enhanced by flower gardens and veg-etable gardens, shaded arcades and benches. Unlike the sacred hut

6.5 Home as neighborhood modeled on the pre-industrial village. Raymond Unwin, sketch of a cooperative quadrangle, 1902.

6.6 Barry Parker, sketch of a cooperative quadrangle, 1912. This is very similar to examples built at Welwyn, Letchworth, and Hampstead in England; it recalls the cloisters of Oxford and Cambridge colleges.

houses of the early twentieth century that shared some of these materials and details, the quadrangles of the Garden City designers attempted to recreate the scale of larger social institutions, recognizing that the rural subsistence farmstead could no longer be the unit of aesthetic expression.

While the Garden Cities influenced planners all over the world, and one of Howard's favorite architectural styles—Tudor revival—became popular with architects all over the United States, the program for the cooperative quadrangle was not part of the set of ideas fully realized in England and widely exported. In the United States, between 1910 and 1940, several housing developments were influenced by the Garden Cities approach. The concepts of neighborhood planning at Forest Hills, New York, developed by Grosvenor Atterbury in 1911, included the provision of an apartment hotel structure for singles and the elderly in a town square at the railroad station, as well as clusters of attached houses. Clarence Stein and Henry Wright, the designers of several major projects, began developing what they called the superblock in 1924 at Sunnyside, Long Island, where they created a small park at the heart of a moderate income housing development. In 1929 at Radburn, New Jersey, Stein and Wright designed a garden city "for the motor age," restricting the domain of the automobile by developing pedestrian courtyards leading to a larger park system running through the project.

COURTYARDS AND GREENS

Finally, one project synthesized the influence of Jefferson's academical village, the feminist experiments, and the Garden Cities. The Baldwin Hills Village in Los Angeles, where Clarence Stein served as consultant to Robert Alexander and the other local architects, opened in 1942.[57] A leisurely walk through the three parks of this project reveals mature trees, tended flowers, an expansion and contraction of landscaped spaces that is in striking contradiction to awareness that one is in the heart of a major city, in the center of a low-cost housing complex.[58] Each housing unit, small or large, also has a private garden or balcony. Serpentine walls enclosing the gardens recall Jefferson's influence. Like Markelius in

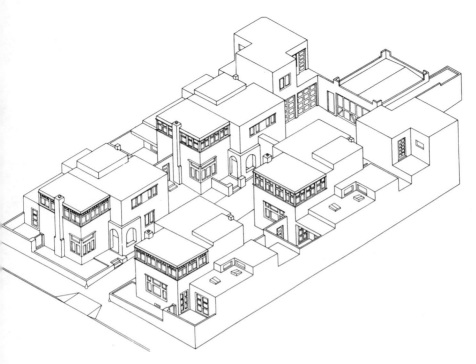

6.7 Irving Gill, Horatio West Courts, Santa Monica, 1919, axonometric drawing. (Courtesy Margaret Bach)

Stockholm and Howard at Homesgarth, some of the designers
moved into this project themselves to reiterate the connections
between personal lifestyle and political beliefs so lacking in many
other housing designers' work.

Irving Gill was another brilliant designer in the American tradition who found low-cost housing with shared courtyards an interesting architectural problem. Trained in the office of Louis Sullivan,
Gill was the son of a building contractor from Syracuse, New York.
He tried to find a way to develop a vernacular style suited to Los
Angeles and San Diego. He admired the adobe structures, arcades,
and courtyards of the Spanish colonial style, but redefined these
traditions with a pure geometry of cubes and circles. He used an
innovative technological approach, with concrete walls poured in
place in the ground and raised into position in the manner of traditional barn raising. If ever a designer was prepared to resolve the

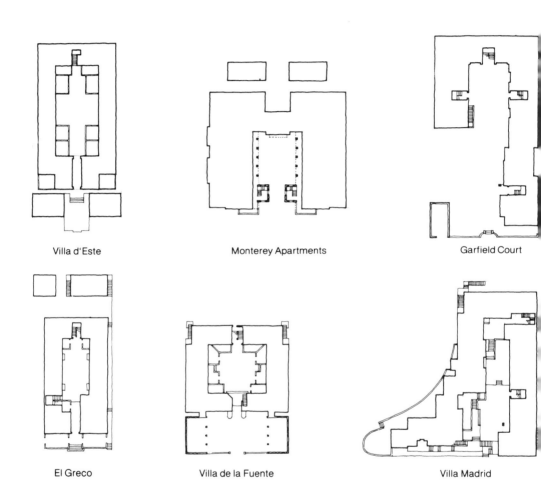

Villa d'Este   Monterey Apartments   Garfield Court

El Greco   Villa de la Fuente   Villa Madrid

6.8 Organizational diagrams of courtyard housing built in Southern California between 1920 and 1930. (From Polyzoides, Sherwood, and Tice, *Courtyard Housing in Los Angeles,* University of California Press, 1981) aesthetic and technical ambiguities of the twentieth century, it was Gill. His Horatio West Court in Santa Monica and his Lewis Courts in Sierra Madre both display his genius for manipulating shared spaces. The Lewis Courts were especially successful, so the client decided that middle-class rents could be charged for what started as a low-income housing project. In each case Gill also drew from the bungalow courts and courtyard housing schemes of Los Angeles as the strongest local tradition for multifamily housing design. Projects such as Bowen Court in Pasadena in the Craftsman style by the Heinemann brothers, or the Andalusia in Hollywood, in the Mediterranean revival style by Arthur and Nina Zwebel, expressed many of the same commitments in program as Gill's work, but were a bit more aesthetically flamboyant.[59] In each case the use of lush landscaping and of local ceramic tiles heightened the sense of place. Los Angeles is the American city with the most interesting multi-family housing stock on the courtyard model, and the best projects are still worth studying.

COHOUSING

Courtyard housing is the strongest typological response to the need to balance privacy and community. In the European tradition, as we have seen, a good many designers struggled to graft the ideas of the feminist exponents of the neighborhood strategy onto multifamily housing projects with extensive facilities for child care, shared meals, and community facilities. While the early-twentieth-century collective houses, apartment hotels, and family hotels of Scandinavia provided some good examples of the neighborhood strategy explored in terms of the machine aesthetic, a Danish hous-ing project, Tynggarden, by the architectural firm, Vankunsten, car-ried on the social tradition of these experiments in the 1970s, and added new courtyards.[60] Each family gave up 10 percent of its allo-cated interior square footage to create a shared neighborhood cen-ter for ten to fifteen families. They shared a courtyard that con-tained the mailboxes, the washing machines and dryers, a commu-nity kitchen, and a large two-level space for activities planned by the residents, from child care to classes to political meetings. The project's combination of private and shared facilities provided an

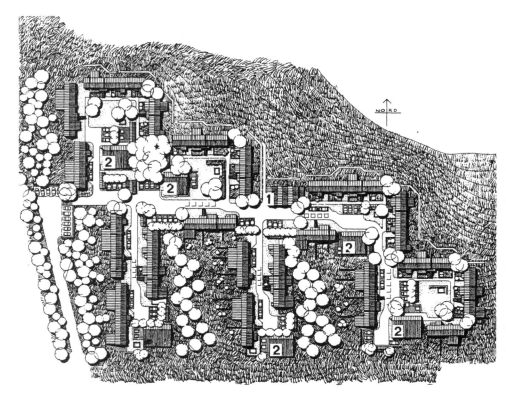

6.9 Tynggarden, outside of Copenhagen, Denmark. Site plan showing six courtyards housing about fifteen families each. (1) Central building with café and sports facilities; (2) multipurpose community buildings.

early example of cohousing. The designers also developed plans for the eventual expansion of the private units, to permit future flexibility for adding rental units or units for elderly dependents.

The designers liked the large red and cream-colored Danish barns in the agricultural area surrounding the project, and favored similar massing, color, and wood siding. To these forms they added a few metallic materials, so that a Citroën "Deux Chevaux" car fit right in. Adventure playgrounds filled the active courtyards, while grass, flowers, and vines grew in the quiet courtyards. In addition to the neighborhood centers, the project had a community center with a café.

In 2002, Tynggarden continues as a successful project. It draws on the agricultural building types of the region, but goes beyond the recalling of stylistic details or the sacred-hut mentality to make a new community comfortable with a mixture of old and new spatial and

6.10

6.11

6.12

6.13

6.14

6.10 Tynggarden, view of community building, side view showing porch with mailboxes. Each family gave up 10 percent of their interior private space to help make this community building; 6.11 Tynggarden, view of courtyard with adventure playground; 6.12 Tynggarden, courtyard with grass; 6.13 Tynggarden, town house; 6.14 Tynggarden, parking.

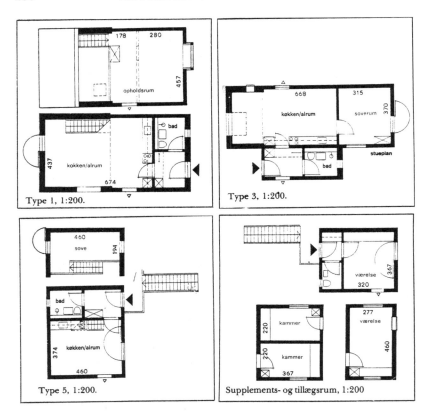

6.15 Tynggarden. Plans of typical town houses. The living spaces include kitchens. Types 1 and 5 have loft bedrooms. The "supplements" are rooms that can be added later.

technical forms: row houses and apartments, metal stairs, corrugated metal roofs, cars. The skyline of a village is simulated in the shed roofs of the community centers, with their place for solar panels, and their exaggerated, tall chimneys. What could be more sociable than a

6.16 Tynggarden. Plan of community building located in each courtyard, a two-level space with kitchen, laundry, and bath on the lower level; open space for classes, meetings, day care, or work on the upper level. The porch area next to the entrance includes mailboxes.

6.17 Aldo Van Eyck, The Mothers' House, Amsterdam, 1980, elevation of the street facade showing its integration with existing buildings.

large front porch lined with mailboxes? Unlike the cooperative quad-rangles of the Garden Cities movement, which look a bit corny in their Tudor half-timbering, the courtyards of Tynggarden look back-wards and forwards at the same time, carrying a complex social pro-gram and cultural agenda into a stylistic expression.

TRANSITIONAL HOUSING

Another European project of great interest is Aldo Van Eyck's courtyard housing complex for single mothers in Amsterdam, Holland.[61] Van Eyck gave care and attention to both social pro-gram and aesthetic realization. In this commission his client was an institution that had long served unmarried mothers. Van Eyck removed the stigma. He made housing for children, housing for parents, counseling spaces, and a common dining facility in addi-tion to offices and outdoor space. "The Mothers' House" suggests what can be done to make institutional housing a truly supportive setting in aesthetic as well as social terms. A rainbow of colors ani-mates the building; the courtyard is beautiful and serene. The kib-butz-like nature of the child-rearing spaces may seem too commu-nal for many households, but the project helps these single parents make a transition, rather than offering them a permanent resi-dence. The Mothers' House is a project that helps sustain a new

family form—the single-parent family—in urban society, rather
than a model of a permanent collective settlement, such as the
Israeli kibbutzim or American communes of the nineteenth and
twentieth centuries, which go beyond a neighborhood strategy
into a shared communal life.

NEW DENSITIES FOR THE TWENTY-FIRST CENTURY

The neighborhood aesthetic can be borrowed by speculative
developers. In the United States in the 1960s and 1970s, Planned
Unit Developments (PUDs) appeared to offer a way to imitate

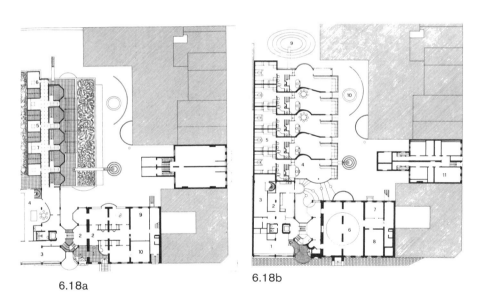

6.18a

6.18b

6.18 The Mothers' House, plans. BASEMENT (6.18a): (1) Bicycles and prams;
(2) laundry; (3) larder; (4) play areas in groups for children ages 1–6; (5) bedrooms for groups of children; (6) living; (7) lobby; (8) store room; (9) outdoor
play area with sculptured hill; (10) sand box; (11) office space. MEZZANINE
(6.18b): (1) entrance; (2) hall; (3) dining room; (4) kitchen; (5) guest room; (6)
night assistant; (7) niches for playing; (9) meeting room; (8 and 10) administration. FIRST FLOOR (6.18c): (1) hall; (2) work rooms; (3) doctor; (4) children
1–6; (5) loggia; (6) janitor's lodge. SECOND FLOOR (6.18d): (1) hall; (2)

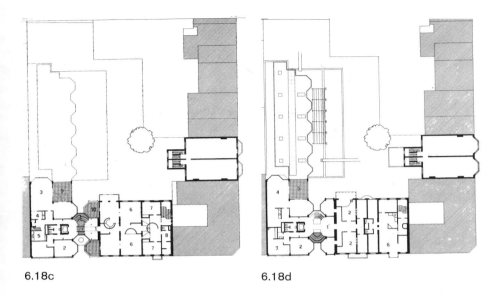

6.18c

6.18d

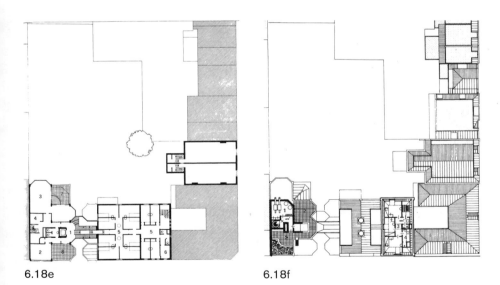

6.18e

6.18f

work rooms (3) babies' housing; (4) kitchen serving babies; (5) tableware; (6) parents' living rooms; (7) parents' bedrooms; (8) bathroom; (9) loggia; (10) terrace. THIRD FLOOR (6.18e): (1) entrance; (2) meeting room; (3) babies; (4) sick bay; (5) parents' bedrooms; (6) bathroom; (7) loggia; (8) terrace. ATTIC (6.18f): (1) heating system; (2) terrace; (3) bedrooms; (4) bathroom.

some of the better low-rise, high-density European housing developments, and, at the same time, a way to sell attached housing
units cheaper than tract houses, or rent them more expensively
than garden apartments. Such projects were quite correctly presented as a way to save the natural landscape while regrouping
housing units at higher densities than the typical single family residence (R-1) tract.[62] But town houses and condominiums often
looked more like Disneyland than any local neighborhood. New
England fishing village condos appeared in Phoenix,
Mediterranean hill-town condos arose in Kansas City, Georgian
squares arrived in Florida. In almost every case the automobile
wrecked the pre-industrial vernacular style (however unsuited to
the site and climate) by its scale. Two or three cars per unit became
standard parking requirements. So scraps of Old World building
forms sat in between streets sized for the turning radii of new
American cars.

Gone were the powerful arcades or pedestrian circulation systems crucial to this approach to programming and design. All the
afterthoughts—carriage lamps, bollards, and artificial lakes—
could not redeem awkward juxtapositions of old and new.
Prospective buyers were often encouraged to join the condominium "community" by purchasing a unit, but the community
facilities tended to be a tennis court, a swimming pool, or a card
room rather than child care or other services connected to the
basic needs of life. When one Los Angeles company (the Ring
brothers) did experiment with day care in rental apartments, they
quickly found it was far too complex to make profits, and
switched back to mundane community card rooms in their next
projects. Of course part of the charm of the monastic model or
the pre-industrial village lies in the variety of economic activities
that make such a complex self-sufficient. The condo development
without small shops and small gardens has little chance of this
aesthetic effect. Town houses need a town.

In 1981 the U.S. Department of Housing and Urban
Development and the Urban Land Institute produced a report,
*The Affordable Community: Growth, Change and Choice in the
80s,* that endorsed condominiums and the concept of "urban villages."[63] The examples of good practice shown in the booklet
reverberated with the stylistic anxieties of condominiums trying

to look like the old neighborhood, the Big Bad Wolf dressed as Grandma and waiting for Red Riding Hood. This reworking of the neighborhood strategy was agreed to by a committee composed of both developers and elected officials; it was not a call for better public housing design or better social service planning. The report defined "affordable housing" as multifamily condominiums, plus mobile homes (manufactured housing); houses without side yards (zero-lot-line housing); and four-family houses (four-unit cluster housing). Unfortunately the call for these choices was couched in terms of easing zoning and planning regulations to permit private developers to build cheaper space and sell it more profitably. With what planner Daniel Lauber criticized as a "distinct developer bias," the authors of the report urged that the power of eminent domain be given to private or quasi-public organizations. They also proposed that projects be allowed to proceed before all permits were awarded. And, on the topic of affordable rental housing, Lauber contended, "George Orwell would have been proud of the doublespeak."[64]

CAMPAIGNS FOR AFFORDABLE HOUSING

Large, for-profit developers provide most of the commissions for American architects interested in multifamily housing and urban design, but nonprofit developers have been doing important projects as well. In 1995, architect Michael Pyatok published an important volume with dozens of case studies of affordable housing developments built largely by nonprofits.[65] He also argued for the inclusion of more work spaces in housing developments. In 2001, an Internet catalog of many excellent examples of affordable housing went online at the University of Illinois, Chicago.[66]

THE CHARTER OF THE NEW URBANISM

In 1993, a number of architects and planners organized the Congress of the New Urbanism and developed the "Charter of the New Urbanism," a document that revitalized debates about housing and urban design. They called for better housing, neighborhoods, and regional planning. Among the authors were Elizabeth Plater-Zyberk and Andres Duany, whose Miami firm, DPZ, had designed the small town of Seaside, Florida and the housing development of Kentlands, Maryland. Peter Calthorpe, whose firm, Calthorpe Associates, was based in Berkeley, California, was the designer of Laguna West, and the author of *The Next American Metropolis*, published in 1993.[67] The New Urbanists espoused pedestrian neighborhoods connected to public transit. They proposed to keep the automobile in its place and build narrower streets, wider sidewalks, and small-scale retail adjacent to housing.

No one could fault these ideas, shared by most architects, although these goals were hard to achieve for designers working for developers in car-dependent suburbs, where traditional zoning and traffic engineering rules prevailed. Calthorpe also worked on conservation, live/work houses, and urban growth boundaries. His 2001 book, *The Regional City*, co-authored with California planner William Fulton, marks him as an environmentalist interested in public policy. The Urban Growth Boundaries he espouses have been tested in Portland and Seattle, where local officials have drawn a line around the metropolitan area. They expect suburban neighborhoods inside the boundary to densify with the addition of public transit.[68]

Unlike Calthorpe, Duany and Plater-Zyberk favored the revival of historic styles of architecture along with traditional neighborhood development (TND). They revived the front porch and included accessory apartments at Seaside, which was constructed according to very strict building and planning codes developed by the architects to encourage the vernacular of the Florida Panhandle as well as pedestrian scale. When Seaside took off as a resort of second homes, the designers claimed that this was because they had "created places where people want to be." In their 2000 book, *Suburban Nation: The Rise of Sprawl and the Decline of the American Dream*, they argued that increased home prices validated their neighborhood approach.[69] By 2001, very small, neotraditional wooden bungalows at Seaside were selling for $700,000—very expensive second homes! DPZ has also done master planning for many towns, and has advocated new approaches to zoning overlays to achieve pedestrian-friendly neighborhoods in many different contexts. They stress historical studies of the urban fabric in different regions of the U.S.

Both Calthorpe and Ray Gindroz, whose firm, Urban Design Associates, is based in Pittsburgh, have also designed public housing under the HOPE VI program, discussed in chapter 7. Their public housing projects emphasize traditional street grids and the chance to give tenants—now in mixed-income neighborhoods—a better address. By 2001, DPZ and Calthorpe were engaged in major projects across the country and had many followers.

Could New Urbanism be seen as a new neighborhood strategy for women? The neighborhood strategy depends on a social and economic program of mutual accountability, not merely on swimming pools, sidewalks, or porches as symbols of community. It requires interdependencies of a more fundamental kind. In the twenty-first century, some Americans may want fewer cars, more public transit, and stronger pedestrian spaces, but a nation with more cars than children, and no child-care policy, will have a hard time shoe-horning itself into New Urbanist housing based on the image of a small town of the 1920s. Some additional attempts to reconnect housing with social services and economic activity are necessary to improve neighborhoods for women, yet these are the very decisions large real estate developers are often unwilling to make, since they involve nonmarket as well as market activities. A comparison of New Urbanist projects with recent European ones aimed at women's equity suggests the difference lies in public services for women. New Urbanists have championed the residential neighborhood and need to focus on economic equality within it.

EUROPEAN CHARTER FOR WOMEN IN THE CITY

In 1994, the Equal Opportunities Unit of the Commission of the European Communities drafted its "European Charter for Women in the City." With the goal of achieving gender parity (*parité*) in democracy, this group encouraged Europeans to "Rediscover the city through women's eyes, abolish stereotypes." The European Commission began to provide funding for action-oriented research on gender issues in programs for mobility and urban safety, as well as new housing experiments and neighborhood organizations.[70] It drew on a wide range of existing networks and examples. In Vienna, Austria, the "Frauenbüro," or office of women, was composed of a

dozen geographers, architects, and planners, as part of city government. They were already far along with plans for several hundred
units of social housing designed by women architects. The Viennese
officials noted that women comprised 53 percent of Vienna's population, and said that it was about time that women got their share as
taxpayers. Their new complex, opened in the mid-1990s, includes
housing, child care, open space, and a police station with specially
trained staff to assist victims of rape or domestic violence.[71] In
Barcelona, Spain, the European Commission funded the Fundació
Maria Aurèlia Capmany, which organized a coalition of women's
trade unions, neighborhood organizations, academics, and architects
to prepare a manual of projects on women in the city.[72]

Working along similar lines in Canada, Gerda Wekerle documented a network of women's housing cooperatives as well as a citizen group called Women Plan Toronto.[73] In an international
framework, architect and urban planner Hemalata Dandekar
organized a 1992 conference at the College of Architecture and
Urban Planning at the University of Michigan. The conference led
to a volume, *Shelter, Women, and Development: First and Third
World Perspectives*, with several dozen essays commenting on
existing conditions and women's demonstration projects around
the world.[74] The United Nations took up women's shelter issues as
a part of economic development and began to list best practices for
demonstration projects on their Web site.[75]

CONSTRUCTION OR RECONSTRUCTION?

Beecher, Bebel, and Peirce all stamped their conceptual models of
home with the fears and desires of the mid-nineteenth century.
The architectural programs derived from that time are all anachronistic: the hope of seclusion embodied in the hut, the fantasy of
efficiency attached to the machine, and the nostalgia for the intact
pre-industrial village expressed in the neighborhood model. Yet
each of these mid-nineteenth-century architectural programs has
persisted into the twenty-first century. Dream houses equipped
with new computers are one prospect. High-rises of 300-square-
foot efficiencies are another. Housing developments disguised as
eighteenth-century Yankee villages are a third. The New Urbanists

have pushed for better physical planning. The European Charter for Women in the City holds out a different prospect, advocating both urban design and housing policy tied to equality for women. Could these programs be effective in the U.S.?

How can Americans adapt the 102.8 million units standing in the United States, as well as design for new realities? Architect Roger Montgomery has argued that "Conservation, recycling in currently fashionable jargon, perforce goes slowly, piecemeal, in very small scale units. To be in tune with the future, house architects and landscape architects will have to practice in equivalently small and piecemeal ways."[76] Yet if the scope of reconstruction is to be national, the needs to be met are larger than ever when political and environmental questions are taken seriously. As the Soviets put it in 1926, "a new life demands new forms." Americans are often living the new life, with the two-earner family, while not yet making the spatial changes that will provide new forms. Can Americans, having splurged on houses as havens, afford new forms? Can the U.S. afford the intensive reconstruction necessary to make dream house tracts into better neighborhoods for women?

Part III

Rethinking
Public Life

SOME KINDS OF CARE FOR
OTHERS CANNOT BE
BOUGHT OR SOLD. BUT
THEY CAN BE
STRENGTHENED — OR
WEAKENED — BY THE WAY
WE ORGANIZE OUR
ECONOMY.

—Nancy Folbre

Chapter 7

Reconstructing Domestic Space

Dody Green got national press in 1981 at a zoning meeting in Springdale, Connecticut, where she and her husband had lived for eighteen years. "There have been a lot of changes in the suburbs, most of them for the worse," she said. "But now they are trying to carve up the American Dream itself—the family home—and I'm going to fight it."[1] The mayor of Springdale wanted to legalize small accessory apartments created within the three- and four-bedroom houses of her neighborhood. Mrs. Green told William Geist of the *New York Times* that she did not like it: "They are doing this in the name of the elderly, and for the struggling young couple. But I do not see this. I see greedy neighbors who are trying to make a few dollars off of a housing shortage and I see officials looking the other way. We have to fight it. They bring in experts to tell us how wonderful this is for everyone. Well, I have had experience in this, and it isn't as nice as they say. Apartments are a sign of deterioration. It takes the sparkle out of the American Dream just knowing there are apartments on the block."

On either side of Mr. and Mrs. Green's house, neighbors had built rental units within their houses. Across the United States, hundreds of builders have remodeled attics, basements, or garages to make apartments, altering the character of their property and their neighborhoods. In many ways, the new apartments make sense. Sometimes they are legal. Never before has the single-family house been so expensive. Never before has owning a house involved such high property taxes. Ownership is always somewhat inflexible. It can be difficult to sell a single-family house in order to accommodate a life change, divorce, relocation, retirement, or to realize one's equity to meet other expenses. There is more housing space per capita in this country than anywhere else in the world, more rooms per person, more rooms per household, and more land per household. Now Americans need more adaptable spatial designs, with fewer inducements to achieve greater residential satisfaction by moving.

House sizes for new construction have almost tripled in the last fifty years, from 800 square feet and one bath, to 2,250 square feet and two and a half baths.[2] Meanwhile average household size has decreased, from 3.37 persons in 1950 to 2.62 persons in 1998.[3] The misfit between buildings and families represents both a problem and an opportunity. One elderly woman interviewed by planner Patrick Hare complained, "I do not want to spend my golden years cleaning three bathrooms."[4] At the same time that the elderly are seeking smaller units, the demand for smaller homes is also increasing among the young. Division of the existing housing stock seems desirable, yet the ideal of the intact one-family home dies hard. As Dody Green protested at her zoning meeting: "This was my dream, a house on a quiet street in the suburbs. There have been enough changes, now they want to undermine the foundation of the dream itself, the house, by subdividing it. We will fight them to the finish." Mrs. Green's phrases, "take the sparkle out of the American Dream," and "carve up the American Dream," reflected her fearful assessment of the situation. One could observe, more optimistically, that renovations create commitment to house and neighborhood, to staying with the American dream and updating it. Commitment means looking again at the usefulness of houses, as opposed to their theoretical market prices. It involves examining the basic shelter needs of households, as opposed to the rising costs of building materials and energy. It involves reappraising the mutual assistance families give (or do not give) to their neighbors, as opposed to the costs of new commercial services or government services. A leading ecologist has noted, "There is theoretical love and then there's applied love."[5] There is the theoretical dream of the one-family house, wearing a bit thin, and the applied one, that depends on continued ingenuity, resourcefulness, and neighborliness. American citizens and designers need a way to balance new needs with high standards for change.

Is it possible to improve American housing to satisfy many different constituencies, and give the phrase "American dream" new meaning? This would involve replanning single-family neighborhoods where there is pressure for accessory apartments. At the same time, it would require improvements in the programming of new housing for new household types as well as rehabilitation of the existing public housing stock. For all this to happen, a coalition of planners, designers, citizens, and political leaders would need to emerge to regulate the efforts of the building industry and encourage both market and nonmarket solutions.

THE BUILDERS' APPROACH — GREENFIELD CONSTRUCTION

During the administrations of Ronald Reagan and George Bush, Sr., various housing task forces and policy advisers took the position that the building industry could provide the solution to American social and economic needs. While there might be good reason to build on the model of such innovative designs as Myrdal and Markelius' Stockholm project, the Nina West Homes, or the Danish experiment at Tynggarden, this is not what most American builders have wanted to do. Developers, banks, realtors, and government officials have proposed much less subtle solutions. The 1982 *Report of the President's Commission on Housing* came to a single conclusion: that builders should be free to create tracts of smaller units, including mobile homes, placed closer together, on any land they liked, and to transfer many infrastructure costs to local governments.[6] The Urban Land Institute's study, *The Affordable Community,* cosponsored by HUD, made the same plea for relaxation of existing controls to favor new construction and new purchases of homes. Yet the grass roots response has been in favor of conservation and adaptive reuse of existing housing. The homeowners of America want to keep their towns the way they are, or increase densities on their own terms. They do not want to see their towns ringed with low-density, cheap construction.

Between 1990 and 2000, the built-up areas of metropolitan regions expanded at an alarming rate, as fields were paved over for new houses, roads, and commercial areas. The National Resources Defense Council published *Once There Were Greenfields* in 1999, explaining these losses.[7] Many Americans began to work in "edge cities," vast new areas of commercial and office space adjacent to highway offramps. When jobs moved to the edge cities, workers decided to commute farther out. By 2000, the fastest growing areas of the United States were on the urban-rural fringe, where small towns with pedestrian-scale centers were often overwhelmed by new automobile-oriented construction. A vast literature has developed on "the costs of sprawl."[8] Economists attempt to quantify both infrastructure costs and less easily measured costs such as time lost in traffic on crowded freeways, deteriorating air quality, or destruction of the local sense of place.[9]

For example, in the 1980s, officials in Madison, Wisconsin calculated the city's cost of sanitary sewers, storm drainage, water mains, and local streets at $16,500 per acre of new development, excluding schools, fire stations, and arterial streets.[10] Under Republican Mayor Pete Wilson, San Diego estimated overall costs to the city of one new detached suburban house at $13,500 and began billing this infrastructure charge to startled developers.[11] Fairfield, California, estimated that total tax revenues from new housing development would cover half the cost of police services and nothing more. By 2001, infrastructure costs had tripled in many places and were often discussed in the popular press.[12] When profit-making developers ask towns and cities to pay for the infrastructure to support new building, most mayors are wary. Taxpayers often do not want to absorb these costs.

Most of the towns and cities of the United States simply cannot afford rampant new development: not the infrastructure cost, or the service cost, or the energy cost. New housing requires neighborhood planning where housing is coordinated with jobs, services, transportation, and landscaping. Some planners call this approach "smart growth." What may be of greatest advantage to a neighborhood, town, or region will not be the same package favored by developers.[13] As economist David Morris has observed, many cities should deal with the problem of unequal resource flows in and out of a specific area by developing a "domestic" policy and a "foreign" policy, much as if these were "balance-of-payments" questions.[14] Local economic planning at the level of the city and the neighborhood is necessary if regional development is to be balanced and equitable overall.

ALTERNATIVE APPROACHES OF INFILL AND RECONSTRUCTION

While greenfield construction is favored by developers and designers, infill is the more practical, locally oriented route to change. Infill offers the potential for citizens to end the owner-speculation on one-family houses, halt the flood of new commercial products and services that do little to support family life, and create local economic development instead.

No one wants to be tied into the lockstep of a completely planned social and economic regimen, but when resources are finite, new economic incentives emerge. What are the precedents for neighbors to organize and make new agreements about how to reuse the residential landscape? Existing mutual aid groups are already present in most suburban and urban neighborhoods, as well as small-scale economic activities of the kind that enhance neighborhood options. There are neighbors involved with making vacant lots into parks and playgrounds. There are baby-sitting co-ops and car pools that represent agreements for shared labor, usually by parents of children of the same age. There are some centers where newspapers, tin cans, glass bottles, and used appliances are recycled. Garage sales are also recycling efforts. In addition, there are small, licensed day-care providers, and homemakers who run catering, cosmetics, or Tupperware businesses. There are professionals who work at home—typists, editors, freelance writers, graphic designers, doctors, architects, and lawyers. There are always teenagers who want to earn money after school or on vacations. All of these bits and pieces of economic activity can be developed into more coherent patterns and related to existing social service programs.

What would be the scope of a practical program for change? A program broad enough to transform housework, housing design, and the economics of residential neighborhoods must, first, support women's and men's participation in the unpaid labor associated with housekeeping and child care on an equal basis; second, support women's and men's participation in the paid-labor force on an equal basis; third, reduce residential segregation by income, race, and age; fourth, minimize wasteful energy consumption; fifth, maximize real choices about recreation and sociability; and sixth, retain privacy in housing while adding new dwellings and new service options. While there are many partial reforms that can support these goals, a piecemeal strategy alone cannot achieve them because of the split between private and public life which is at the heart of the problem. Reorganization of the built environment involves both economic and architectural restructuring.

Demonstration projects from our own culture and from other countries provide models and offer experience about what may work, and what may not. Nonprofit groups play a key role in developing alternatives to the market or the state. Most adults in the United States are not interested in moving toward communal groups, nor are they interested in having new bureaucracies run family life. They desire community services to support the private household, rather than an end to private life altogether. They also desire solutions that reinforce their economic independence and enhance personal choices about child rearing and sociability. They want homeownership to remain an American tradition, albeit one that can be improved and expanded.

Each of the alternatives to new speculative housing involves a different set of planning issues and a slightly different constituency. Three possibilities need examination: first, adding accessory apartments to homes in existing single-family neighborhoods; second, rehabilitating existing public housing with fewer units but more space for jobs and services; and third, constructing new kinds of multifamily housing to meet the needs of diverse household types.

ACCESSORY APARTMENTS IN SINGLE-FAMILY NEIGHBORHOODS

Citizens and planners have three choices about how to proceed with the existing single-family housing stock. It can be remodeled illegally, on a piecemeal basis; it can be remodeled legally, on a piecemeal basis; or it can be remodeled legally within the context of replanned blocks. In towns choosing the third option, it would be possible to encourage incremental changes with accessory apartments, while planning for the whole to become more than the sum of the parts. Instead of updating our single-family houses as primitive sacred huts, Americans can coax, push, and nudge whole blocks toward the model of the neighborhood, where accountability is a stronger value than privacy. This could be done by refusing zoning variances and building permits to owners who wish to build accessory apartments unless they comply with an agreed-upon neighborhood improvement plan. For instance, owners who add a rental unit to their property could be assessed for additional amenities such as street trees, underground wiring, off-street parking, and community green space.

While planners in some towns and cities have encouraged accessory apartments, others have chosen to ignore them, or to wink and look the other way.[15] Planners may argue that changing the traditional R-1 zoning is difficult politically. They may feel that calling attention to the problem will decrease the supply of affordable housing and even cause hardship to families where the second unit is intended for an elderly parent (who might otherwise be in a nursing home), or a young daughter or son (whose alternative is a rental unit where grandparents cannot baby-sit for them). Some planners estimate that there are already up to two and a half million illegal conversions, however, and at this scale, piecemeal remodeling in suburbia causes planning problems: loss of acoustical privacy, strain on existing utilities, fire hazards, and lack of street parking.

Certain planners have attempted to attack the issues by introducing legislation favoring the new units. According to Patrick

Hare's report *Accessory Apartments: Using Surplus Space in Single-Family Houses*, areas actively promoting the legal conversion of excess space in one-family houses into rental units in 1982 included Portland, Oregon; New Castle, Babylon, and Lydenhurst, New York; Weston, Connecticut; Montclair and Princeton, New Jersey; Fairfax, Virginia; Concord and Lincoln, Massachusetts; Belvedere and San Anselmo, California. In these towns, in neighborhoods ranging from working class to upper class, with housing stock ranging from Victorian mansions to post–World War II split-levels, conversions were legal under certain circumstances.

These conversions were restricted to houses of a certain size (Portland) or to lots of a certain size (Princeton) or to houses of a certain age (Montclair). This last provision discouraged new houses in one-family districts designed for instant conversion to two-family houses. Accessory apartments may also be restricted to owner-occupied houses (Portland and New Castle) or even restricted to relatives of the homeowners (Fairfax and Montclair). They may be subject to intensive review processes—by neighbors, zoning boards, or special accessory apartment boards. Particular concerns include adequate off-street parking (Lincoln), adequate sewage facilities, and maintaining indicators of one-family neighborhood character, such as keeping only one front entrance visible from the front yard (Babylon, New York and Brookline, Massachusetts).[16] To many citizens and planners, these legal restrictions and review processes have guaranteed a smooth transition from old-fashioned single-family neighborhoods to neighborhoods with better housing resources. Some towns even required yearly code of occupancy reviews. The most sensitive planners offered a little extra flexibility in physical design requirements to encourage barrier-free conversions for the handicapped.[17]

Even so, the legally restricted remodeling of single-family houses was not an answer to the full range of planning, design, and landscaping needs embodied in the housing problem, nor was it a full exercise of the opportunities available in these districts. The relaxed zoning laws suggested how short-term private investments of time and money could be used to support homeowners' longer term investments, and they provided safeguards for neighbors who did not want the quality of their neighborhoods to deteriorate.[18] By 2001, these new laws were common.[19] Yet, the house-by-house approach denied that, over several decades, most of the single-family housing stock and most of the neighborhoods might change to reflect basic demographic shifts.

Legalizing house-by-house conversions not only denied the scale of demographic change, it denied the economics. While some of the ordinances prohibited absentee owners from gaining the appreciation in property values a rental unit provided, none dealt with the economic question of the owner-speculator who saw the rental unit as a way to increase the value of his or her own property at the expense of neighbors' property values, represented by low densities and quiet, traffic-free streets. Some cities, such as Davis, California and Washington, D.C., did restrict the owner-speculator in the early 1980s. In Davis, no one could buy a single-family home unless he or she was willing to live in it as a principal place of residence for one year. In Washington, D.C., a graduated capital gains tax penalized those who bought and sold property quickly.[20] Santa Cruz, California, acknowledged the plight of the renter by requiring that accessory apartments be rented only to low and moderate income tenants. When Dody Green complained about "greedy neighbors who are trying to make a few dollars off of a housing shortage," she targeted the problem of the owner-speculators in Springdale, Connecticut.

To develop a broader perspective, citizens, planners, and designers must cast an interested eye on the whole suburban and urban landscape, and begin to think at the scale of the block, the neighborhood, and the city or town. The time horizon for this broader analysis extends two or three decades, not two or three years. Just as some cities now bill infrastructure charges or demand other amenities be built by large-scale commercial developers operating within their bounds, so some neighborhoods will scrutinize the public costs and private benefits of what homeowners want to do, and bill them accordingly.

THE CONSTITUENCY FOR ACCESSORY APARTMENTS

Who might become part of an effort to transform residential neighborhoods? Who could lobby for more comprehensive planning efforts, including changes in zoning, incentives to local economic development, and reorganization of local social services? Planner Patrick Hare identified one constituency, older homeowners: "They are politically unassailable and would be acting out of legitimate self-interest. A related group would be the sons and daughters of older homeowners who cannot take their parents into their own homes, but do not want to see them forced into nursing homes or other institutions."[21] (He conceded that there were problems with the grown children as lobbyists because they might not live in the same towns as their parents; this, he believed, would lead to lobbying at the county, state, and national level for zoning changes.) Hare argued that elderly homeowners could acquire new bargaining power in American society through their creative concern for the unused space in their homes. In 1982, residents over 65 controlled "the nation's largest untapped housing resource," which Hare estimated as 14 percent of the owner-occupied housing stock. In 1999, this had risen to 25 percent.[22]

Many sociologists have observed that the elderly do not choose to move from their homes, even when their health or financial situation becomes precarious. Many elderly cannot bear the psychological consequences of losing ties to their dwellings and communities. For elderly homeowners, changing the ways the existing housing stock is used would be appropriate. In addition, the elderly in good health may want accessory apartments either for income or for tenants who could help with home maintenance. Their children often want zoning permission for apartments or "elder cottages" for the frail elderly.[23]

A second constituency for change consists of young people who are now tenants of apartments and their middle-aged parents who are owners. Many young single people and young childless couples cannot afford to buy houses in the towns where they grew up. Their parents are empty-nesters. They would like to be near their grown children and help their children economically. In the past, the parents might have provided their children with the down payment on a small house near their own; now, all they can provide is an accessory apartment in their own home. By accommodating more young single people and more young couples, as well as the single elderly, neighborhoods can house diverse age groups and diverse household types to bring more varied family ties and friendships into the lives of suburban residents.[24] New kinds of financial arrangements and architectural arrangements might make it more attractive for younger people to live in or near their parents' homes, while preserving privacy and autonomy as young adults. If they could, for instance, become co-owners of private spaces within their parents' houses, rather than heirs, it might add to the attraction of living in a separate apartment in the same dwelling.

A third potential constituency consists of single parents, male and female, and their children. The national association, Parents Without Partners, seeks housing options for its members. In his book, *Going It Alone*, sociologist Robert Weiss noted that housing has always been a major problem for this group.[25] Some single parents have tried shared housing—two parents inhabiting a single-family house—but this has met with mixed success. The existing housing stock in suburbia needs to be modified architecturally to meet single parents' needs for privacy as well as support. Shared housing programs have to overcome the significant spatial conventions most of us carry with us. These are not so much a function of square footages as much as a need for gradual spatial transitions from community to privacy. A house designed for one family cannot accommodate two families unless these physical transitions are redesigned.

Women form a fourth constituency.[26] Women often bear the burden of maintaining kinship ties across generations. They also have a special interest in developing day care as a community service, and in creating local jobs to ease commuting for employed mothers.

A fifth constituency consists of environmental activists. In such an effort, conservation-minded citizens and small designers, carpenters, and builders might find common interests.[27]

A sixth constituency is people of color, both owners and renters, who have experienced difficulties in finding, renting, buying, and reselling suburban dwellings. The research of Robert Lake and Thomas Clark has shown that racial discrimination has limited minority participation in the capital accumulation that many white homeowners have achieved, although the number of blacks in suburbia has increased since the 1970s.[28] When people of color, as owners and renters, are more committed to certain neighborhoods, they are a potential constituency for projects that play down the role of the owner-speculator in favor of greater neighborhood improvements available to the community. They also form a potential constituency to combat gentrification.

A seventh potential constituency consists of the Dody Greens of America, who cannot stand noise, too many cars, or greedy neighbors. Mr. and Mrs. Green were living in a rapidly changing neighborhood, fighting a rear guard action. The alternative for them, and for other homeowners concerned about the amenities of their neighborhoods, was to insist that changes be made to the highest standards of quality in planning and design. The benefits to people like the Greens of joining forces to replan their neighborhood, rather than simply fighting those who want it to be rezoned, are substantial. The planners and designers who care about quality need the Greens on their team to speak up in favor of quiet, trees, and public transportation, and to fulminate against owner-speculators. This last constituency of house-proud owners is key, if their high standards can represent zeal for quality rather than resistance to change.

REORGANIZING THE DREAM HOUSES

Consider a stereotypical tract of the 1950s and 1960s. A modest suburban block will have been divided into plots of a quarter to half an acre each. If there are thirteen houses, then thirteen driveways might be used by twenty-six cars; thirteen garden sheds, thirteen swings, thirteen lawn mowers, and thirteen outdoor dining tables begin to suggest the repetition of amenities. Yet, in the existing design, there are few transitions between the public streets and the private homes—no community park, no space to socialize with neighbors—because space is either strictly private or strictly public. The typical one-family houses—ranch, split level, or colonial—will probably include three bedrooms and den, two and a half baths, a laundry room, and a two-car garage.

It is easy to see how such suburban single-family houses could be remodeled. Hattie Hartman developed a handbook to show many variations. A 2,000 square-foot house can become a duplex or triplex, with a two-bedroom unit; a one-bedroom unit; and perhaps an efficiency unit for a single person. The three units can

7.1 A typical tract of single-family houses without any common space, 1970s. Imagine every house becoming a duplex or a triplex as accessory apartments are added, legally or illegally.

share a porch and entry hall. While the remodeled apartments are small (400 to 800 square feet), they are not as tiny as some that developers have proposed or even executed as new construction.[29] Many experiments can take place with regard to the sizes and shapes of new apartments. They can be in the garage, extending into the backyard, under the roof, or at the bottom levels of a split-level design. A good architect can make many of these plans work. Designing for acoustical privacy is especially important.

Architect Renée Chow's elegant book, *Suburban Spaces: The Fabric of Dwelling*, suggests that "while suburban houses pretend to be independent from one another, it is their interrelationship that needs to be acknowledged and designed." She emphasizes "weaving of a fabric for dwelling" in the suburbs by "describing relations not just within but between houses." Her research methods involve meticulous measurements of both traditional house types and multifamily designs around the country, to show that "private and public are not seen as opposing, but as reciprocal." She looks for "an alternative view of single detached housing that supports diverse choices of ways to live; that provides desired private outdoor space, but does not waste it; and that allows opportunities for individuals and households to build their own sense of community that can change over time."[30]

RELANDSCAPING THE DREAM NEIGHBORHOODS

Unless the entire block is landscaped to create more common green space, the conversion of one house to two or three apartments will not be especially pleasant in its connection of indoor and outdoor spaces. A minimum recommendation would be to provide private outdoor space for each unit. Preferably this would be a small garden, but porches and decks could serve first- and second-floor apartments. Aesthetically the neighborhood as a whole would be improved if empty front lawns were replaced with diverse, small, private gardens, and new front porches. But an even greater aesthetic impact can be achieved if residents start to create new common land by joining parts of their yards. Many American suburban blocks are large enough to accommodate private gardens and new common land as well. Pedestrian paths and sidewalks can be created to link housing with such central spaces. Private porches, garages, and tool sheds could also be more intensely utilized as semipublic or public spaces. Precedents for this approach were proposed in the post–World War II era, as well as in more recent years.

In redefining the American suburban block spatially, there are two alternatives: a zone of greater activity at the street or at the center of the block. Urban neighborhoods may wish to emphasize the public aspects of street life; Raquel Ramati's book *How to Save Your Own Street* suggested this for Manhattan.[31] In suburbia, there are great advantages to turning the block inside out for

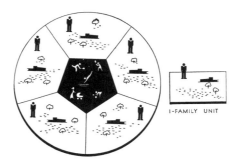

7.2 Architect's diagram from the 1940s proposing suburban community with shared child care and recreation space. The roles were traditional but not the land use.

community use away from the auto. Clarence Stein clearly delin-
eated this second approach as better design for "the motor age,"
with cars segregated from residents' green spaces and spaces for
children. At Radburn, New Jersey, and in the Baldwin Hills
Village in Los Angeles, Stein achieved remarkably luxurious
results (at a density of about seven units to the acre) by this
method, since multiple-unit housing always bordered a lush park-
land without automobile traffic.[32] A revitalized suburban block
with lots as small as a quarter of an acre could be reorganized to
yield a similar effect. Shared green space of this kind is also the
tradition in some of the most expensive and exclusive row house
blocks in New York.

Some neighborhoods will find the model of the traditional village greens of New England a powerful inspiration, and many
Americans could have town greens again, by literally carving out
the heart of every converted suburban block for shared open space
where new neighborhood activities could be accommodated. The
experiences of one European city and one American city demonstrate the various ways in which backyard rehabilitations have
been accomplished.

The work of architect Hans Wirz of Zurich, Switzerland exploited the potential of his city's backyards, alleys, and service
entrances, and provided an extensive, urban case study of how to
relandscape residential blocks. Wirz succeeded in getting his city
to vote $300,000 in funds to sponsor such projects, as well as to
establish a city agency to "encourage, motivate, and coordinate
involved property owners," to conduct the often lengthy negotia-
tions, and participate in the design and construction process. By
1979, his efforts resulted in twenty completed block rehabilitations
of backyard spaces in Zurich.

With the city agency providing technical, legal, and financial
assistance to groups of homeowners, tenant organizations, and
housing cooperatives, the projects proceeded with voluntary participation and private initiative. Four basic categories developed.
In projects emphasizing private and semipublic space, private
yards were reduced in depth to half their size, and the remaining
land was developed as a cooperatively owned central open space
accessible to each private yard. In other neighborhoods, the
whole backyard area was turned into common space accessible to

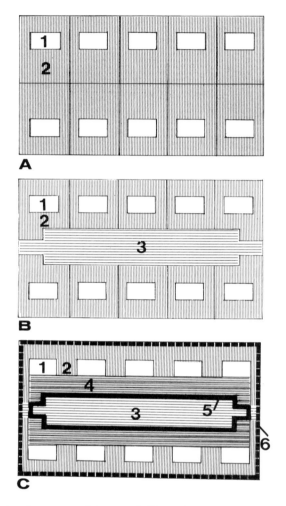

7.3 Diagram showing some of the possibilities of reorganizing a typical suburban block through rezoning, rebuilding, and relandscaping. A, ten single-family houses (1) on ten private lots (2); B, the same houses (1) with smaller private lots (2) after a backyard rehabilitation program has created a new village green (3) at the heart of the block; C, the same houses (1) and many small private gardens (2) with a new village green (3) surrounded by a zone for a new services and accessory apartments (4) connected by a new sidewalk or arcade (5) and surrounded by a new border of street trees (6). In figure C, (4) can include space for such activities as day care, elderly care, laundry, and food service as well as housing, while (3) can accommodate a children's play area, vegetable or flower gardens, and outdoor seating. (5) may be a sidewalk, a vine-covered trellis, or a formal arcade. The narrow ends of the block can be emphasized as collective entrances with gates (to which residents have keys), leading to new accessory apartments entered from the arcade or sidewalk. In the densest possible situations, (3) may be alley and parking lot, if existing street parking and public transit are not adequate.

all. A third type of project involved making community services, such as day-care centers, in new common spaces. The most urbanized, mixed-use areas with both retail and housing required that expensive, underground parking be constructed in the rear yards. Commercial uses helped to finance construction of an accessible roof deck over the parking lot as a common space.

Wirz has noted that his main obstacle was "the skepticism of home owners that an agreement can be reached among the neighbors regarding the legal, financial, and other design considerations involved." He believed that "it was essential for" a third party—such as Zurich's special agency for rear yard rehabilitation—to be available to channel and coordinate individual interests and initiatives.[33] Wirz noted that the United States has great potential. There are similar problems but even greater opportunities given more generous lot sizes. Either a town's planning and zoning agency or a neighborhood association could undertake such activities.

Cheyenne, Wyoming provides another model of how some groups might build upon Wirz's work. For the last twenty-five years, solar greenhouses run by a community development corporation have generated income from a commercial nursery, food from a community garden, and environmental education for all. Building and gardening activities develop a sense of citizen accountability for the young, the middle-aged, and the old. The Cheyenne project began in 1976 as a program employing fifteen low-income community youths to build three small solar greenhouses on vacant lots. The youths worked on these as an alternative to going to jail. The greenhouses provided food for a group home of thirty-five handicapped people. The success of the small greenhouses led to a larger community undertaking in 1977, involving the design and construction of a three-stage, three-growing-climate, 5,000-square-foot greenhouse. In spite of heavy snow and long winters, the greenhouse produced its first harvest in May, 1978. Director Gary Garber reported that the project attracted about eighty gardeners ranging in age from ten to ninety-two, including retirees and the handicapped.

What seems most distinctive about the Cheyenne system, as compared with the outdoor community gardens found in Santa Monica, California, or many other towns where city residents cultivate private plots and socialize across the plot lines, is that the cultivation proceeds collectively. The greenhouse's paid staff select plantings, make up work schedules, and assign jobs to participants. Harvesting is more remarkable: "individuals simply take what they need. In some cases, people who may work at the greenhouse three or four days a week for several hours a day may choose to take little or nothing, while an individual with less time to spend but more need might take whatever is ready to pick." According to Garber, there were no problems with this system of distribution, because people got to know each other through working side-by-side in the structure, and developed bonds of mutual understanding and respect. Garber noted that, "This has been one of the least anticipated and most heartening aspects of the project."[34]

Yields constantly increased; two sections of the greenhouse produced foods such as tomatoes, onions, spinach, and herbs in two growing seasons, while the third was used for commercial production of plants to generate income. Environmental education was also essential. As Garber said, "A visitor at the greenhouse may be greeted by a retired school teacher, a little girl, or a weather-beaten old cowboy. Any of them will gladly conduct a tour and explain how everything works. A visitor will see a cross-section of the community—young and old, rich and poor—working side-by-side. Some are there to socialize, some to learn, while others need the food." Garber concluded that his project was "an alternative energy park where people can learn not only how to save energy, but how to create it." By 2001, the project had been replicated in a city park, with Shane Smith, a horticulturist, directing the activities of the renamed Cheyenne Botanic Garden. Garber, meanwhile, went on to become marketing director for a nonprofit, member-owned electrical cooperative, working on renewable energy projects all over Wyoming.[35]

Homeownership has long been associated with the "each farmer on his own farm" sort of territoriality, translated into fences and guard dogs in some suburban areas. New neighborhood densities are certain to cause friction. While financial need will be pressing some owners to accept new densities, the American nonverbal conventions of personal space attached to suburban homeownership may generate resistance. Yet a closer look at homeownership, in comparison with other forms of domestic proprietorship, suggests it can be renegotiated.

Homeownership in Limited-Equity Cooperatives

In 2000, John Emmeus Davis documented nonprofit or "third sector" housing initiatives as successful projects: privately owned, price restricted, and socially oriented.[36] As Davis argues, homeownership is a powerful national inducement for any policy change, whether it is wielded in favor of those who want to retain it or those who want to achieve it. There is nothing wrong with homeownership, if it is available to all without regard to gender or race, if owners do not receive tax benefits unavailable to renters, and if owners do not speculate on their homes and deprive the next generation of a chance for ownership. An alternative version of current forms of homeownership is the limited-equity cooperative. Such an organization holds a blanket mortgage on housing units, maintains them, takes care of the common land. Owners receive all personal income tax deductions that single mortgage holders do, but they sell their shares back to the co-op when they leave, rather than selling a unit on the open housing market. The rate of appreciation is determined in their membership agreement. In many neighborhoods, a limited-equity cooperative association concerned with taking care of buildings and common land could be a way to nurture commitment to a specific place, to encourage accountability to a group, to educate the young about the necessary work of society, and to carry out the responsibilities every generation has to those older and younger.

In neighborhoods dealing with accessory apartments on a long-term basis, forming a limited-equity cooperative of owners would assure that the housing—whether old units or new ones—would remain affordable. This strategy is fair to present owners, but discourages absentee landlords and speculators. Here is how such an arrangement might develop in a neighborhood with a long-term landscape plan and a policy of strict enforcement of zoning and building codes. Let's say that Owner A wants a permit to convert excess space in a $170,000 house into an extra apartment. Suppose the tough local planning board offers owner A two choices. First: Owner A can subdivide the house into a legal duplex, and sell the second unit for the market price, $55,000, provided that both Owner A and the new duplex owner then enter into a limited-equity cooperative association, which fixes the future appreciation of each unit and handles neighborhood improvements. Second: Owner A can subdivide the house by making one legal accessory apartment for rental income subject to a special assessment for neighborhood improvements by the neighbors' association. If Owner A wants cash, he or she will subdivide and sell. If Owner A wants income, he or she will subdivide, pay the neighborhood assessment, and collect rent. The second approach can lead to the first after some years. Either way, a local planning authority or a neighborhood association can begin to gain the power to plan more changes over time as owners feel the pressure to make legal conversions to realize part of their equity, or to increase their income. Those who feel the pressure of foreclosure, those who are elderly, and those who are getting divorced or separated would be most likely to sell part but not all of their property. Households with extra space or households needing help with maintenance, babysitting, or elderly care would be more likely to rent.

The Route Two Cooperative in Los Angeles provides a model for the shared ownership of existing houses by new types of households, although it is not a model of how to start such a process, because it all began with a proposal for a freeway. In the pressure to expand the Los Angeles freeway system of the 1960s, Caltrans, the California transportation agency, condemned 124 small single-family houses and 90 apartment buildings containing 350 units, in order to build a 2.4-mile extension of Route 2 called the Glendale Freeway. For fourteen years, the low- and moderate-income housing units sat, deteriorating, in the projected path of the freeway. When the freeway extension was held up by protest groups, Caltrans rented them on a temporary basis. Finally, the freeway plan was abandoned and the state proposed to resell the housing units at market prices. The former owners argued that years had gone by and they could not afford to repurchase their own houses. The tenants joined them in protest.[37]

After an heroic organizing drive over several years, aided by the Los Angeles Community Design Center, the Route Two Cooperative won support for a different proposal. Caltrans agreed to rehabilitate these properties and to offer all the tenants (and former owners) the first chance to purchase them. But, because a public agency was involved, everyone agreed that they had to produce affordable units and prohibit speculation in order to keep them affordable. House prices ranged from $25,000 to $60,000; apartments in a limited-equity cooperative on scattered sites cost about $20,000. The FHA insured mortgages arranged by a consortium of local lenders. After years of being threatened by eviction, the dream of homeownership came true—but without the possibility of speculative profit. The resale of any unit was restricted to other low- and moderate-income families.[38]

A limited-equity cooperative structure has several other advantages besides easing the psychological and economic transition from lower to higher densities. It also solves maintenance problems for common land and it can introduce new economic activities to combine jobs and services with housing. Any new suburban parks, courtyards, or greens imply shared maintenance, or proprietorship, as Ronald Fleming and Lauri Halderman point out in *On Common Ground*.[39] Their concept of proprietorship is derived from New England Puritan covenant communities. In each town's covenant, the greens were established as common lands by the original settlers, called the proprietors. Proprietorship can mean many different forms of ownership, management, and concern, but any shared space needs care by its owners or users. If the shared space includes shared economic and social activities, even more organization is required. How much are neighbors capable of doing together? Gradual involvement in projects that provide real gains to an entire neighborhood can reassure neighbors that the struggle to organize and work collectively actually produces results that are worth the long meetings, economic risks, and social challenges.

PUBLIC HOUSING: MAKING IT MORE LIKE HOME

Public housing represents a relatively small part of the American housing stock, but it is a crucial area for improvement in the combination of housing, jobs, and services for residents. The majority of public-housing tenants are female-headed families. In 1998, the 2.8 million Public Housing Authority tenants earned, on average, 17 percent of median U.S. family income. Almost 60 percent of the households were people of color, while 33 percent were elderly.[40]

These households suffer from all of the restrictions on women's earning capability and independent movement in the city that have been explored.

In the late 1940s, severe cost restrictions were placed on public housing by legislators, and very bad buildings resulted. Grim projects were planned without any local employment for women or day-care services. In the worst cases, these projects were also located away from urban centers, such as Boston's huge Columbia Point housing project, seven miles from downtown on the site of an old garbage dump. The residents of these projects were usually expected to subsist on such programs as Aid to Families with Dependent Children (AFDC) and Food Stamps, programs that simulated the traditional family with the welfare mother as home-maker, cooking meals and minding children all day long, even though the male breadwinner was often absent.

Forward-looking social service administrators who wished to find ways to locate jobs and day care in subsidized housing, and

7.4 Public housing, Columbia Point, Dorchester, Massachusetts, before renovation as Harbor Point. Many aging housing projects remain in need of job development programs for women residents and services such as child care, as well as renovation.

progressive housing administrators who wished to integrate more services with dwellings, found obstacles in the myriad rules, regulations, and prohibitions set up by HUD and HHS (the Department of Health and Human Services) that made the spatial connection of housing, jobs, and services a nightmare to administer.[41] Enterprising tenants, such as women who tried to make money serving dinners to their neighbors in the Williamsburg Houses in Brooklyn, were also frustrated by the charge that such businesses were illegal when run in housing space. In the 1980s, when tenant groups suggested removing units to make room for child care and jobs, their efforts were not appreciated at first, but they soon became influential.

In the 1990s, a new HUD approach to Consolidated Planning, and new programs such as HOPE VI (Housing Opportunities for People Everywhere, sixth phase) began to change the physical design of public housing to promote the connection of new dwellings with existing neighborhoods. Some obsolete public housing units were demolished. Others were revitalized. There was new construction. New site plans stressed low-rise housing with yards and porches fronting streets connected to local neighborhoods. The new projects attempted to attract market-rate tenants as well as subsidized ones, in order to create mixed-income neighborhoods. While this improved neighborhood quality, it forced many public housing tenants to be relocated.

In the mid-1990s, while HUD was working on HOPE VI, HHS attempted to reform welfare by replacing AFDC with jobs or job-training programs. However, the economic activities of residents were not always addressed on the sites of the housing projects. In contrast to earlier public housing programs that pushed the worlds of "home" and "work" farther apart, some designers of new projects have seen local economic development as an essential part of public housing reform.

The HOPE VI program included one project in Indianapolis, Indiana that focused on the construction itself as an opportunity for local economic development. Concord Village, administered by Eugene Jones as the Executive Director of the Indianapolis Housing Authority, was designed by Clyde Woods of Indianapolis and Tise, Hurwitz, and Diamond of Boston.[42] As part of a broad local economic development strategy, planners, architects, and organizers trained small local contractors to construct sections of a 220-unit public housing project, by designing the project so it could be built house by house. They worked at the scale of the older houses in an African-American neighborhood that had once been a streetcar suburb. Instead of contracting the whole project to a large builder, they enable very small builders to create new one- and two-family units to fit in with the existing neighborhood, extending its narrow streets and replicating its front porches in new construction. For the professionals involved, like project architects Daniel Glenn and Olon Dotsun, it meant tough, unglamorous work, with lots of organizing. By helping the local contractors to take part in a large federal project, and expand their skills and experience, the architects empowered the people in the neighborhood in ways that most HOPE VI projects never attempted.

Housing on Congregate Models for the Elderly, Singles, and Families

While single-family living appeals to most Americans, some groups benefit from more sociable settings. The route to independent living for many frail elderly people has required rethinking the standard house or apartment. This means integrating apartments with unobtrusive support services such as meals on wheels, health care, personal services, and counseling. Sometimes this is called "assisted living." While hotel chains have moved into serving this market, there are also nonprofit examples built by church groups or local governments. Like the frail elderly, healthy, young singles may also want spatial changes to support fuller social lives. Some families with young children are also attracted to cohousing.

Programming housing to suit new needs is a complex task, whether it leads to new construction or renovation. A few architectural examples suggest how important shared facilities can be.[43]

An Inn for the Elderly in New England

New Canaan, Connecticut, is one affluent town where residents struggled to meet the housing needs of the elderly who could no longer afford to live alone in their houses, or who could not manage the driving or physical maintenance that suburban houses required. When townspeople assessed the situation in 1981, they saw that there were few moderately priced rentals, and only one small inn in town taking a few elderly guests. As one man summed up the situation: "Many of our older citizens, who had contributed so much to the town, had had to move elsewhere in their later years. Or they had continued to live alone in their own homes, coping as best they could with problems of safety, loneliness, isolated locations, maintenance of their properties, and meal preparation. Our desire was to provide a conveniently located residence for seniors where they could live comfortably under one roof, but with dignity, privacy, and independence." So town residents decided to establish the New Canaan Inn as a nonsectarian, nonprofit corporation without any government funding.

A new building was designed by architect James Evans of Stamford as an inn with forty separate apartments (thirty-five studios and five one-bedrooms). An Episcopal church provided the land and initial financing. It is a short walk to shops and the post office. A retired librarian moved in to be in the center of things happening in town. Residents come together in the dining room, library, living room, and recreation areas. Residents enjoy three meals a day and invite guests for meals when they like. The Inn has a twenty-four-hour staff. The Friends of the Inn is a group of more than one hundred local volunteer drivers, helpers, and companions. The average age is ninety-one, and the oldest resident is ninety-nine. Residents can also obtain assisted living services from Nursing and Home Care, Inc., a local provider. The Inn celebrated its twentieth anniversary in 2001.[44] When asked if they could improve anything, a staff member suggested eliminating studio apartments in favor of one bedrooms.

Congregate Housing Designed for Privacy and Community

A similar project in Massachusetts operates with a state subsidy. At Captain Clarence Eldridge House in Hyannis, a New England sea captain's house was rehabilitated and extended to become congregate housing for the elderly. Architect Barry Korobkin, sociologist John Zeisel, and associated architects Donham and Sweeney

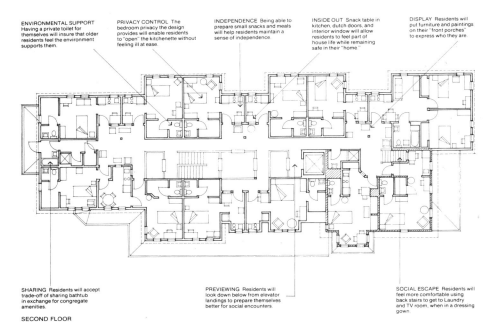

ENVIRONMENTAL SUPPORT Having a private toilet for themselves will insure that older residents feel the environment supports them.

PRIVACY CONTROL The bedroom privacy the design provides will enable residents to "open" the kitchenette without feeling ill at ease.

INDEPENDENCE Being able to prepare small snacks and meals will help residents maintain a sense of independence.

INSIDE OUT Snack table in kitchen, dutch doors, and interior window will allow residents to feel part of house life while remaining safe in their "home."

DISPLAY Residents will put furniture and paintings on their "front porches" to express who they are.

SHARING Residents will accept trade-off of sharing bathtub in exchange for congregate amenities.

PREVIEWING Residents will look down below from elevator landings to prepare themselves better for social encounters.

SOCIAL ESCAPE Residents will feel more comfortable using back stairs to get to Laundry and TV room, when in a dressing gown.

SECOND FLOOR

7.5a

7.5b

7.5 Captain Clarence Eldridge House, Hyannis, Massachusetts, 1981; floor plan, second floor (a), and view (b). Residents share the front porch, laundry, TV room, living and dining areas, but individual kitchenettes, bed-sitting rooms, and toilets maximize privacy. (*Progressive Architecture*, August 1981, photo courtesy Reinhold Publications) developed the design for the state's Office of Communities and Development, the sponsor of over a dozen similar projects. As an architect-sociologist collaboration, patterns of activity were researched before any decisions were made about private spaces and shared facilities. To keep costs down, the units were very small, but the project is adjacent to a town center.

The entrance to the Captain Clarence Eldridge House is placed for easy visibility from Main Street in Hyannis, so residents "will not feel it is a long walk" home. A waiting room with windows overlooking the entry allows for comfortable, indoor seating next to the automobile drop-off. Nearby is the main office, unobtrusively sited. All entrances and the dining room open onto a shallow front porch that wraps the extended sea captain's dwelling in a familiar architectural symbol of home, amenity, and comfort. Inside, on the ground floor, two main rooms of the original house (at the lower left in the plans), serve as informal living rooms for the residents. The designers call this a "backstage" where they can watch TV, chat, or wait for their laundry to be done in a nearby room with washer and dryer. The social spaces next to this living area include a formal dining room where residents eat one meal per day together. A large kitchen includes a table and chairs in an alcove for "homeyness," or sitting around chatting and drinking coffee, as well as space for the efficient preparation of the meals to be served next door.

Circulation within the building is designed to balance sociability and privacy, exercise and ease. The front stair is formal. The back stair connects apartments to the "backstage" and allows residents to watch TV in dressing gowns and slippers. An elevator is stationed in the most sociable space next to the dining room. Seating nearby is overlooked by both a midstair landing and an elevator landing so residents can "preview" the social scene and "decide if they want to join activity below."

The eighteen private apartments are tiny. Two-person units include a dining area, small kitchenette, dining table, full bath, and two bedrooms. One-person units provide a bed/sitting room, half-bath, kitchenette, and dining area. Independence is stressed by making it possible for residents to eat alone, yet the private dining tables are placed next to interior windows opening onto the corridor, to simulate a very small "front porch." Probably the residents would have preferred more generous one-bedroom units.

The delicate balancing of private space, space shared by residents, and semipublic space shared with outsiders must go on all the time in housing design. New designs that make unexpected trade-offs—say a shared bathtub room in return for private kitchenettes—explore the sense of what is socially and architecturally possible. Ultimately, the goal should never be to enforce communal living against the residents' wishes. Rather it is to reinforce autonomy and privacy by providing support in the form of social services. The arrangement is not unlike a college dormitory or a modest hotel. Some of these ideas may be applicable to housing for young families with children needing child care or to single young people, as well as to the frail elderly.

Rehabilitation for Singles and Small Households

The remodeling of larger one-family houses can also take place under the control of a sensitive preservationist, developer, or architect with a special interest in new kinds of households and their needs. Of course, there is the disadvantage of segregating singles, be they young or old, from families with children or other household types, but some argue that the new facilities provided outweigh the disadvantages. A community of people of a common age or situation in life can be more congenial than having grandmothers next to young singles.

Existing tax incentives for historic preservation have encouraged entrepreneurs to create more shared space within housing. Catherine Davis of Los Angeles, California, a preservationist, took advantage of the Economic Recovery Tax Act of 1981 by acquiring historic houses, restoring them, and renting them. She began by helping a friend create a shelter for battered wives and their children. Then she explored how to find new kinds of tenants for large old houses—young single professionals or two or more families. She argued that traditionalists like to live in fine old houses—the sense of history pleased them. Renting to a group of single adults generates more income. Transitional neighborhoods can be strengthened for further preservation efforts, by permitting slow appreciation rather than quick resale. Davis's projects have included: "A Craftsman house in Pasadena, designed by Greene and Greene. It's home to a group of art students. They use the airy living room as a gallery, the inglenook as a drafting room, the sleeping porches as a sculpture studio and an upstairs bathtub for soaking their watercolor paper." She rehabilitated a Mediterranean villa of the 1920s in the Hollywood Hills, where young professionals shared the large living and dining rooms and terraces for entertaining, and turned a Colonial Revival mansion in Dallas into a duplex.[45] Davis gave new life to physical settings designed for large affluent households by redesigning for moderate-income single adults. She offered homes that went beyond the options usually available to singles: efficiencies, shared apartments, or the singles complex. She also created a social context with both privacy and community for adults who might not have the capital, the skills, or the time to commit to such preservation projects themselves.

Gwen Rønø Noyes, a developer and architect in Cambridge, Massachusetts, undertook the restoration and expansion of a nineteenth-century parsonage on Harvard Street. Ten people bought small, private condominiums, some as residences, others as rental properties. Rønø created a guest room that all residents could use for visitors, a popular option. Rønø and her husband then went on to develop a larger project, forty-one units for residents from ages one to eighty-nine, located at 175 Richdale Avenue, Cambridge.[46] The new project is part of a movement called Cohousing, launched in Denmark in the early 1970s with projects like Tynggarden (discussed in chapter 5). Cohousing projects generally are planned and managed by residents. Often they include complete private apartments or townhouses in a complex where there is also a community building and shared outdoor space. Similar projects in the U. S. are located in Amherst, Massachusetts, Davis and Emeryville, California, and Bainbridge Island, Washington. Members hold an annual convention where housing design and management skills are shared. Kathryn McCamant and Charles Durrett have documented many of these projects in their 1994 book, Cohousing. Karen Frank and Sherry Ahrentzen have discussed the range of new housing types emerging for new households. Jacqueline Leavitt, Charles Hoch, and others have analyzed some of the subtle difficulties and substantial rewards in Under One Roof.[47]

IMPLEMENTING CHANGE IN THE BUILT
ENVIRONMENT: TAKING THE LONG VIEW

Architecture cannot bring about revolution; spatial change by itself can't effect social change. American housing reform movements over the last two centuries have often been blessed with a multitude of good ideas and cursed with a lack of economic power. Until land and residential buildings are no longer treated as commodities in this society and government policies such as depreciation allowances and other tax breaks favoring real estate developers are ended, the United States will always have housing problems. Yet, it seems crucial to reiterate the underlying potential. Concerned citizens, local officials, planners, and designers have provided leadership for transformation. The demonstration projects discussed here show how citizens can gain a clearer sense of their spatial needs.

The story of "Lonelyville" explores another transformation in historical terms. In the years just after the Civil War, affluent young New Yorkers confronted a housing crisis, a dilemma somewhat similar to our own suburban crisis. At that time, the preeminent model of an urban dwelling for a middle-class family and their servants in New York City was a brick row house with a basement, two or three additional habitable floors, and an attic. In many ways this house form promoted good urban design because row houses joined with others to form graceful urban streets and, in the best situations, row houses formed handsome squares or crescents. In other ways, this house form was overgenerous, because it was based on a zoning law of 1811 that decreed a grid of 25-by-100 lots covering the best part of Manhattan Island "to facilitate the buying and selling of land." Large backyards complemented the row houses' unified street fronts, and the unified fronts also provided the face-to-face contact between households that was important for social continuity. The manners cherished by Henry James and Edith Wharton were rooted here. But the system was too expensive to sustain in the face of post–Civil War industrial and commercial development.

Young couples in Manhattan found that they could not afford to buy lots of this size and build three-story houses on them as their parents and grandparents had. While they might have liked the same amount of space, they confronted a shortage of servants to maintain the space. They also had smaller families and more modern ideas about how to entertain. One obvious physical solution was to divide row houses horizontally, but the young couples considered this socially unacceptable. The middle-class social strictures against having anyone live above or below oneself—sharing a horizontal surface such as a floor or ceiling—seem quaint now, but they caused panic then. Families simply could not imagine life without the row houses they knew and loved, but they would not subdivide them.

Another spatial option was sharing land costs with other families to build multifamily buildings with common services, but this was even less agreeable. It suggested working-class poverty, the unrespectable, bohemian life of flats and hotels, or European-style apartment houses. Another, temporary alternative for a young couple was boarding somewhere until they could afford to buy a row house or build one, but this simply postponed the problem. The last resort was to move to "Lonelyville," as one young wife called it, the remote suburbs reached by railroad (or perhaps streetcar) where land was cheaper: "The busy men leave on early trains and are at once plunged into the rush of their accustomed life among their usual associates, while the suburban woman remains at home, standing behind the struggling young vines of her brand new Piazza."[48]

Despite women's reservations, affluent Lonelyvilles proliferated in response to the row house crisis. Other changes evolved over time. After several decades new housing types such as apartments became somewhat acceptable for Manhattan's middle-class families. At the same time, some families began to subdivide the large old row houses into small apartments, or into apartments, office, and shops. Some became slums. Eventually the row houses began to be recycled for smaller families and new uses. They form districts in New York that include some of the most sought-after housing today. However small the row house apartments are, when these neighborhoods are well cared for, they are still among the most desirable of all urban and suburban areas anywhere.

The context of this story cannot be overemphasized: the years of that housing crisis for the upper classes and upper-middle classes of Manhattan were also the years of the greatest slum problems, when immigrants huddled six to a room in tenement districts, and densities in New York's slums were among the highest in the world, close to today's densities in places like Calcutta. The middle-class fears of social ostracism based on shared spaces not only seem silly to us now; those fears also seemed silly to the poor of the 1870s.

In 2002, the housing problem has a similar social and economic context. The middle-class ideal of the detached, single-family suburban house has become less affordable. Prime inner-city properties are priced sky-high. The solutions for suburbanites—moving to remote exurban locations (new Lonelyvilles) or sharing houses with other families—seem equally undesirable to many young couples. Like the affluent Manhattan residents in the 1870s, suburbanites lack a sense of the world context of their housing problems. Their two-car garages are often larger than basic shelter for a family in a developing country.

The question of how to sustain or divide our seven-room suburban houses is not the problem itself, but a symptom of a larger, underlying demographic shift. Americans have established a national fabric of single-family housing that needs updating. The adaptation of suburban house forms to new uses is as inevitable as was the adaptation of brick row houses and brownstones and the introduction of mixed uses, higher densities, and new building types that accompanied it. This adaptation can be carried out brilliantly or half-heartedly. Housing stock can deteriorate or it can be correctly preserved; multifamily neighborhoods can create fear and unease or generate a better context for new kinds of units. These choices reverberate with implications for the larger public domain. If reconstructing domestic space will make life easier for American families, domesticating public space is also essential to new forms of private and public life.

Chapter 8

Domesticating Urban Space

If the stock phrase, "woman's place is in the home," has defined housing policy, the query, "What's a nice girl like you doing in a place like this?" has defined attitudes toward women in urban space. Both phrases have their roots in the nineteenth-century split between private and public life. Both are implicit rather than explicit principles of urban planning; neither will be found stated in large type in textbooks on land use. Both attitudes are linked to a set of nineteenth-century beliefs about female passivity and propriety in the domestic setting ("woman's sphere") versus male combativeness and aggression in the public setting ("man's world").

When nineteenth-century men and women argued that a good woman was at home in the kitchen with her husband, they implied that no decent

225

8.1 A temperance banner of the 1850s attacks the male sexual double standard: corseted wife in white offers water; the 'fallen' women in black with loose robes and flowing hair flaunts wine, dice, and cards. While the temperance reformers meant this as a lesson, the male really did not have to choose. (Library of Congress)

woman was out in city streets, going places where men went. A "public woman" was a prostitute, and all women in public places risked being labelled. It was "unladylike" for a woman to earn her own living. Because the working woman was no one urban man's property (her father or her husband had failed to keep her at home), she was every urban man's property. She was the potential victim of harassment in the factory, in the office, on the street, in restaurants, and in places of amusement such as theaters or parks. While the numbers of employed women and women in active public life have increased, many spatial stereotypes and patterns of behavior remain. Haven houses hobble employed women. City space planned on the Victorian double standard causes problems.[1] Men do not escape the problem. As husbands and fathers they share the stresses of the isolated houses and the violent streets they and their wives and children must negotiate. But rarely do men attribute the problems of housing and the city to the Victorian attitudes that reserved urban, public life for men only.[2]

THE FREEDOM OF THE CITY FOR WOMEN

Women never legally enjoyed the medieval right to the freedom of the city that distinguished urban citizens from feudal serfs.[3] The existing literature on urban history and theory conveys this in dozens of titles like *City of Man* or *The Fall of Public Man.* The experiences of women in urban space are absent from the content of many academic studies as well as from the titles.[4] The implicit assumption has been that either respectable women had the same urban experiences as men when they were with men, or else that women had no urban experiences, since their place was in the home. American women of all classes and races challenged this view in the Progressive era, when Frances Willard attacked the double standard as expressed in saloons and the ward-boss political culture of the late nineteenth century and attempted to domesticate the American city as a "homelike world." Daphne Spain's account of *How Women Saved the City* documents these campaigns and many other philanthropic efforts.[5]

8.2 Public space and the male double standard are shown in J. N. Hyde's "Running the Gauntlet," New York City, 1874. A respectable woman walks down the street with ten men ogling as if she were a prostitute. Her body is tense and corseted, her eyes averted. The men lounge and stare boldly, providing a graphic example of what Nancy Henley calls "body politics," the dominance of one race, class, or gender over another shown through positioning of bodies in space.

Some historians and critics have suggested that women failed to establish lasting power in the public sphere in the Progressive era because they failed to develop an urban political theory suited to their needs.[6] Critics who complain of women's lack of "ideology" might first examine definitions of the nature of political theory and political activity. As long as the domestic world remains a romantic haven "outside" of public life and the political economy, politically active women can always be sent back to it, and men can justify the exclusion of women and children from their public debates and analyses. But if women can overcome what Lyn Lofland has called the "thereness" of women, we can transcend what Jessie Bernard has defined as "the female world" of a segregated place.[7]

In order for a political program to overcome the "thereness" of women and win access to safe, public urban space, the presence of women and their children in public space must be established as a political right. Gender stereotypes must be eliminated from architecture, urban design, and graphic design in public space. Such a political program would share many common features with Olmsted's attempt to create public space accessible to women; it would require many new institutions like Jane Addams's Hull-House, a public center for community organizing on the model of a single house; it would link the campaigns of the office workers' Anti-Flirt Club of the 1920s to the feminist "Take Back the Night" marches of the 1970s.

Many professionals in the design fields are ready to support the political struggles necessary to bring domestic standards of amenity and safety into public space. In the recent past, disdainful speculators and politicians have claimed that the men engaged in these causes were not "real men," and the women were "little old ladies in tennis shoes," but on this subject, Lewis Mumford can be very reassuring. Calling for a serious study of resources and settlement design in 1956, Mumford challenged Americans to go beyond the machismo of previous urban development patterns. "This new adventure," he said, "demands psychological maturity as the boyish heroism of the old adventures did not; for it is an exploration in depth, to fathom all the potential resources of a region . . . and to assess its possibilities for continued enjoyment."[8] The ultimate proof of maturity is the ability to nurture and protect human life, to develop public safety, public mobility, and public amenities. Small, common-sense improvements in urban design can be linked to

8.3 Inhospitable environments. Older women wait for a bus while the car culture passes them by; a young women waits for a bus while "Kim" advertises the double standard.

8.4 Charter members of the "Anti-Flirt Club," formed by female office workers to combat street harassment of women, Washington, D.C., 1920s. The problem of comfort in public space continues as women enter paid employment in larger numbers, but are hassled on the streets. (Library of Congress)

larger ideas about nurturing to help end the split between private life and public life.

PUBLIC SPACE FOR PARENTS

Anyone who has ever cared for babies or small children away from a domestic environment, even for a few hours, knows how little thought has been given to making public space friendly to parents. Parents find that having a baby puts great spatial limits on their public, urban life. Although a first priority is to have adequate infant care and day care in residential neighborhoods for parents, it is also necessary to make it easier for adults to move in public space with their children. In Denmark, banks provide children's play areas with small furniture and toys; in New Zealand, department stores offer day care to customers.[9] Some American examples of this kind exist as well. The Swedish furniture store, IKEA, offers a "ball room" for customers' children in its U.S. branches. Hairdressing salons, clothing boutiques, and other stores catering to women also stock toys to keep tots entertained.

Developing public facilities with the expectation that parents and grandparents with babies and young children will be using them is not a technically difficult task. It requires a little imagination. Baby-changing spaces should be a standard feature in both men's rooms and women's rooms. Well-located seating and small children's furniture in stores can suggest that children are expected and welcomed with their fathers or mothers. High chairs signal child-friendly restaurants. Windows at children's eye levels, as well as adults', are attractive in spaces where children represent a substantial number of users. Such changes in scale to accommodate children add liveliness and diversity to the urban scene. Concern for building materials and interior finishes neither too fragile nor too rough also helps define places that children can use. Play spaces can add a sense of joy for people of all ages, especially when they are organized to incorporate trees and flowers, public art, or local landmarks. Cities such as San Francisco, Portland, and Seattle have developed programs to support child-friendly city spaces. Public space for children is, at its best, not only warm and educational but also fun. Linda Hollis's

1980 exhibit, "Kidspace," alerts parents and designers to the potential of both planned and spontaneous possibilities, as does the work of Colin Ward, Robin Moore, and Clare Cooper in more scholarly ways.[10]

GREENLIGHTS AND SAFEHOUSES

Many adult Americans are afraid of public urban space. In 1967, the U.S. President's Commission on Law Enforcement and the Administration of Justice concluded that "one-third of a representative sample of all Americans say it is unsafe to walk alone at night in their neighborhoods."[11] Six out of ten Canadian women were fearful of walking alone in their neighborhoods at night.[12] Another study by sociologists in Chicago found that one-half of all women and 20 percent of all men were afraid to walk alone in their neighborhoods at night.[13] The Greenlight Program developed by the Women's Safety Committee of City Lights in Jamaica Plain, Massachusetts, and the Safehouse Program created by Tenderloin Tenants for Safer Streets in San Francisco were two programs designed to bring a greater sense of security into the lives of citizens in the 1980s. As one reporter put it, "Safehouses, the traditional refuges of intelligence agents, fugitive radicals—and more recently havens for battered wives—now are being established for senior citizens."[14] Both programs attempted to extend a sense of domestic security into the public realm. Greenlight aimed to protect women from mugging and rape. Any house in the neighborhood showing a green light in the window was a place where a frightened woman could find shelter, a telephone, and emergency counseling. The Safehouse program, identified by signs showing a peaked roof and a dove, operated in stores, bars, and hotels in a district of San Francisco. People in distress were welcome to enter and ask for safety, help in getting to the hospital, or assistance from the police. The group distributed maps of the area to show the locations of the refuges, and encouraged residents to patronize them. Obviously, neither green lights nor safehouse signs can prevent crime. However, these two efforts suggested how citizens and planners can begin to give public space a more homelike quality, and were copied widely.

Rape Prevention, Public Transportation, and Women's Safety

In 1995–96, the National Violence Against Women Survey estimated that one woman in three in the United States experiences an attempted or completed rape in her lifetime.[15] Of course, if most citizens, including politicians and police officers, believe that a woman's place is in the home to begin with, they will not necessarily be concerned about unsafe streets. Instead, they may blame the rape victim for being in urban public space. Good public transportation is a key factor in rape prevention. Several innovative transportation projects, documented by Rebecca Dreis and Gerda Wekerle, have met the demand for greater safety on the streets by adding flexible transportation. In 1973, the Madison, Wisconsin Women's Transit Authority began serving 1,000 women per month. They operated two cars, seven nights a week, on a fixed-route shuttle service plus a flexible service within a four-mile radius of the University of Wisconsin campus. Volunteers drove; the university, city, and county paid the costs of the vehicles. In Whitehorse, Alaska, the Yukon Women's Minibus Society reached an even broader constituency. Women concerned about access to public space and about security created a system of four minibuses with sixteen seats that served seven hundred passengers per day. The women's project provided the first bus system for the whole community.[16]

Public transportation not only provides safe access to public space, it can also educate riders through adult education classes on commuter trains and exhibits in key places—in bus shelters and subway stations, and on buses and subways. Riders can be united as a constituency for better services. *Dolores's Dilemma,* a romantic comedy produced on the Los Angeles buses by the Bus Riders' Union Teatro, was one of twelve skits used to organize thousands of riders in 2000. On the bus, Dolores is waiting in her wedding gown for the groom, but he never joins her because his bus never comes. As actors and riders continue discussion after the skit, riders learn about organizing for better service.[17]

ADVERTISEMENTS, PORNOGRAPHY,
AND PUBLIC SPACE

Americans need to look more consciously at the ways in which the public domain is misused for spatial displays of gender stereotypes. These appear in outdoor advertising, and to a lesser extent in commercial displays, architectural decoration, and public sculpture. While the commercial tone and violence of the American city are often criticized, crude stereotypes still appear in public, urban spaces as the staple themes of advertising. Most Americans have long been accustomed to seeing giant females in various states of undress, smiling and caressing products such as whiskey, food, and records.

Male models also sell goods, but are often active and clothed. Ad campaigns of the 1980s aimed at gay men were the first major exception. By 2000, displays of male bodies were more common. Several geographers have suggested that men are most often shown playing sports or posed in the great outdoors; women are shown in reflective postures responding to male demands in interior spaces. As the nineteenth-century sexual double standard is preserved by urban advertising, many twentieth-century urban men behave as if good women are at home while bad ones adorn the billboards and travel on their own in urban space. At the same time, urban women are encouraged to think of emotionlessness as natural to the Marlboro cowboy and every other male adult.

This double standard is the result of advertising practices, graphic design, and urban design. Sanctioned by the zoning laws, billboards are approved by the same urban planning boards who will not permit child-care centers or mother-in-law apartments in many residential districts. But the problem with billboards is not only aesthetic degradation. By presenting gender stereotypes in the form of nonverbal body language, fifty-feet long and thirty-feet high, billboards turn the public space of the city into a stage set for a drama starring enticing women and stern men.

Imagine two women on an urban commuting trip along the Sunset Strip in Los Angeles. Standing on a street corner, the two women are waiting for a bus to go to work. The bus arrives, bearing a placard on the side advertising a local night club. It shows strippers doing their act, their headless bodies bare from neck to crotch except for a few blue sequins. The two women get on the bus and find seats for the ride along Sunset Boulevard. They look out the windows. As the bus pulls away, their heads appear

8.5 The male double standard: pedestrian passing a billboard for *The Bitch*, a movie starring Joan Collins, Los Angeles, 1981. Vulgar graffiti has been inflicted on "the bitch." This kind of advertising makes urban space dangerous for all women.

8.6 The same problem abroad: *Beau Père,* movie ad, Paris, 1981.

incongruously above the voluptuous cardboard female bodies displayed on the side. They ride through a district of record company headquarters and film offices, one of the most prosperous in L.A.

Their first views reveal rows of billboards. Silent Marlboro man rides the range; husky, khaki-clad Camel man stares at green hills; gigantic, uniformed professional athletes catch passes and hit home runs on behalf of booze. These are the male images. Then, on a billboard for whiskey, a horizontal blonde in a backless black velvet dress, slit to the thigh, invites men to "Try on a little Black Velvet." Next a billboard shows a well-known actress, reclining with legs spread, who notes that avocadoes are only sixteen calories a slice. "Would this body lie to you?" she asks coyly, emphasizing that the body language that communicates blatant sexual availability is only meant to bring attention to her thin figure.

Next the bus riders pass a club called the Body Shop that advertises "nude girls." Two reclining, realistic nudes, one in front of a moonlit cityscape, the other bathed in orange sunlight, stretch their thirty-foot bodies along the sidewalk. This is the same neighborhood where a billboard advertising a Rolling Stones' record album called *Black and Blue* made news in the 1970s, when a manacled woman with torn clothes proclaimed, "I'm Black and Blue

from the Rolling Stones and I love it!" Members of a group called
Women Against Violence Against Women (WAVAW) arrived with
cans of spray paint and climbed the scaffolding to make small,
uneven letters of protest: "This is a crime against women."
Demonstrations and boycotts eventually succeeded in achieving
the removal of that image, but not in eliminating the graphic
design problem. *Black and Blue* was replaced by James Bond in a
tuxedo, pistol in hand, viewed through the spread legs and but-
tocks of a giant woman in a bathing suit and improbably high heels,
captioned *For Your Eyes Only*.

When the two women get off the bus in Hollywood, they experience more stereotypes as pedestrians. First, they walk past a
department store. In the windows, mannequins suggest the pre-
vailing ideals of sartorial elegance. The male torsos lean forward,
as if they are about to clinch a deal. The female torsos, pinheaded,
tip backward and sideways, at odd angles, as if they are about to be
pushed over onto a bed. Next, the women pass an apartment building. Two neoclassical caryatids support the entablature over the
front door. Their breasts are bared, their heads carry the load. They
recall the architecture of the Erechtheum on the Acropolis in
Athens, dating from the 5th century B.C., where the sculptured
stone forms of female slaves were used as support for a porch in
place of traditional columns and capitals. This is an ancient image
of servitude.

After the neoclassical apartment house, the commuters approach
a construction site. Here they are subject to an activity traditionally called "running the gauntlet," but referred to as "girl watching"
by urban sociologist William H. Whyte. Twelve workers stop whatever they are doing, whistle, and yell: "Hey, baby!" The women put
their heads down, and walk faster, tense with anger. The construction workers take delight in causing exactly this response: "You're
cute when you're mad!" Whyte regarded this type of behavior as
charming, pedestrian fun in his article "Street Life," where he even
took pleasure in tracing its historic antecedents. He had never been
whistled at, hooted at, or had the dimensions of his body parts analyzed out loud on a public street.[18] Finally, these women get to the
office building where they work. Their journey has taken them
through an urban landscape filled with images of men as sexual
aggressors and women as submissive sexual objects.

The transient quality of male and female interaction in public streets makes the behavior provoked by billboards and other public images particularly difficult to attack. Sociologist Erving Goffman has analyzed both print ads and billboards as *Gender Advertisements*, concluding that art directors use exaggerated body language because consumers buy not products, but images of masculinity or feminity.[19] If passersby are driving at fifty miles per hour, these gender cues cannot be subtle. *In Ways of Seeing*, art historian John Berger describes the cumulative problem that gender stereotypes in advertising create for woman as "split consciousness."[20] While many women guard themselves, some men assume that ogling is part of normal life. Women are always wary, watching men watch them, and wondering if and when something is going to happen to them.

Urban residents encounter even more explicit sexual images. Tawdry strip clubs, X-rated films, "adult" bookstores, and sex shops are common sights, as are pornographic magazine and video stores. Pornography is a bigger, more profitable industry in the United States than all legitimate film and record business combined.[21] It spills over into soft-porn, quasi-porn, and tasteless public imagery everywhere. In the midst of this sexploitation, if one sees a real prostitute, there is mild surprise. Yet soliciting is still a crime. Of course, the male customer of an adult prostitute is almost never arrested. The graphic designer, the urban designer, and the urban planner never even come under suspicion for their contributions to a commercial public landscape that preserves the sexual double standard in a brutal and vulgar way.

Feminist Laura Shapiro has called the U.S. a "rape culture."[22] Surely most Americans do not deliberately accept public space given over to commercial exploitation, violence, and harassment of women. The success of campaigns against obscenity in films or music lyrics suggests how a few activists have been able to tap public concern about commercialized sexuality, albeit in a narrow, antihumanist way. In contrast, the example of the Women's Christian Temperance Union under Frances Willard's leadership, and the parks movement under Olmsted's, show that religious idealism, love of nature, and concern for female safety were activated into Progressive-era urban reform movements that enlarged domestic values into urban values, instead of diminishing them into domestic pieties.

Worldwide, many cultures have denied women the freedom of the city. In 1961, Lewis Mumford wrote: "the prime need of the city today is for an intensification of collective self-knowledge, a deeper insight into the processes of history, as a first step toward discipline and control: such a knowledge as is achieved by a neurotic patient in facing a long buried infantile trauma that has stood in the way of his normal growth and integration."[23] He was referring to a male infatuation with automobile technology and metropolitan expansion, but his metaphor of urban citizens as neurotic patients can be applied to the Victorian double standard of male and female behavior. Until girls and boys, men and women, achieve equal citizenship in the city which is created and sustained by the labors of both sexes, Mumford's metaphor will remain valid. When women, men, and children of all classes and races can identify the public domain as the place where they feel most comfortable as citizens, Americans will finally have homelike urban space.

Chapter 9

Beyond the
Architecture
of Gender

I REMEMBERED THE END OF MY FIRST SEMESTER AT PENN WHEN, AFTER MONTHS OF TALK IN OUR HOUSING COURSE, LEARNING UNFAMILIAR ACRONYMS AND DIGESTING STRANGE STATISTICS, I FINALLY REALIZED THAT ALL THE TALK AND ALL THE FIGURES SUGGESTED NO REMEDY, BUT MASKED THE SCANDAL THAT AMERICANS WITH HOUSES DON'T CARE ABOUT THOSE WHO DON'T HAVE THEM. "BUT WHAT ARE YOU GOING TO DO?" "I DON'T KNOW," SAID WHEATON, DOYEN OF HOUSERS, WALKER OF WASHINGTON CORRIDORS, DRAFTER OF LEGISLATION: "WHAT ARE YOU GOING TO DO?"

—*Denise Scott Brown*

One or two decades ago, American cities appeared to be wealthy enough to sustain their unique spatial structure. In addition to having the highest rate of homeownership, the U.S. had some of the tallest skyscrapers in the world. Spatial patterns—skyscrapers downtown and detached single-family houses in suburbia—were imitated from Paris to Nairobi. Both the skyscrapers and the suburban houses reflected patterns of building—one too big and one too small—that made neighborhoods difficult to sustain. For improved urban design, better neighborhoods are central. Homeowners and tenants concerned about the costs of sprawl now engage these issues. While the Congress for the New Urbanism has generated broad public debate, the *European Charter for Women in the*

239

City has provided feminist inspiration. The next step for Americans is to address economic and gender equality in the context of urban design for neighborhoods and for metropolitan regions.

REUNITING HOME AND WORK, SUBURB AND CITY

Before planners, designers, citizens' groups and local officials can form an effective constituency for better housing, two ideas must be held in common. First, housing issues must include "work" as well as "home." Better spatial design requires concern for employment patterns and household work as the basic economic issues connected to residential neighborhoods. Private life and public life, private space and public space, are bound together despite all the cultural pressures to separate them. Privacy is indeed a crucial element in our personal lives. At the same time, a much richer and more complex set of spaces and activities is required to support the transition between private life and public life effectively. Women do most of this informal work, and they must be involved as users and designers. Second, suburban neighborhoods are part of urban problems. The American spatial patterns of deteriorated ghettos, skyscraper congestion, and low-density dream houses are inextricably related to land speculation and depreciation. To deal with these broad problems, Americans need sophisticated federal, state, and local policies as well as better skills in design.

Correcting the artificial split between "home" and "work" requires a new approach to economics. To change patterns of land speculation and building depreciation, it would be necessary to reform the underlying taxation policies that are at the core of banking and real estate development. Currently the federal government subsidizes developers and homeowners with mortgage arrangements, and auto manufacturers with roads. Myron Orfield's recent book *Metropolitics* outlines an additional problem: poorer residents in older suburban areas are often taxed heavily by states to support infrastructure in affluent new suburbs.[1]

Citizen activity on the local level must include a very accurate critique of gender inequality, hidden subsidies, poverty, and sprawl in order to move concerned Americans toward effective solutions. To distinguish simplistic partial solutions from significant ones, one can ask these questions of any new proposal. Does it recognize both paid and unpaid work? Does it deal with housing construction as an economic process important to workers as well as developers and banks? Does it support racial and ethnic diversity as well as gender equality? Does it strengthen the connection between house and neighborhood? Does it reconnect the suburbs to the metropolitan region?

Simplistic corporate solutions to our housing crisis are framed in the rhetoric of marketing directors' new products. They include: introducing tiny houses, condominiums, and apartments; advocating mobile homes as cheap housing; promoting home computers to make traditional homes seem modern and technologically sophisticated; and selling new commercial services to make housewives feel they are dealing efficiently with their double workload. Examples of such commercial services include fast food, profit-making nursing homes, and franchise day-care systems.

Simplistic political solutions, however well intentioned, are also too close to the old economic models and real estate models. The proposals of labor, environmental groups, civil rights, and women's groups are often too narrow. It is not helpful to argue for new construction to make more jobs available to building trades workers without making efforts to bring women and people of color into these unions. It is shortsighted to promote solar design without considering larger patterns of energy consumption. It is too simple to advocate role reversals for women and men without looking at gender roles in terms of time and space. It is not enough to advocate racial integration of white, male homeowner culture without examining the quality of that culture. Neither the simple corporate responses nor the simple political responses will work. Single-issue proposals need to be studied for their fullest implications for class, race, and gender. Activists who can weave these issues together, rather than pit one group's partial solution against another group's partial solution, will be in demand.

URBANISM: MAKING ECONOMIC, SOCIAL, AND ARCHITECTURAL IDEAS WORK TOGETHER

Housing involves a complex, interlocked set of economic, social, and physical design components. Many innovative groups have tried to build creative projects, such as the Women's Development Corporation, or Tynggarden. Each group managed to create an ingenious package that was more than the sum of its parts. Taken together, these experiences suggest the rewards for national, state, and local governments that support small, self-sustaining projects. The results are infinitely preferable to million-dollar tax write-offs for slumlords.

In the area of social planning, we have also seen ingenious attempts to renegotiate the boundary between private life and public life. While a national day-care policy—one that also covers after-school hours—is desperately needed, a social service approach alone is not enough. Many women spend their lives trying to reconnect the divided city; more original approaches should reach out to jobs, housing, transportation, child care, and care of the elderly as parts of a better solution.

What are the design components of better proposals? In the area of architecture and planning, no great changes can occur until the economic and social policies already discussed have been agreed upon. Architects and planners know that different kinds of residential neighborhoods will require different design solutions. In aging tracts of single-family houses as well as deteriorated public housing projects, intensive reprogramming and renovation efforts are needed. New housing construction requires integration with transportation, jobs, and social services. In public space, child-friendly projects should be encouraged, and the excesses of outdoor advertising regulated. Public safety must also be a priority along with the preservation of local history and culture.

THE CITY OF WOMEN'S EQUALITY

Between any urban context and any new urban design lies a long negotiating process. Many local city councils and planning boards consist of responsible, progressive people who care about their towns and know the day-to-day needs of their citizens. Yet those officials are often pressured by real estate interests who want to promote unchecked development. Some elected officials resist growth-oriented lobbying groups, while others serve these interests all too well. With focused citizen support, both planners and politicians can handle these pressures and deal with gender issues more effectively.

Denise Scott Brown has suggested that the United States is a country where people "with houses don't care about those who don't have them," but in recent decades, environmentalists, women, people of color, single parents, and retired persons have taken on housing issues.[2] Americans recognize the need to solve our housing problems room by room and block by block, starting with existing dwellings. But we need to go beyond modifying each lot by adding inventions, such as an organic garden, an aquaculture pond, a movable granny-house on wheels, or an accessory apartment in the attic. The entire fabric needs to change to encourage neighborliness while preserving family privacy.

Can women vote these changes into being? Women voters do decide some elections, but housing and urban design ultimately represent labor issues—not lifestyle issues—for women. Strikes are labor's traditional source of political clout. From the wildcat strikes of small groups of workers spontaneously agreeing to lay down their tools, to the general strikes that are often a prelude to revolution, the paid workers of the world have used this technique. Terms like "rent strike" show how tenants have borrowed this concept to explain the withholding of rent in equally forceful terms. In the 1970s, a new form of strike appeared that was particularly promising for social movements dealing with housework, housing, and urban design. The Women's Strike for Equality on August 26, 1970, celebrated the fiftieth anniversary of women's suffrage, and its nationwide demonstrations were the largest since the suffrage movement. Fifty thousand marchers moved down Fifth Avenue in New York City, demanding day care, abortion rights, equal jobs, and equal access to education. Slogans like "Don't Iron While the Strike is Hot," emphasized

9.1 Thousands of women on Fifth Avenue in New York City during the Women's March for Equality, August 26, 1971. The previous year, fifty thousand had marched to celebrate the fiftieth anniversary of women's suffrage. (Photograph by Bettye Lane)

housewives' labor. This event established women's liberation as a widely recognized social movement and set off many local organizing efforts.[3]

While this event suggests the power that organized women can have, the experience of a European group that mounted a general strike of women is even more suggestive. In 1975, the women of Iceland organized a general strike—housewives, nurses, secretaries, architects, cabinet ministers. Family life stopped, offices stopped, factories stopped. Twenty-five thousand women, old and young, flooded into the main square of the capital city, Rekjavik, to demonstrate for equal rights. It was the first nationally organized general strike of women citizens anywhere in the world. It lasted but one day. Yet the image remains. The news photographs of that day are astonishing.

For the last two centuries, the quintessential American intellectual, political, and architectural dilemma has been: dream house or ideal city? We have seen how Americans have wavered over these alternatives, and how costly this hesitation has been for an urban society. Yet Americans can find the roots of housing solutions, as well as the roots of the housing problem, within our own culture. The common sense of Charlotte Perkins Gilman, the urban visions of Bernice Johnson Reagon, the political energy of the feminist campaigns of the municipal housekeeping advocates, the settlement workers, and the material feminists offer precedents. Other societies such as Denmark, Sweden, England, and Holland also provide examples of complex, innovative approaches to nurturing and earning, but no country has yet created an urban fabric and an urban culture to support men and women on equal terms as citizens and workers. As Janet Abu-Lughod wrote in 1974, "The city we seek as women is a human city in which all will share in the pleasures and pains, where women will be neither dolls nor drudges, and where the role specializations so idealized in the past—females nurturing and males laboring—will give way to whole and cooperating humans."[4]

The world awaits the city of women's equality. Demonstration projects offer glimpses of its streets and rooms. Its architecture will combine professional craft and political activism. Its social life will blend nurturing and services. Its neighborhoods will be vibrant when Americans' diverse households transcend the architecture of gender to define for themselves their future patterns of housing, work, and family life.

Notes

Chapter 1. Housing and American Life

1. "Designed for 24 Hour Child Care," *Architectural Record* (March 1944), 86.
2. "Nation's Biggest Housebuilder," *Life* (May 22, 1950), 75–76; "Up From the Potato Fields," *Time* (July 3, 1950), 68.
3. William Levitt in an interview with the *Saturday Evening Post* (Aug. 7, 1954), 72. For a full study of this company and its policies, see Herbert Gans, *The Levittowners: Ways of Life and Politics in a New Suburban Community* (1967; New York: Columbia University Press, 1982).
4. Gwendolyn Wright, *Building the Dream: A Social History of Housing in America* (New York: Pantheon, 1981), 247–248; Esther McCoy, "Gregory Ain's Social Housing," *Arts and Architecture* 1 (Winter 1981), 66–70; Kenneth T. Jackson, *Crabgrass Frontier: The Suburbanization of the United States* (New York: Oxford University Press, 1985), 190–230; 241.
5. "Vanport City," *Architectural Forum* (Aug. 1943), 53.
6. William Levitt, in an interview with Eric Larrabee, "The Six Thousand Houses That Levitt Built," *Harper's* (Sept. 1948), 84.
7. "Houses Off the Line: Burns and Kaiser Throw the Switch," *Architectural Forum* (Oct. 1946), 10.
8. Clarence Stein, *Toward New Towns for America* (1957; Cambridge, Mass.: MIT Press, 1971), 188–216, 218.
9. *Ibid.*, 209–210.
10. Leverett Richards, "And So a City Died," *Oregonian* (Dec. 3, 1975); Kate Huang, "Women, War, and Work," unpublished paper, 1982. The Northwest Women's History Project in Portland, Oregon, has done some oral history and a slide show on shipyard workers. Sherna Gluck of California State University, Long Beach, has also researched an extensive oral history, *Rosie the Riveter Revisited: Women, the War and Social Change* (Boston: Twayne Publishers, 1987), and produced a documentary film, *Rosie the Riveter.*
11. U.S. Bureau of the Census, "Detailed Tables for Total Occupied Housing Units," *American Housing Survey*, 1999, October 2000, http://www.census.gov/hhes/www/housing/ahs/99dtchart/tab2-1.html (June 2001); U.S. Bureau of the Census, "Average Population per Household and Family: 1940 to the Present," *Current Population Survey*, December 1998, http://www.census.

gov/population/socdemo/hh-fam/htabHH-6.txt (June 2001); U.S. Bureau of the Census, "Profile of General Demographic Characteristics for the United States: 2000," Census 2000, May 2001, http://www.census.gov/Press-Release/www/2001/cb01cn67.html (June 2001).

12. Allan Heskin, *Tenants and the American Dream* (New York: Praeger, 1983); U.S. Bureau of the Census, "Homeownership Rates for the United States, by Age of Householder and by Family Composition," *Housing Vacancies and Homeownership Annual Statistics: 2000,* February 2001, http://www.census.gov/hhes/www/housing/hvs/annual00/ann00t15.html (June 2001).

13. National Association of Realtors, "Existing Home Prices, 1989–2000," February 2000, http://www.nahb.com.facts/economics/existing_home_prices.html (June 2001).

14. Martin Wachs, *Transportation for the Elderly: Changing Lifestyles, Changing Needs* (Berkeley and Los Angeles: University of California Press, 1979).

15. Carol Brown, "Spatial Inequalities and Divorced Mothers," paper delivered at the American Sociological Association Annual Meeting, San Francisco, Sept. 6, 1978; Jacqueline Leavitt, "Aunt Mary and the Shelter-Service Crisis for Single Parents," paper delivered at the Association of Collegiate Schools of Planning Annual Meeting, Chicago, Oct. 21–24, 1982; Robert Weiss, *Going It Alone: the Family Life and Social Situation of the Single Parent* (New York: Basic Books, 1979).

16. "Burning the House to Roast the Pig: Unrelated Individuals and Single Family Zoning's Blood Relation Criterion," *Cornell Law Review* 58 (1972), 138–165.

17. Rita A. Calvan, "Children and Families—the Latest Victims of Exclusionary Land Use Practices," in Frank Schnidman and Jane Silverman, eds., *Management and Control of Growth: Updating the Law,* vol. 3 (Washington, D.C.: Urban Land Institute, 1980), 283–289.

18. Patrick Hare, "Rethinking Single Family Zoning: Growing Old in American Neighborhoods," *New England Journal of Human Services* (Summer 1981), 32–35; Wendy Schuman, "The Return of Togetherness," *New York Times,* Mar. 20, 1977, 1. Also see Martin Gellen, "Underutilization in American Housing," and "A Home in Every Garage: The Economics of Secondary Units," Working Papers, U. C. Berkeley College of Environmental Design, 1982.

19. Kathryn P. Nelson, "Recent Suburbanization of Blacks: How Much, Who, and Where," *American Planning Association Journal,* 46 (July 1980), 287–300; J. John Palen, "Minorities in Suburbia: New Realities," in *The Suburbs* (New York: McGraw-Hill, Inc., 1995), 116–152.

20. Martha Burt and Laudan Aron, "America's Homeless II: Populations and Services, 1996," February 2000, http://www.urban.org/housing/homeless/numbers/index.htm (June 2001).

CHAPTER 2. FROM IDEAL CITY TO DREAM HOUSE

1. Joseph Giovannini, "Sex Stereotyping in Design," *New York Times* (Dec.16, 1982), C1.

2. Wright, *Building the Dream*, 3–17.

3. Ronald Lee Fleming and Lauri Halderman, *On Common Ground* (Harvard, Mass.: Harvard Common Press, 1982).

4. Dolores Hayden, *Seven American Utopias: The Architecture of Communitarian Socialism*, 1790-1975 (Cambridge, Mass.: MIT Press, 1976).

5. Catharine E. Beecher and Harriet Beecher Stowe, *The American Woman's Home* (New York: J.B. Ford, 1869); Catharine E. Beecher, "How to Redeem Woman's Profession from Dishonor," *Harper's* 31 (Nov. 1865), 712; Dolores Hayden, "Catharine Beecher and the Politics of Housework," in S. Torre, ed., *Women in American Architecture: An Historic and Contemporary Perspective* (New York: Whitney Library of Design, 1977), 40–49.

6. Walt Whitman, "Song of the Broad-Axe," in *Complete Poetry and Selected Prose*, ed. James E. Miller, Jr., (Boston: Houghton Mifflin, 1959), 136, 141.

7. *Ibid.*, 138, 141, 142.

8. Walt Whitman, "Poem of Remembrance for a Girl or Boy of These States," in *Complete Poetry*, 393.

9. Walt Whitman, "In the New Garden, in All Its Parts," in *Complete Poetry*, 399.

10. Walt Whitman, "I Dream'd in a Dream," in *Complete Poetry*, 96.

11. Walt Whitman, *Democratic Vistas*, in *Complete Poetry*, 462.

12. Frederick Law Olmsted, *Public Parks and the Enlargement of Towns* (Cambridge, Mass.: American Social Science Association, 1870).

13. Olmsted, *Public Parks*, 7–9. See, for background, Laura Roper, *FLO: A Biography of Frederick Law Olmsted* (Baltimore: Johns Hopkins University Press, 1973); Francesco Dal Co, "From Parks to the Region," in G. Ciucci, M. Tafuri, F. Dal Co, *The American City* (Cambridge, Mass.: MIT Press, 1977); Albert Fein, *Frederick Law Olmsted and the American Environmental Tradition* (New York: Braziller, 1972).

14. Dolores Hayden, *The Grand Domestic Revolution: A History of Feminist Designs for American Homes, Neighborhoods, and Cities* (Cambridge, Mass.: MIT Press, 1981); Peirce, "Cooperative Housekeeping II," *Atlantic Monthly* 22 (Dec. 1868), 684; Zona Gale, "Shall the Kitchen in Our Home Go?" *Ladies' Home Journal* 36 (Mar. 1919), 35.

15. Ruth Bordin, *Women and Temperance: The Quest for Power and Liberty, 1873–1900* (Philadelphia: Temple University Press, 1972), 33.

16. *Ibid.*, 29–30.

17. *Id.*

18. *Id.*

19. Frances Willard, quoted in Sheila Rothman, *Woman's Proper Place: A History of Changing Ideals and Practices, 1870 to the Present* (New York: Basic Books, 1978), 67.

20. *Id.*; Marlene S. Wortman, "Domesticating the American City," in Jack Salzman, ed. *Prospects: An Annual of American Cultural Studies* (New York: Bert Franklin and Co., 1977), 531–572.

21. Florence Kelley, ed., *Hull-House Maps and Papers* (1895; New York: Arno, 1975).

22. Sam Bass Warner, Jr., *The Urban Wilderness* (New York: Harper and Row, 1972); David Gordon, "Capitalist Development and the History of American Cities," in W. Tabb and L. Sawyers, eds., *Marxism and the Metropolis* (New York: Oxford University Press, 1978), 25–63; Richard Walker, "The Suburban Solution," Ph.D. dissertation, Department of Geography, Johns Hopkins University, 1977, and "A Theory of Suburbanization: Capitalism and the Construction of Urban Space in the United States," in Michael Dear and Allen Scott, eds., *Urbanization and Planning in Capitalist Society* (New York: Methuen, 1981), 396–400.

23. For a good account of the Red Scare in this period, see J. Stanley Lemons, *The Woman Citizen: Social Feminism in the 1920s* (Urbana, Illinois: University of Illinois Press, 1973), 209–227.

24. Barbara Ehrenreich and Deidre English, *For Her Own Good: 150 Years of the Experts' Advice to Women* (Garden City, N.Y.: Anchor/Doubleday, 1978), 134.; Industrial Housing Associates, *Good Homes Make Contented Workers*, (Philadelphia: Industrial Housing Associates, 1919); the last of these quotes is printed on an old textile used in a quilt. A review essay covering many approaches to homeownership is Nancy G. Duncan, "Home Ownership and Social Theory," in *Housing and Identity*, ed. James Duncan (London: Croom Helm, 1981), 98–134.

25. Daniel Luria, "Suburbanization, Ethnicity, and Party Base: Spatial Aspects of the Decline of American Socialism," *Antipode* 11 (Fall 1979), 76–79.

26. Stuart Ewen, *Captains of Consciousness: Advertising and the Social Roots of the Consumer Culture* (New York: McGraw Hill, 1976).

27. Christine Frederick, *Selling Mrs. Consumer* (New York: Business Bourse, 1929), 244–245, 388–394.

28. Reports from *The President's Conference on Home Building and Home Ownership*, (Washington, D. C.: U.S. Government Printing Office, 1932).

29. R. Slitor, "The Federal Income Tax in Relation to Housing Research," *Report No. 5, National Commission on Urban Problems* (Washington, D.C.: U.S.G.P.O., 1968). On public housing initiatives in this era, see Catherine Bauer, *Modern Housing* (Boston: Houghton Mifflin, 1934); Gail Radford, *Modern Housing for America: Policy Struggles in the New Deal Era* (Chicago: University of Chicago Press, 1996); Timothy L. McDonnell, *The Wagner Housing Act* (Chicago: Loyola University Press, 1975); and Eugenie Ladner Birch, "Woman-made America: The Case of Early Public Housing Policy," in Donald A. Krueckeberg, ed. *The American Planner: Biographies and Recollections* (New York: Methuen, 1983), 149–175.

30. Luria, "Suburbanization," 79.

31. *Survey of AFL-CIO Members' Housing, 1975* (Washington, D.C.: AFL-CIO, 1976), 16.

32. U.S. Bureau of the Census, *Historical Statistics of the United States, Colonial Times to 1970* (Washington, D.C., U.S.G.P.O., 1975), Part 1, 8; U. S. Bureau of the Census, "Profile of General Demographic Characteristics for the United States: 2000," *Census 2000*, May 2001, http://www.census.gov/Press-Release/www/2001/cb01cn67.html (June 2001).

33. U. S. Bureau of the Census, "Detailed Tables for Total Occupied Housing Units," *American Housing Survey: 1999*, October 2000, http://www.census.

gov/hhes/www/housing/ahs/99dchrt/tab2-3.html (June 2001); Dolores Hayden, "Revisiting the Sitcom Suburbs," *Landlines: Newsletter of the Lincoln Institute of Land Policy* (March 2001), 1–3.

34. Fred J. Napolitano, "Housing—A Priority to Preserve the American Dream," *Newsweek* (Sept. 13, 1982), 20.

Chapter 3. Awakening from the Dream

1. U.S. Department of Labor, Bureau of Labor Statistics, "Employment Characteristics of Families in 2000," April 2001, http://stats.bls.gov/news rels.htm (June 2001); U.S. Bureau of the Census, "Living Arrangements of Children Under 18 Years Old: 1960 to Present," http://www.census.gov/pop-ulation/socdemo/ms-1a/tabch-1.txt (June 2001).

2. Susanne Greaves, "Levittown Revisited," *New York Herald Tribune Magazine,* (Aug. 16, 1964), 9–12; "Same Rooms, Varied Decor," *Life* (Jan. 14, 1952), 90–93.

3. Wright, *Building the Dream*, 251.

4. Barbara Miller Lane, *Architecture and Politics in Germany, 1918–1945* (Cambridge, Mass.: Harvard University Press, 1968), 206–210.

5. Hayden, *Grand Domestic Revolution*, 228–265.

6. Dolores Hayden, "Model Houses for the Millions," in Elizabeth A. T. Smith, ed., *Blueprints for Modern Living: History and Legacy of the Case Study Houses* (Los Angeles: Museum of Contemporary Art: 1989), 197–211.

7. For a sampling of the critiques of suburbia, see: Philip C. Dolce, ed., *Suburbia: The American Dream and Dilemma* (Garden City, N.Y.: Doubleday Anchor, 1976); Robert Goldstone, *Suburbia: Civic Denial* (New York: Macmillan, 1970); Charles Haar, *The End of Innocence: A Suburban Reader* (Glenview, Illinois: Scott, Foresman, 1972); Bennett M. Berger, *Working Class Suburb: A Study of Auto Workers in Suburbia* (Berkeley, Calif.: University of California Press, 1971); William Michelson, *Environmental Choice, Human Behavior, and Residential Satisfaction* (New York: Oxford University Press, 1977); Donald N. Rothblatt, Daniel J. Garr, and Jo Sprague, *The Suburban Environment and Women* (New York: Praeger, 1979); Robert A.M. Stern, "The Suburban Alternative for the 'Middle City,'" *Architectural Record* (Aug. 1978), 98–100. For a more extensive bibliographical review, see the essay by Muller listed in the bibliography.

8. Lewis Mumford, "Planning for the Phases of Life," *The Urban Prospect* (New York: Harcourt, Brace, Jovanovich, 1968), 34–35.

9. Recent critiques of this bias of location theory include Ann R. Markusen, "City Spatial Structure, Women's Household Work, and National Urban Policy," in C. Stimpson, et al., eds., *Women and the American City* (Chicago: University of Chicago Press, 1981). Also see Gerda Wekerle, ed., *New Space For Women* (Boulder, Colorado: Westview Press, 1980); Suzanne Keller, ed., *Building For Women* (Lexington, Mass.:Lexington Books, 1981); Susana Torre, ed., *Women in American Architecture* (New York: Whitney Library of Design, 1977).

10. Chester Hartman and Michael E. Stone, "A Socialist Housing Program for the United States," in Marcus G. Raskin, ed., *The Federal Budget and Social Reconstruction* (Washington, D.C.: Institute for Policy Studies, 1979).

11. U. S. Department of Energy, Energy Information Administration, "World Population, 1990–1999," http://www.eia.doe.gov/emeu/iea/tableb1.html (June 2001) and "World Primary Energy Consumption, 1990–1999," http://www.eia.doe.gov/emeu/iea/tablee1.html (June 2001).

12. Hayden, *Grand Domestic Revolution*, 314, n. 33.

13. U. S. Department of Transportation Federal Highway Administration, "Summary of Travel Trends: 1995 Nationwide Personal Transportation Survey," December 1999, http://www.cta.ornl.gov/npts/1995/Doc/trends_report.pdf (June 2001); U.S. Bureau of the Census, "Means of Transportation to Work for the U.S.," 1990 Census, http://www.census.gov/population/soc demo/journey/ustime90.txt (June 2001).

14. Helga Olkowski and William Olkowski, "Urban Agriculture: A Strategy for Transition to a Solar Society," in Gary J. Coates, ed., *Resettling America: Energy, Ecology, and Community* (Andover, Mass.: Brick House Publishing Company, 1981), 339. For a solar dream house, see Malcolm Wells, "Mac Well's Summertime Blues," *New Shelter* 2 (May/June 1981), 60–69; and David Bainbridge, Judy Corbett, and John Hofacre, *Village Homes Solar House Designs* (Emmaus, Pa.: Rodale Press, 1979).

15. Ray Reece, *The Sun Betrayed* (Boston: South End Press, 1979).

16. U.S. Department of Labor, Bureau of Labor Statistics, "Employment Characteristics of Families in 2000," April 2001, ftp://ftp.bls.gov/pub/news/release/famee.txt (June 2001); Patricia Mainardi, "The Politics of Housework," in R. Morgan, ed., *Sisterhood is Powerful* (New York: Vintage, 1970), 447–454.

17. Michele Zimbalist Rosaldo, "Women, Culture, and Society: A Theoretical Overview," in *Women, Culture and Society*, ed. Michele Zimbalist Rosaldo and Louise Lamphere (Stanford, Calif.: Stanford University Press, 1974).

18. Bonnie Loyd, "Women, Home, and Status," in *Housing and Identity*, ed. James Duncan (London: Croom Helm, 1981), 181–197.

19. Anne S. Kasper, "Women Victimized by Valium," *New Directions for Women* 8 (Winter 1979–80), 7.

20. Betty Friedan, *The Feminine Mystique* (New York: W. W. Norton, 1963).

21. Adrienne Rich, "A Primary Ground," in *Poems: Selected and New, 1950–1974* (New York: W. W. Norton, 1975), 203–204.

22. Adrienne Rich, "The Fourth Month of the Landscape Architect," in *Poems*, 224–225.

23. Bernice Johnson Reagon, "My Black Mothers and Sisters, or On Beginning a Cultural Autobiography," *Feminist Studies* 8 (Spring 1982), 81–96.

24. Susan Anderson-Khleif, "Housing Needs of Single-Parent Mothers," in Suzanne Keller, ed., *Building for Women* (Lexington, MA: Lexington Books, 1981), 21–38.

25. Anne Cools, "Emergency Shelter: The Development of an Innovative Women's Environment," in G. Wekerle, et al., eds., *New Space for Women*, 311–318. Also see: Lois Ahrens, "Battered Women's Refuges: Feminist

Cooperatives vs. Social Service Institutions," *Radical America* 14 (May–June 1980), 40–47; Ann Withorn, "Helping Ourselves: The Limits and Potential of Self Help," *Radical America* 14 (May–June 1980), 24–39; and Reneé Scott, "Notes on Race, Mothering, and Culture in the Shelter Movement," *Radical America* 14 (May–June 1980), 48–50.

26. Donna E. Shalala and Jo Anne McGeorge, "The Women and Mortgage Credit Project: A Government Response to the Housing Problems of Women," in Keller, ed., *Building for Women*, 39–46.

27. Killearn Estates, Tallahassee, Florida. I am indebted to Martin Pawley for this phrase, "owner-speculator," used in his *Home Ownership* (London: Architectural Press, 1978), 135.

28. Constance Perin, *Everything in Its Place: Social Order and Land Use in America* (Princeton, N.J.: Princeton University Press, 1977), 32–80.

29. Jon Douglas, Beverly Hills, California, realtors.

30. On the Federal Housing Administration, see Wright, *Building the Dream*, 247-248. Levitt was quoted in the *Saturday Evening Post*, Aug. 7, 1954, page 72: "As a Jew, I have no room in my mind or heart for racial prejudice. But, by various means, I have come to know that if we sell one house to a Negro family, then 90 to 95 percent of our white customers will not buy into the community. That is their attitude, not ours. We did not create it and cannot cure it. As a company, our position is simply this: we can solve a housing problem, or we can try to solve a racial problem. But we cannot combine the two." For a discussion of what happened when a Black family did move into the second Levittown, see Gans, *The Levittowners*, 375.

31. Emily Card, "Women, Housing Access, and Mortgage Credit," *Signs: A Journal of Women in Culture and Society* 5 (Supplement, Spring 1980), S215–S219; U. S. Bureau of the Census, "Homeownership Rates for the United States by Age of Householder and by Family Composition," *Housing Vacancies and Homeownership Annual Statistics: 2000*, February 2001, http://www.census.gov/hhes/www/housing/hvs/annual00/ann00t15.html (June 2001), and "Homeownership Rates by Race and Ethnicity of Householder," http://www.census.gov/hhes/www/housing/hvs/annual00/ann 00t20.html (June 2001).

32. *Los Angeles Times* (Nov. 21, 1982), VII, 24; National Association of Realtors, "Existing Home Prices, 1989–2000," February 2001, http://www.nahb.com/ facts/economics/existing_home_prices.html (June 2001).

33. Federal National Mortgage Association, "The Baby Boom is Househunting," *Smithsonian* 11 (Nov. 1980), 151; Urban Land Institute and Council on Development Choices for the 1980s, *The Affordable Community: Growth, Change, and Choice in the 80s* (Washington, D.C.: U.S.G.P.O., 1981), 3.

34. U. S. Census Bureau, "Mortgage Debt Outstanding by Type of Property and Holder," and "Consumer Credit Outstanding and Finance Rates," *Statistical Abstract of the United States: 2000*, Section 16, Banking, Finance, and Insurance, http://www.census.gov/prod/2001pubs/statab/sec16.pdf (June 2001).

35. Eric Schmitt, "Census Data Show a Sharp Increase in Living Standard," *New York Times* (August 6, 2001), A1. Schmitt quotes Robert Lang, who works for the Fannie Mae Foundation. Fannie Mae (Federal National Mortgage

Association) itself is in the secondary mortgage market and 97 percent of their holdings are single-family homes.

CHAPTER 4. NURTURING: HOME, MOM, AND APPLE PIE

1. Ellen Malos, ed., *The Politics of Housework* (London: Virago Press, 1980); Nancy Folbre, *The Invisible Heart: Economics and Family Values* (New York: The New Press, 2001); Arlie Russell Hochschild, *The Second Shift* (1989; New York: Avon Books, 1997), includes a bibliography of recent scholarship.

2. Lily Braun, *Frauenarbeit und Hauswirtschaft* (Berlin, 1901); Hayden, *Grand Domestic Revolution*, 291–305.

3. Hartmann has pioneered the analysis of women's labor time in the home, as the basis for her analysis of the family as a site of class and gender conflict usually ignored by liberal theorists. Heidi I. Hartmann, "The Family as the Locus of Gender, Class, and Political Struggle: The Example of Housework," *Signs: Journal of Women in Culture and Society* 6 (Spring, 1981), 366–394.

4. Laura Balbo, "The Servicing Work of Women and the Capitalist State," in *Political Power and Social Theory* (New York: Basic Books, 1981); Laura Balbo, "Crazy Quilts: Rethinking the Welfare State Debate From a Woman's Perspective," mimeographed, GRIFF, Milan, Italy, 1981; Laura Balbo and Renate Siebert Zahar, *Interferenze* (Milan: Feltrinelli, 1979).

5. Erma Bombeck, *The Grass is Always Greener Over the Septic Tank* (New York: Fawcet, 1977), 5. Billed as "the exposé to end all exposés—the truth about the suburbs," this book can be read as a bunch of little jokes, or as an unconscious but revealing indictment of numerous planning and design failures, and housewives' struggles to overcome them. A more serious attack is John Keats, *The Crack in the Picture Window* (Boston: Houghton Mifflin, 1957).

6. Literature on the family is reviewed in Hartmann, "The Family as the Locus of Gender, Class, and Political Struggle," 365–368.

7. Among the traditional family's defenders is Christopher Lasch, *Haven in a Heartless World: The Family Besieged* (New York: Basic Books, 1976).

8. William O'Neill, *Everyone Was Brave: A History of Feminism in America* (1969; New York: Quadrangle, 1971), 358.

9. Betty Friedan, *The Second Stage* (New York: Summit, 1981), 43, 83.

10. August Bebel, *Women Under Socialism*, tr. Daniel De Leon (1883; New York: Schocken, 1971), 338–339; V. I. Lenin, *The Emancipation of Women* (New York: Progress Publishers, 1975), 69.

11. Hayden, *Grand Domestic Revolution*, 3–5.

12. Bebel, *Women Under Socialism*, 338–339.

13. Jane Cunningham Croly, letter to Elizabeth Cady Stanton, printed in *The Revolution* 3 (May 27, 1869), 324.

14. Melusina Fay Peirce, "Cooperative Housekeeping II" (second of five articles), *Atlantic Monthly* 22 (Dec. 1868), 684.

15. Melusina Fay Peirce, "Cooperative Housekeeping III," *Atlantic Monthly* 23 (Jan. 1869), 29–30.

16. Mari Jo Buhle, "A Republic of Women: Feminist Theory in the Gilded Age," paper read at the 1981 meeting of the American Historical Association, 4–7; also *Lake Placid Conference on Home Economics, Proceedings* (Lake Placid, N.Y., 1903, 1907).

17. Thomas Kuhn, *The Structure of Scientific Revolutions* (1962; Chicago: University of Chicago Press, 1973); "Second Thoughts on Paradigms," in *The Essential Tension: Selected Studies in Scientific Tradition and Change* (Chicago: University of Chicago Press, 1977), 293–319.

18. Susan Strasser, *Never Done: A History of American Housework* (New York: Pantheon Books, 1982), is an excellent work.

19. Ruth Schwartz Cowan, "The 'Industrial' Revolution in the Home: Household Technology and Social Change in the 20th Century," *Technology and Culture* 17 (Jan. 1976), 1–23.

20. Carol Miles, "The Craftsman Ideal of Home Life," unpublished paper, 1981.

21. Christine Frederick, *Household Engineering: Scientific Management in the Home* (Chicago: American School of Home Economics, 1920), 92.

22. Edith Mendel Stern, "Women Are Household Slaves," *American Mercury* (Jan. 1949), 71.

23. Jo Anne Vanek, "Time Spent in Housework," *Scientific American* (Nov. 1974), 116–120.

24. "U.S. Dines Out Despite Prices," *Boston Globe* (Oct. 25, 1978), 75; Eric Schlosser, *Fast Food Nation: The Dark Side of the All-American Meal* (Boston: Houghton Mifflin, 2001), 3.

25. Kentucky Fried Chicken Website, http://www.kfc.com/about/kfcfacts.htm (June 2001); Edith Evans Asbury, "Col. Harland Sanders, Founder of Kentucky Fried Chicken Dies," *New York Times* (Dec. 17, 1980), 29.

26. Kinder Care Web site, http://www.kindercare.com (June 2001); "A Big, Big Business," *Southern Exposure* 8 (Fall 1980), 36–40; Joseph Lelyveld, "Drive-in Day Care," *New York Times Magazine* (June 5, 1977), 110.

27. Barbara Ehrenreich, *Nickel and Dimed: On [Not] Getting By in America* (New York: Metropolitan Books, 2001), 72.

28. U.S. Department of Labor, "FMLA Compliance Guide," http://www.dol. gov/esa/public/regs/compliance/whd/1421.htm (July 2001); "U.S. Maternity Plans Pale in Comparison to Other Nations," *Washington Post* (Feb. 15, 1998), http://www.chron.com/content/chronicle/nation/98/02/16/maternityleave.2-0.html (July 2001).

29. Kristin Moore and Sandra Hofferth, "Women and Their Children," in R. Smith, ed., *The Subtle Revolution: Women At Work* (Washington, D.C.: Urban Land Institute, 1979), 125–58; U.S. Department of Labor, Bureau of Labor Statistics, "Employment Characteristics of Families in 2000," April 2001, ftp://ftp.bls.gov/pub/news.release/famee.txt (June 2001); Nancy S. Barrett, "Women in The Job Market: Unemployment and Work Schedules," in Smith, ed., *The Subtle Revolution*, 88–90.

30. Sheila B. Kamerman, "Work and Family in Industrialized Societies," *Signs* 4 (Summer 1979), 644–645; Statistics Sweden, "Employment Rates for EU Member States, 1999," March 2001, http://www.scb.se/eng/omscb/eu/syssel

sattning.asp (June 2001); Ann Crittenden, *The Price of Motherhood*, (New York: Metropolitan Books, 2001), 244–246.

31. Ari Korpivaara, "Play Groups for Dads," and Alison Herzig and Jane Mali, "Oh, Boy! Babies!" in *Ms.* 10 (Feb. 1982), 52–58.

32. Sarah Fenstermaker Berk, "The Household as Workplace," in G. Wekerle, ed., *New Space For Women*, 70; Nona Glazer-Malbin, "Review Essay: Housework," *Signs* 1 (Summer 1976), 905–22; Nadine Brozan, "Men and Housework: Do They or Don't They?" *New York Times* (Nov. 1, 1980), 52; Clair Vickery, "Women's Economic Contribution to the Family," in Smith, ed., *The Subtle Revolution*, 159–200; Arlie Hochschild and Anne Machung, "Afterword" to the 1997 edition of *The Second Shift* (1989; New York: Avon, 1997), 279; Nona Glazer, *Women's Paid and Unpaid Labor: The Work Transfer in Health Care and Retailing* (Philadelphia: Temple University Press, 1993); Hartmann, "The Family as the Locus of Gender, Class, and Political Struggle," 383.

33. Hartmann, "The Family as Locus," 380; Crittenden, *The Price of Motherhood*, 22.

34. Mainardi, "The Politics of Housework," in Morgan, ed., *Sisterhood Is Powerful*, 447–454.

35. The majority of American men stop paying child support within two years of a divorce settlement, according to Kathryn Kish Sklar, "Women, Work, and Children, 1600–1980," paper read at the Third Annual Conference on Planning and Women's Needs, UCLA, Urban Planning Program, Feb. 21, 1981.

36. Bebel, *Women Under Socialism*, 344–349.

37. Vladmir I. Lenin, *The Great Initiative*, quoted in Vladimir Zelinski, "Architecture as a Tool of Social Transformation," *Women and Revolution* 11 (Spring 1976), 6–14.

38. Anatole Kopp, "Soviet Architecture Since the 20th Congress of the C.P.S.U.," paper delivered at the Second World Congress of Soviet and East European Studies, 1980, 12–13.

39. Michael Paul Sacks, "Unchanging Times: A Comparison of the Everyday Life of Soviet Working Men and Women Between 1923 and 1966," *Journal of Marriage and the Family*, 39 (Nov. 1977), 793–805.

40. Alice H. Cook, *The Working Mother: A Survey of Problems and Programs in Nine Countries*, 2nd ed. (1978; Ithaca, N.Y.: New York State School of Industrial and Labor Relations, 1975), 8.

41. Carollee Benglesdorf and Alice Hageman, "Women and Work," in "Women in Transition," special issue of *Cuba Review* 4 (Sept. 1974), 9.

42. I was shown this project by planners in April 1980 when I visited China as a guest of the Chinese Architectural Society.

43. Heidi Steffens, "A Woman's Place," *Cuba Review* 4 (Sept. 1974), 29.

44. Geoffrey E. Fox, "Honor, Shame, and Women's Liberation in Cuba: Views of Working-Class Emigrée Men," in A. Pescatello, ed. *Female and Male in Latin America*, (Pittsburgh: University of Pittsburgh Press, 1973). I visited Cuba in 1979 and also observed male refusal to do housework in many situations.

45. Delia Davin, *Woman-Work: Women and the Party in Revolutionary China*

(Oxford, England: Clarendon Press, 1976); Elisabeth J. Croll, "Women in Rural Production and Reproduction in the Soviet Union, China, Cuba, and Tanzania: Case Studies," in *Signs*, special issue on Development and the Sexual Division of Labor, 7 (Winter 1981), 375–399.

46. Hayden, *Grand Domestic Revolution*, 66–89, 208–227, 266–277.

47. Charlotte Perkins Gilman, *Women and Economics* (Boston: Maynard and Small, 1898), Hayden, *Grand Domestic Revolution*, 182–205. An early translation of Gilman in an architectural journal is "La Maison de Demain," *La Construction Moderne* 5 (Nov. 1914), 66–68.

48. Erwin Muhlestein, "Kollektives Wohnen gestern und heute," *Architese* 14 (1975), 4–5.

49. Otto Fick, "The Apartment House Up To Date" *Architectural Record* 22 (July 1907), 68–71.

50. Dick Urban Vestbro, "Collective Housing Units in Sweden," *Current Sweden*, Svenska Institutet, Stockholm, publication no. 234 (Sept. 1976), (6), 6–7.

51. *Id.*

52. "Sweden's Model Apartments: Stockholm Building is Wonderful for Wives Who Work," *Life* 18 (Mar. 12, 1945), 112–114.

53. Muhlestein, "Kollektives," 6–8; Vestbro, "Collective Housing," 8–11.

54. Hayden, *Grand Domestic Revolution*, 230–237.

55. Clementina Black, *A New Way of Housekeeping* (London: W. Collins Sons, 1918).

56. Lawrence Wolfe, *The Reilly Plan* (London: Nicholson and Watson, 1945).

57. Hayden, *Grand Domestic Revolution*, 251–261.

58. Ann Oakley, *Woman's Work: The Housewife Past and Present* (New York: Pantheon, 1974), 227–229.

59. Kay Hanly Bretnall, "Should Housewives Be Paid a Salary?" *American Home* 37 (Feb. 1947), 15–16.

60. Wages for Housework Collective, *All Work and No Pay* (London: Falling Wall Press, 1975), 5; also see Malos, *The Politics of Housework*, for a full analysis of this movement.

61. Gary B. Trudeau, *Doonesbury*, "And Now, Here's Nichole," in Ann E. Beaudry, ed. *Women in the Economy* (Washington, D.C.: Insitute for Policy Studies, 1978), 61.

62. Nona Glazer, Lindka Mjaka, Joan Acker, Christine Bose, *Women in a Full Employment Economy* (1977), mimeo.

63. Melusina Fay Peirce, "Cooperative Housekeeping," *Atlantic Monthly* 23 (March 1869), 297.

Chapter 5. Economics: Getting and Spending

1. Helvi Sipila, *The State of the World's Women, 1979* (New York: United Nations, 1979); United Nations Development Programme, *Human Development Report, 1995*, quoted in Ann Crittenden, *The Price of*

Motherhood: Why the Most Important Job in the World is Still the Least Valued (New York: Metropolitan Books, 2001), 78.

2. See also a special issue of *Signs*, "Development and the Sexual Division of Labor," 7 (Winter 1981).

3. Jan Peterson, speaking at a conference at Smith College, Northampton, Mass., Oct. 1981.

4. Markusen, "City Spatial Structure," 27; Crittenden, *The Price of Motherhood*, 8.

5. Heidi Hartmann, "Capitalism, Patriarchy, and Job Segregation by Sex," *Signs* 1 (Spring 1976), 137–169; Hartmann, "The Family as the Locus of Gender, Class and Political Struggle," 370–372, 377.

6. Nancy S. Barrett, "Women in the Job Market: Occupations, Earning, and Career Opportunities," in Smith, ed. *The Subtle Revolution*, 31–62.

7. Mary Witt and Patricia K. Naherny, *Woman's Work—Up from 878: Report on the DOT Research Project* (Madison, Wisconsin: University of Wisconsin Extension, Women's Education Resources, 1975); U. S. Department of Labor, Bureau of Labor Statistics, "1999 National Occupational Employment and Wage Estimates: Personal Care and Service Occupation," March 2001, http://stats.bls.gov/oes/1999/oes_39Pe.htm (June 2001).

8. Alice Amsden, ed., *The Economics of Women and Work* (New York: St. Martin's Press, 1980).

9. Robert Goodman, *The Last Entrepreneurs: America's Regional Wars for Jobs and Dollars* (New York: Simon and Schuster, 1980), 38; Yen Le Espiritu, *Asian American Women and Men: Labor, Laws and Love* (Thousand Oaks, Calif.: Sage Publications, 1997), 63, 74.

10. William Gauger, "Household Work: Can We Add It to the GNP?" *Journal of Home Economics* (Oct. 1973), 12–15; Folbre, *The Invisible Heart*, 12, shows that Marshall was no feminist.

11. Paul Samuelson, *Economics: An Introductory Analysis*, 5th ed. (New York: McGraw Hill, 1961), 212–237.

12. Gauger, "Household Work," 12–15.

13. Folbre, *The Invisible Heart*, 51.

14. Kay Lehman Schlozman, "Women and Unemployment: Assessing the Biggest Myths," *Women: A Feminist Perspective*, ed. Jo Freeman, 2nd ed. (Palo Alto, Calif.: Mayfield Publishing, 1979), 290–312; Nancy S. Barrett, "Women in the Job Market," 64–79.

15. Rae Andre, *Homemakers: The Forgotten Workers* (Chicago: University of Chicago Press, 1981), 186–206.

16. Nancy M. Gordon, "Institutional Responses: The Social Security System," in Smith, ed., *The Subtle Revolution*, 223–256. Also see "The Future of Social Security: An Exchange," *The New York Review of Books* 30 (March 17, 1983), 41–57.

17. "Social Security Survivors' Benefits," http://www.ssa.gov/pubs/10084.html (June 2001).

18. Markusen, "City Spatial Structure," 27.

19. Gerda Wekerle, "Review Essay: Women in the Urban Environment," in C. Stimpson, ed., *Women and the American City*, 206.

20. Melanie Archer, "Public Policy and Access to Opportunity: A Time-

Geographic Analysis of Constraints on Women's Activity Patterns," M.A. Thesis, Architecture and Urban Planning, University of California, Los Angeles, 1980; Risa Palm and Allan Pred, "A Time-Geographic Perspective on Problems of Inequality for Women," Working Paper no. 236 (Berkeley, Calif.: Institute of Urban and Regional Development, 1974).

21. Markusen, "City Spatial Structure."

22. Martin Wachs, "Issues in Transportation for Women," text of talk at Second Annual Conference on Planning and Women's Needs, UCLA, 1981, 2.

23. Sandra Rosenbloon, "Trends in Women's Travel Patterns," in *Women's Travel Issues: Proceedings from the Second National Conference*, October 1996, http://www.fhwa.dot.gov/ohim/womens/chap2.pdf (June 2001).

24. Jane Holtz Kay, *Asphalt Nation: How the Automobile Took Over America* (New York: Crown Publishers, 1997); Edith Perlman, "Kicking the Car Habit: Why It's Up to Women," *Radcliffe Quarterly* 67 (Dec. 1981), 25–26.

25. Wachs, "Issues."

26. Helena Znaniecki Lopata, "The Chicago Woman: A Study of Patterns of Mobility and Transportation," *Signs* 5 (Supplement, Spring 1980), S161–S169.

27. Wachs, "Issues."

28. My account of this incident is based on a personal conversation with Prof. Rosenbloom in 1979.

29. Michael Freedberg, "Self-Help Housing and the Cities: Sweat Equity in New York," in Gary J. Coates, ed., *Resettling America*, 272.

30. *Ibid.*, 264, 280.

31. Gabrielle Brainard, interview with Michael Freedberg, June 28, 2001; Gabrielle Brainard, interview with Andrew Reicher, July 9, 2001; Urban Homesteading Assistance Board Website, http://www.uhab.org (June 2001).

32. Jacqueline Leavitt and Susan Saegert, *From Abandonment to Hope: Community Households in Harlem* (New York: Columbia University Press: 1990).

33. "Bridge Over Troubled Water," *Architects' Journal* (London, Sept. 27, 1972), 680–684; personal interview by the author with Nina West, 1978; Gabrielle Brainard, interview with Eve Schwartz, manager of Nina West Nurseries, July 2, 2001.

34. Women's Development Corporation, Providence, R. I., mimeographed statement, 1980.

35. Joan Forrester Sprague, *More than Housing: Lifeboats for Women and Children* (Boston, Mass.: Butterworth-Heinemann, 1991).

36. Folbre, *The Invisible Heart*, 231–232.

Chapter 6. Architecture: Roof, Fire, and Center

1. Kenneth Frampton, *Modern Architecture: A Critical History* (London: Thames and Hudson, 1980), 9.

2. Ada Louise Huxtable, "Some Handsome Housing Mythology," *Kicked a Building Lately?* (New York: Quadrangle, 1976), 33.

3. Kathleen Anne Mackie, "An Exploration of the Idea of Home in Human Geography," M.A. Thesis, University of Toronto, 1981, 33. This outstanding essay reviews a wide variety of literature, including Cooper, Jung, Gibran, Raglan, Heidegger, Eliade.

4. *Ibid.*, 33–57, see also Clare Cooper, "The House as Symbol of the Self," in Proshansky, et al., eds., *Environmental Psychology* (New York: Holt, Rinehart, and Winston, 1976).

5. Francesco Dal Co, *Abitare Nel Moderno* (Rome: Laterza, 1982).

6. Joseph Rykwert, *On Adam's House in Paradise: The Idea of the Primitive Hut in Architectural History* (New York: Museum of Modern Art, 1972).

7. John Brinckerhoff Jackson, "The Westward Moving House," *Landscapes* (Amherst: University of Massachusetts Press, 1970), 10–42.

8. Adrienne Rich, "A Primary Ground," in *Poems: Selected and New* (New York: W. W. Norton, 1975), 203–204.

9. William Nowlin, *The Bark-Covered House, or Back in the Woods Again* (1876; New York: Readex Microprint, 1966).

10. Hayden, "Catharine Beecher and the Politics of Housework," 40–49.

11. Amos Rapoport, *House Form and Culture* (Englewood Cliffs, N.J.: Prentice Hall, 1969), 54, shows the Herrgottswinkel.

12. Charlotte Perkins Gilman, *The Home*, 100.

13. Carol Barkin, "Electricity Is Her Servant," *Heresies* 11 (1981), 62–63.

14. Eric Larrabee, "The Six Thousand Houses That Levitt Built," *Harper's* (Sept. 1948), 84.

15. "Housing: Up From the Potato Fields," *Time* (July 3, 1950), 67.

16. Research by Scott Kinzy, discussed in Philip Langdon, "Suburbanites Pick Favorite Home Styles," *New York Times* (Apr. 22, 1982), Home Section, 1.

17. Tom Wolfe, *From Bauhaus to Our House* (New York: Farrar, Straus and Giroux, 1981), 69.

18. Bill Owens, *Suburbia* (San Francisco: Straight Arrow, 1973).

19. Denise Scott Brown and Robert Venturi, *Signs of Life: Symbols in the American City* (Washington, D.C.: Aperture, Inc., 1976).

20. Manufactured Housing Institute, "Quick Facts: The Latest Trends and Information on the Manufactured Housing Industry, 2000–2001," http://www.manufacturedhousing.org/quick_facts/2000/index.html (June 2001).

21. Patrick H. Hare, "Why Granny Flats Are a Good Idea," *Planning* 18 (Feb. 1982), 15–16; Larry Agran, "Rethinking the Single-family Home," *Los Angeles Times Home Magazine* (Feb. 14, 1982), 24; Jack Birkinshaw, "Granny Housing Act Weighed in County," *Los Angeles Times*, Westside (Dec. 20, 1981), 1.

22. Henry James, *The American Scene* (1904; Bloomington, Ind.: Indiana University Press, 1968), 11.

23 *Ibid.*, 10.

24. Thorstein Veblen, *The Theory of the Leisure Class: An Economic Study of Institutions* (1899; New York: The Modern Library, 1934), 153–154.

25. Robert Woods Kennedy, *The House and the Art of Its Design* (New York: Reinhold Publishing Co., 1953), 42.

26. R. Buckminster Fuller, "The Dymaxion House," *Architectural Forum* 70 (1932); "The 8000 Lb. House," *Architectural Forum* 84 (1946); Elliott Erwhitt, "A House That Thinks for Itself," *House and Garden* (July 1976), 52–57. For a really extreme example of high-tech sacred huts, see Gerard O'Neill, *The High Frontier: Human Colonies in Space* (New York: William Morrow, 1977).

27. Terence Riley, *The Un-Private House* (New York: Museum of Modern Art, 1999), 56–59.

28. Joseph Deken, *The Electronic Cottage: Everyday Living with Your Personal Computers in the 1980's* (New York: Morrow, 1981).

29. Stephen Doheny-Farina, *The Wired Neighborhood* (New Haven: Yale University Press, 1996).

30. Robin Evans, "Bentham's Panopticon," *Architectural Association Quarterly* 3 (Apr.–July 1971), 21–37.

31. Taylor Stoehr, *Nay-Saying in Concord* (New Haven: Archon Books, 1978), 100.

32. Bauer, *Modern Housing*, 119–141.

33. Frampton, *Modern Architecture*, 137–138.

34. Competition prospectus, quoted in Vladmir Zelinski, "Architecture as a Tool of Social Transformation," 6–14. See also Barbara Kreis, "The Ideal of the *Dom-Kommuna* and the Dilemma of the Soviet Avant-Garde," *Oppositions* 21 (Summer 1980), 52–77; Victor Buchli, *An Archaeology of Socialism* (Oxford, UK: Berg, 1999).

35. Filippo Marinetti, "Foundation Manifesto of Futurist Architecture," 1909, quoted in Ian Todd and Michael Wheeler, *Utopia* (New York: Harmony Books, 1978), 131. For another translation, see *Marinetti: Selected Writings*, ed. and tr. R. W. Flint, (New York: Farrar, Straus and Giroux, 1971), 41–42.

36. Alexandra Kollontai, *Women's Labor in Economic Development*, quoted in Zelinski, 10.

37. Kopp, "Soviet Architecture," 26.

38. Le Corbusier, *Towards a New Architecture* (1927; London: The Architectural Press, 1946), 269. See also Peter Serenyi, "Le Corbusier, Fourier, and the Monastery of Ema," *Art Bulletin* (Dec. 1967), 277–286.

39. Nicholas John Habraken, *Supports: An Alternative to Mass Housing* (Cambridge, Mass.: MIT, 1964).

40. Dolores Hayden, "What Would a Non-Sexist City Be Like?" in Stimpson, et. al., eds., *Women and the American City*, 179.

41. SITE, *Highrise of Homes* (New York: Rizzoli, 1982).

42. Department of the Environment, *Space in the Home* (London: Her Majesty's Stationery Office, 1972), 4–8.

43. Glenn Robert Lym, *A Psychology of Building: How We Shape and Experience Our Structured Spaces* (Englewood Cliffs, N.J.: Prentice Hall, 1980), 20–29.

44. *Ibid.*, 45–48.

45. Virginia Woolf, *A Room of One's Own* (1929; San Diego: Harcourt, Brace, Jovanovich, 1957), 24.

46. Torsten Malmberg, *Human Territoriality* (The Hague: Mouton, 1980).

47. Margaret Mead, *Sex and Temperament in Three Primitive Societies* (1935; New York: Morrow Quill, 1980), is a pioneering example.

48. Catherine Bauer, "The Dreary Deadlock of Public Housing," *Architectural Forum* (May 1957), 140ff.

49. Charles Jencks, *The Language of Post-Modern Architecture* (New York: Rizzoli, 1977), 9; see also Lee Rainwater, *Behind Ghetto Walls* (Chicago: Aldine, 1970), and "Fear and the House-as-Haven in the Lower Class," *AIP Journal* (Jan. 1966), 23–31.

50. Personal conversation with Charles Jencks, 1982.

51. Jan Wampler, Columbia Point Project, *Progressive Architecture* (Jan. 1973), 74–75.

52. Charles Jencks, *The Language of Post-Modern Architecture*, 79–82.

53. Hayden, *Grand Domestic Revolution*, 50–63.

54. *Ibid.*, 64–114.

55. *Ibid.*, 151-179.

56. Ebenezer Howard, *Garden Cities of To-Morrow* (1902; Cambridge, Mass.: MIT Press, 1970); Hayden, *Grand Domestic Revolution*, 230–237.

57. Stein, *Toward New Towns for America*, 188–216.

58. *Ibid.*, 210.

59. Esther McCoy, *Five California Architects* (New York: Praeger, 1975), 58–100. See also Stefanos Polyzoides, Roger Sherwood, James Tice, and Julius Schulman, *Courtyard Housing in Los Angeles* (Berkeley and Los Angeles: University of California Press, 1982).

60. Tynggarden was built by Tegnestuen Vandkunsten of Copenhagen with Svend Algren, Jens T. Arnfred, Michael S. Johnsen, Steffen Kragh, and Karsten Vibild.

61. Francis Strauven, "A place of reciprocity: home for one parent families in Amsterdam by Aldo Van Eyck," *Lotus* 28 (1980), 22–39.

62. Roger Montgomery, "High Density, Low-Rise Housing and Changes in the American Housing Economy," in Sam Davis, ed., *The Form of Housing* (New York: Van Nostrand Reinhold, 1977), 83–111.

63. U.S. Department of Housing and Urban Development, *The Affordable Community: Growth, Change and Choice in the 80s* (Washington, D.C.: U.S. G.P.O., 1981).

64. Daniel Lauber, "Nothing New in This Housing Report," *Planning* 48 (June 1982), 26.

65. Michael Pyatok, Tom Jones, William Pettus, eds., *Good Neighbors: Affordable Family Housing* (New York: McGraw-Hill, 1995).

66. Internet catalog of outstanding affordable housing design in the U.S., sponsored by the City Design Center at the University of Illinois, Chicago, http://affordable.housing.aa.uic.edu (June, 2001).

67. Peter Calthorpe, *The Next American Metropolis: Ecology, Community, and the American Dream* (New York: Princeton Architectural Press, 1993).

68. Peter Calthorpe and William Fulton, *The Regional City: Planning for the End of Sprawl* (Washington, D.C.: Island Press, 2001). Includes "Charter of the New Urbanism" as appendix.

69. Andres Duany, Elizabeth Plater-Zyberk, and Jeff Speck, *Suburban Nation: the*

Rise of Sprawl and the Decline of the American Dream (New York: North Point Press, 2000), 107.

70. Equal Opportunities Unit, Commission of the European Communities, *European Charter for Women in the City* (Brussels: European Commission, 1994), 14.

71. Frauenbüro (Office of Women's Affairs), City of Vienna, Women in Vienna, unpublished document, 1991; Joanne McCrystal, "Urban Planning in Austria—Do Women Have a Voice?" unpublished paper, n.d.; http://www.unesco.org/most/wenteu19.htm (August 2001).

72. "Women and the City," Fundació Maria Aurèlia Capmany, Rambles, 81 baixos, 08002, Barcelona, http://www.fmac.org/fmac/ciutat and http://www.fmac.org/fmac/eurowoman.

73. Gerda R. Wekerle, "Responding to Diversity: Housing Developed By and For Women," *Canadian Journal of Urban Research* (Dec. 1993), 95–113; Gerda R. Wekerle and Carolyn Whitzman, *Safe Cities: Guidelines for Planning, Design, and Management* (New York: Van Nostrand Reinhold, 1995).

74. Hemalata Dandekar, *Shelter, Women, and Development: First and Third World Perspectives* (Ann Arbor, MI: G. Wahr Publishing, 1993).

75. United Nations, Women in Human Settlements Development Programme, http://www.unesco.org/most/bpwomen.htm (August 2001).

76. Montgomery, "High Density," 110–111.

Chapter 7. Reconstructing Domestic Space

1. William E. Geist, "A Suburban Tempest," *New York Times* (Dec. 8, 1981), B2.

2. George Sternlieb and James Hughes, *America's Housing: Prospects and Problems*, 26–27; National Association of Home Builders, "Characteristics of New Single-Family Homes, 1987-1999," http://www.nahb.com/facts/forecast/sf.html (June 2001).

3. U.S. Bureau of the Census, "Average Population per Household and Family: 1940 to the Present," *Current Population Survey*, December 1998, http://www.census.gov/population/socdemo/hh-fam/htabHH-6.txt (June 2001).

4. Andrée Brooks, "Wide Appeal for Accessory Apartments," *New York Times* (Jan. 3, 1982), Real Estate Section, 6; Patrick Hare, "Carving Up The American Dream," *Planning* (July 1981), 14–17.

5. Bill McLarney, quoted by Amory Lovins, in Coates, ed., *Resettling America.*

6. *The Report of the President's Commission on Housing* (Washington, D.C.: U.S.G.P. O., 1982), xxxiv.

7. F. Kaid Benfield, Matthew D. Raimi, Donald D. T. Chen, *Once There Were Greenfields: How Urban Sprawl is Undermining American's Environment, Economy, and Social Fabric* (Washington, D.C.: National Resources Defense Council, 1999).

8. Transit Cooperative Research Program, Report 39, *The Costs of Sprawl—Revisited* (Washington, D. C.: National Academy Press, 1998).

9. Benfield, et. al., *Once There Were Greenfields*, 89–116.

10. David Morris, "Self-Reliant Cities: The Rise of the New City States," in Coates, ed., *Resettling America*, 248.

11. Robert Lindsey, "Southern California Sets An Example of How to Grow Old in the Sunbelt," *New York Times* (July 10, 1982), 7.

12. David Morris, "Self-Reliant Cities," 248; William Nolan, "Urban Growth: Too Much of a Good Thing?" *Better Homes and Gardens* (April 2001), 92.

13. Robert Goodman, *The Last Entrepreneurs*, 52–75.

14. Morris, "Self-Reliant Cities," 243.

15. Patrick H. Hare, with Susan Conner and Dwight Merriam, *Accessory Apartments: Using Surplus Space in Single-Family Houses*, PAS Report no. 265 (Chicago, Illinois: American Planning Association, 1982).

16. *Ibid.*, 9–19.

17. *Ibid.*, 6.

18. Patrick H. Hare, "Accessory Apartments for Today's Communities," *Planning Commissioner's Journal* (Nov./Dec. 1991), 14–15.

19. Patrick H. Hare, "Accessory Apartment," The Supportive Housing Connection Website, http://www.aoa.gov/Housing/Accessory.html (July 2001).

20. Morris, "Self-Reliant Cities," 243.

21. Patrick H. Hare, "Rethinking Single-Family Zoning," 34.

22. Patrick H. Hare, "The Nation's Largest Untapped Housing Resource," *Christian Science Monitor* (Aug. 19, 1981); U.S. Bureau of the Census, "Data Chart for Occupied Units with an Elderly Householder," *American Housing Survey: 1999*, April 2001,http://www.census.gov/hhes/www/housing/ahs/99ed chrt/ahs99e.html (June 2001).

23. Hare, "Rethinking," 33; also see his "Why Granny Flats Are a Good Idea," *Planning* 18 (Feb. 1982), 15–16; Deborah A. Howe, Nancy J. Chapman, Sharon A. Baggett, *Planning for an Aging Society*, PAS Report 451 (Chicago: American Planning Association, Planning Advisory Service, 1994).

24. Nancy Rubin, *The New Suburban Woman: Beyond Myth and Motherhood* (New York: Coward, McCann, and Geoghegan, 1982); Karen Lindsey, *Friends as Family: New Kinds of Families And What They Could Mean For You* (Boston: Beacon Press, 1981).

25. Robert Weiss, *Going It Alone: The Family Life and Social Situation of the Single Parent* (New York: Basic Books, 1979).

26. National Congress of Neighborhood Women, "Women's Leadership and Community Development Program," xerox, 1982.

27. Marshall Runt and David Bainbridge, "The Davis Experience," in Coates, ed., *Resettling America*, 366–374; "Four Families Get Together," *Sunset* (April 1983), 258–259.

28. Robert Lake, *The New Suburbanites: Race and Housing in the Suburbs* (New Brunswick, N.J.: Rutgers, 1981); Thomas A. Clark, *Blacks in Suburbs: A National Perspective* (New Brunswick, N.J.: Rutgers, 1979).

29. Hattie H. Hartman, "Rehabbing the Suburbs: Freedom to Change," M. Arch. thesis, MIT, 1982.

30. Reneé Chow, *Suburban Spaces: The Fabric of Dwelling* (Berkeley: University of California Press, 2002), forthcoming.

31. Raquel Ramati, *How to Save Your Own Street* (Garden City, N.Y.: Dolphin Books, 1981).

32. Stein, *Toward New Towns for America*, 188–216.

33. Hans Wirz, "Backyard Rehab: Urban Microcosm Rediscovered," *Urban Innovation Abroad* 3 (July 1979), 2–3. See also Donald Shoup, "The Economics of Neighborhood Renewal," UCLA Graduate School of Architecture and Urban Planning, Discussion Paper DP 121, May 1979.

34. Gary Garber, "The Cheyenne Community Solar Greenhouse," in Coates, ed., *Resettling America*, 357, 363.

35. Gabrielle Brainard, interview with Gary Garber, June 27, 2001; Cheyenne Botanic Garden, http://www.botanic.org (June 2001).

36. John Emmeus Davis, "Homemaking: The Programmatic Politics of Third Sector Housing," in Charles Geisler and Gail Daneker, *Property and Values: Alternatives to Public and Private Ownership* (Washington, D.C.: Island Press, 2000), 233–258.

37. Sam Hall Kaplan, "From Renters to Owners: A Success Story," *Los Angeles Times* (June 10, 1982), 5, 1.

38. Id.; Elizabeth Virata, "Cooperative Housing in Los Angeles, 1945–1982," unpublished paper, UCLA, 1982.

39. Ronald Lee Fleming and Lauri Halderman, *On Common Ground*, 150. On shared maintenance and its problems, also see Gerda Wekerle, et al. "Condominium Housing: Contradiction in Ownership, Participation, and Control," paper given at Environmental Design Research Association meeting, Tucson, 1978.

40. U.S. Department of Housing and Urban Development, "A Picture of Subsidized Households in 1998," http://www.huduser.org/datasets/assthsg/statedata98/index.html (June 2001).

41. U.S. Department of Housing and Urban Development, "Housing and Social Services," transcript of a roundtable, Oct. 28, 1980.

42. "HOPE VI Program Authority and Funding History," http://www.hud.gov:80/pih/programs/ph/hope6/history_8-8-00.pdf (July 2001); Blair Kamin, "Public Housing in 1999: A Hard Assessment," *Architectural Record* 187 (November 1999), 76-83; Dolores Hayden, "Model Houses for the Millions," http://www.lincinst.edu (June 2001); Gayle Epp, "Emerging Strategies for Revitalizing Public Housing Communities," *Housing Policy Debate* (1996), 582; and Dolores Hayden, interview with Daniel Glenn, August 2000.

43. A detailed examination of new housing typologies is Karen A. Franck and Sherry Ahrentzen, eds., *New Households, Hew Housing* (New York: Van Nostrand Reinhold, 1989).

44. "Inn for the Elderly Proves Workable Idea," *Los Angeles Times* (Jan 17, 1982), VII, 23; Gabrielle Brainard, interview with Jeanne Farrell, executive director, New Canaan Inn, June 28, 2001; *Inn-Side Report*, New Canaan Inn, 73 Oenoke Ridge, New Canaan, CT 06840, Spring/Summer 2001.

45. Catharine Davis, "Business Is Booming," *Historic Preservation* 34 (July/August 1982), 52–53.

46. Gabrielle Brainard, interview with Jean Mason, psychologist who has worked with Gwen Noyes, June 27, 2001.

47. Kathryn McCamant and Charles Durrett, *Cohousing: A Contemporary Approach to Housing Ourselves* (1988; Berkeley, Calif.: Ten Speed Press, 1994); The Cohousing Network, http://www.cohousing.org; Karen A. Frank and Sherry Ahrentzen, eds., *New Households, New Housing* (New York: Van Nostrand Reinhold, 1989); Jacqueline Leavitt, "Designing Women's Welfare: Home/Work," in George C. Hemmens, Charles J. Hoch, and Jana Carp, eds., *Under One Roof: Issues and Innovations in Shared Housing* (Albany: State University of New York Press, 1996), 63–74.

48. Grace Duffield Goodwin, "The Commuter's Wife: A Sisterly Talk by One Who Knows Her Problems," *Good Housekeeping* 49 (Oct. 1909), 363.

CHAPTER 8. DOMESTICATING URBAN SPACE

1. Susan Saegert, "Masculine Cities, Feminine Suburbs: Polarized Ideas, Contradictory Realities," in Stimpson, et al., eds., *Women and the American City*, S96–S111; Adele Chatfield-Taylor, "Hitting Home," *Architectural Forum* 138 (Mar. 1973), 58–61.

2. Ira Katznelson, *City Trenches: Urban Politics and the Patterning of Class in the United States* (Chicago: University of Chicago Press, 1981), discusses the split between "home" and "work" but makes no gender analysis.

3. Henri Lefebvre, *La production de l'espace* (Paris: Anthropos, 1974) suggests the political importance of this demand for men. On women's exclusion, see Christine de Pizan, *The Book of the City of Ladies*, tr. E. J. Richards (New York: Persea Books, 1982).

4. See Wekerle's review essay in Stimpson, et al., eds., *Women and the American City*, S188–S214. Also see Claude Enjeu and Joana Savé, "The City: Off-Limits to Women," *Liberation* 8 (July–Aug. 1974), 9–15; Bodil Kjaer, "A Woman's Place," *Architect's Journal* 176 (Sept. 15, 1982), 87. These last two essays from France and from Denmark (published in England) show that the double standard in public places is an international problem, not simply a result of American housing.

5. Daphne Spain, *How Women Saved the City* (Minneapolis: University of Minnesota Press, 2001); "Gender and the City," special issue, *Historical Geography* 26 (1998).

6. Carl Degler, "Revolution Without Ideology," *Daedalus* 93 (Spring 1964), 653–670, and also his *At Odds: Women and the Family* (New York: Oxford, 1979).

7. Lyn Lofland notes that in urban sociology, for many researchers, women are "part of the locale or neighborhood or area—described like other important aspects of the setting such as income, ecology, or demography—but largely irrelevant to the analytic *action*. They may reflect a group's social organization

and culture, but they never seem to be in the process of creating it. They may be talked about by actors in the scene, but they rarely speak for themselves. They may, like males, suffer from certain structural inequalities, strains or disjunctions, but it is primarily the male figure who struggles against the pain. They may participate in organized groups, but such groups are tangential to the structuring of community life or to the processes of community government. When the researcher's lens pulls back for the wide-angle view, they are lost in the ubiquitous and undifferentiated 'he.' When it moves forward to close, detailed focus, they are fuzzy, shadowy, background figures, framing the male at center stage." "The 'Thereness' of Women: A Selective Review of Urban Sociology," in *Another Voice: Feminist Perspectives on Social Life and Social Science*, ed. M. Milliman and R. M. Kanter (New York: Anchor, 1975); Jessie Bernard, *The Female World* (New York: Simon and Schuster, 1980), takes up the pervasiveness of gender segregation without analyzing this as an explicitly spatial phenomenon, although she is the most perceptive of all feminist sociologists.

8. Lewis Mumford, *The Transformations of Man* (New York: Harper and Row, 1956), 159–161.

9. For a description of one mother's problems in public, see Phyllis Chesler, *With Child: A Diary of Motherhood* (New York: Thomas Crowell, 1979), 149–50, 175.

10. Linda Hollis and Vivian Barry, "Kidspace," Community Design for Family Use exhibit organized in 1980, Capitol Children's Museum, Washington, D.C.; Colin Ward, *The Child in the City* (London: The Architectural Press, 1960).

11. Robert B. Edgerton, *Alone Together: Social Order on an Urban Beach* (Los Angeles: University of California Press, 1978), 4.

12. Gerda Wekerle and Carolyn Whitzman, *Safe Cities: Guidelines for Planning, Design, and Management* (New York: Van Nostrand Reinhold, 1995), 3.

13. Margaret Gordon, Stephanie Riger, Robert K. LeBailly, and Linda Heath, "Crime, Women, and the Quality of Urban Life," in C. Stimpson, et al., eds., *Women and the American City*, 144–160.

14. Philip Hager, "Safehouses Ease Fears of Aged Residents of San Francisco," *Los Angeles Times*, Nov. 21, 1982, 1.

15. Allan Griswold Johnson, "On the Prevalence of Rape in the United States," *Signs: Journal of Women in Culture and Society* 6 (Autumn 1980), 136–146; Patricia Tjaden and Nancy Thoennes, U.S. Department of Justice, National Institute of Justice, "Prevalence, Incidence, and Consequences of Violence Against Women: Findings from the National Violence Against Women Survey," November 1998, http://www.ncjrs.org/pdfffo;es/172837.pdf (June 2001).

16. Gerda Wekerle, "Women's Self-Help Projects in the City: Transportation and Housing," paper presented at conference on Social Practice, UCLA Urban Planning Program, Mar. 2, 1979, 5–7. On women as providers of urban services, also see Galen Cranz, "Women and Urban Parks: Their Roles as Users and Suppliers of Park Services," in Keller, ed., *Building for Women*, 151–171; "Women in Urban Parks," in Stimpson, et al., eds., *Women and the American City*, 79–95.

17. "Organizing and Theater: Bus Riders' Union," Community Arts Network Website, http://www.communityarts.net/concal/busriders.html (July 2001).

18. William H. Whyte, "Street Life," *Urban Open Spaces* (Summer 1980), 2. For a more detailed critique of hassling: Lindsy Van Gelder, "The International Language of Street Hassling," *Ms.* 9 (May 1981), 15–20, and letters about this article, *Ms.* (Sept.1981); and Cheryl Benard and Edith Schlaffer, "The Man in the Street: Why He Harasses," *Ms.* 9 (May 1981), 18–19.

19. Erving Goffman, *Gender Advertisements* (New York: Harper Colophon, 1976), 24–27. Nancy Henley, *Body Politics: Power, Sex, and Nonverbal Communication* (Englewood Cliffs, N.J.: Prentice-Hall, 1977), 30; Marianne Wex, *Let's Take Back Our Space* (Berlin: Movimento Druck, 1979).

20. John Berger, et. al., *Ways of Seeing* (Harmondsworth, England: BBC and Penguin, 1972), 45–64.

21. Tom Hayden, *The American Future: New Visions Beyond Old Frontiers* (Boston: South End Press, 1980), 15.

22. Laura Shapiro, "Violence: The Most Obscene Fantasy," in Freeman, ed., *Women: A Feminist Perspective*, 469–473.

23. Lewis Mumford, *The City in History* (New York: Harcourt Brace, 1961), 526.

Chapter 9. Beyond the Architecture of Gender

1. Myron Orfield, *Metropolitics: A Regional Agenda for Community and Stability*, rev. ed., (Washington and Cambridge: Brookings Institution Press and Lincoln Institute of Land Policy, 1997).

2. Denise Scott Brown, "Between Three Stools: A Personal View of Urban Design Practice and Pedagogy," in *Education for Urban Design*, special issue of *Urban Design International* (Winter 1982), 156.

3. Ruth Rosen, *The World Split Open: How the Modern Women's Movement Changed America* (New York: Viking, 2000), 92–93; Susan Brownmiller, *In Our Time: Memoir of a Revolution* (New York: Delta, 1999), 146–148.

4. Janet L. Abu-Lughod, "Designing a City for All," in Judith Getzels and Karen Hapgood, *Planning Women, and Change* (Chicago: Planning Advisory Service/American Society of Planning Officials, 1974), 42.

Selected Bibliography

Albrecht, Donald, ed. *World War II and the American Dream: How Wartime Building Changed a Nation.* Washington D.C. and Cambridge, Mass.: The National Building Museum and The MIT Press, 1995.

Amsden, Alice, ed. *The Economics of Women and Work.* New York: St. Martin's Press, 1980.

André, Rae. *Homemakers: The Forgotten Workers.* Chicago: University of Chicago Press, 1981.

Ardener, Shirley, ed. *Women and Space: Ground Rules and Social Maps.* London: Croom Helm, 1981.

Bauer, Catherine. *Modern Housing.* Boston: Houghton Mifflin, 1934.

Baxandall, Rosalyn and Elizabeth Ewen. *Picture Windows: How the Suburbs Happened.* New York: Basic Books, 2000.

Bebel, August. *Woman Under Socialism.* 1883. Tr. Daniel De Leon, 1904. New York: Schocken Books, 1971.

Benfield, F. Kaid, Matthew D. Raimi, and Donald D. T. Chen, *Once there Were Greenfields: How Urban Sprawl is Undermining America's Environment, Economy, and Social Fabric.* Washington, D.C.: Natural Resources Defense Council, 1999.

Bernhardt, Arthur D. *Building Tomorrow: The Mobile / Manufactured Housing Industry.* Cambridge, Mass.: MIT Press, 1980.

Blake, Peter. *Form Follows Fiasco: Why Modern Architecture Hasn't Worked.* Boston: Little, Brown, 1977.

—. *God's Own Junkyard: The Planned Deterioration of America's Landscape.* New York: Holt, Rinehart and Winston, 1964.

Birch, Eugenie Ladner, ed. *The Unsheltered Woman: Women and Housing in the 1980s.* New Brunswick, N.J.: Center for Urban Policy Research, 1985.

Bose, Christine and Glenna Spitze, eds. *Ingredients for Women's Employment Policy.* Albany, New York: State University of New York Press, 1987.

Bratt, Rachel G., Chester Hartman, and Ann Meyerson, eds. *Critical Perspectives on Housing.* Philadelphia: Temple University Press, 1986.

Britz, Richard. *The Edible City: Resource Manual.* Los Altos, Calif.: William Kaufmann, Inc., 1981.

Burggraf, Shirley. *The Feminine Economy and Economic Man: Reviving the Role of Family in the Post-Industrial Age*. New York: Addison-Wesley Publishing Co., 1997.

Burns, Leland S. and Leo Grebler. *The Housing of Nations: Analysis and Policy in a Comparative Framework*. London: The Macmillan Company, 1977.

Burns, Scott. *Home, Inc.: The Hidden Wealth and Power of the American Household*. Garden City, New York: Doubleday, 1975. Republished as *The Household Economy: Its Shape, Origins, and Future*.

Calthorpe, Peter. *The Next American Metropolis: Ecology, Community and the American Dream*. Princeton, N.J.: Princeton Architectural Press, 1993.

—and William Fulton. *The Regional City: Planning for the End of Sprawl*. Washington D.C.: Island Press, 2001.

—and Sim Van Der Ryn, eds. *Sustainable Communities: A New Design Synthesis for Cities, Suburbs, and Towns*. San Francisco: Sierra Club Books, 1986.

Card, David E., and Rebecca M. Blank, eds. *Finding Jobs: Work and Welfare Reform*. New York: Russell Sage Foundation, 2000.

Carp, Jana, George C. Hemmens, and Charles J. Hoch, eds. *Under One Roof: Issues and Innovations in Shared Housing*. Albany, N.Y.: State University of New York Press, 1996.

Chauncey, George. *Gay New York: Gender, Urban Culture, and the Making of the Gay Male World, 1890-1940*. New York: Basic Books, 1994.

City and Shelter. *City, Citizenship and Gender*. CD-ROM. Brussels and Antwerp: Humanity Development Library, 1998.

Clark, Thomas A. *Blacks in Suburbs: A National Perspective*. New Brunswick, N.J.: Rutgers University, Center for Urban Policy Research, 1979.

Coates, Gary J., ed. *Resettling America: Energy, Ecology, and Community*. Andover, Mass.: Brick House Publishing Company, 1981.

Coatsworth, Patricia, ed. *Women and Urban Planning: A Bibliography*. Chicago: Council of Planning Librarians, 1981.

Commission of the European Communities, Equal Opportunities Unit, *Proposition for a European Charter for Women in the City*. Paris: Genicot, 1994.

Commoner, Barry. *The Politics of Energy*. New York: Alfred A. Knopf, 1979.

—. *The Poverty of Power: Energy and the Economic Crisis*. New York: Alfred A. Knopf, 1976.

Community Energy Cooperatives: How to Organize, Manage, and Finance Them. Washington, D.C.: Conference on Alternative State and Local Policies, 1983.

Connell, R. W. "Gender as a Structure of Social Practice." *Masculinities*. Cambridge: Polity Press, 1995.

Coontz, Stephanie. *The Way We Never Were: American Families and the Nostalgia Trap*. New York, Basic Books, 1992.

—*The Way We Really Are: Coming to Terms with Americas's Changing Families*. New York, Basic Books, 1997.

Corbett, Michael N. *A Better Place to Live: New Designs for Tomorrow's Communities*. Emmaus, Pennsylvania: Rodale Press, 1981.

Cott, Nancy. *Public Vows: A History of Marriage and the Nation*. Cambridge, Mass: Harvard University Press, 2000.

Cowan, Ruth Schwartz. *More Work for Mother: The Ironies of Household Technology from the Open Hearth to the Microwave*. New York: Basic Books, 1983.

Crittenden, Ann. *The Price of Motherhood: Why the Most Important Job in the World is Still the Least Valued*. New York: Metropolitan Books, 2001.

Dal Co, Francesco. *Abitare nel Moderno*. Rome: Laterza, 1982.

Dandekar, Hemalata C, ed. *Shelter, Women and Development: First and Third World Perspectives*. Ann Arbor, Mich.: George Wahr Publishing Co., 1993.

Darke, Jane, Roberta Woods, and Sue Ledwith, eds. *Women and the City: Visibility and Voice in Urban Space*. New York: St. Martin's Press, 2000.

Davis, Sam., ed. *The Form of Housing*. New York: Van Nostrand Reinhold, 1977.

Deal, Mary, ed. *Planning to Meet the Changing Needs of Women: A Compendium Developed from a National Competition to Identify and Promote Creative Solutions for Women in Urban Environments*. Dayton, Ohio: xerox manuscript, furnished by the editor, 1982.

Deutsch, Francine M. *Halving It All: How Equally Shared Parenting Works*. Cambridge, Mass.: Harvard University Press, 1999.

Deutsch, Sarah Jane. *Women and the City: Gender, Power, and Space in Boston, 1870-1940*. New York: Oxford University Press, 2000.

Doheny-Farina, Stephen. *The Wired Neighborhood*. New Haven: Yale University Press, 1996.

Duany, Andres, Elizabeth Plater-Zyberk, and Jeff Speck. *Suburban Nation: The Rise of Sprawl and the Decline of the American Dream*. New York: North Point Press, 2000.

Duly, Colin. *The Houses of Mankind*. London: Thames and Hudson, 1979.

Duncan, James S., ed. *Housing and Identity: Cross-cultural Perspectives*. London: Croom Helm, 1981.

Edwards, Arthur M. *The Design of Suburbia: A Critical Study in Environmental History*. London: Pembridge Press, 1981.

Ehrenreich, Barbara. *The Hearts of Men: American Dreams and the Flight from Commitment*. New York: Doubleday, 1983.

—*Nickel and Dimed: On (Not) Getting By in America*. New York: Henry Holt and Co, 2001.

Eichler, Ned. *The Merchant Builders*. Cambridge, Mass.: MIT Press, 1982.

Faltermayer, Edmund. *Redoing America: A Nationwide Report on How to Make Our Cities and Suburbs Livable*. New York: Harper and Row, 1968.

Feins, Judith D. and Terry Saunders Lane. *How Much For Housing*. Cambridge, Mass.: Abt Books, 1981.

Fleming, Ronald Lee and Lauri A. Halderman. *On Common Ground: Caring for Shared Land from Town Common to Urban Park*. Harvard, Mass.: The Harvard Common Press, 1982.

Fleming, Ronald Lee and Renata Von Tscharner. *Place Makers: Public Art That Tells You Where You Are*. Cambridge, Mass. and New York: Townscape Institute and Architectural Book Publishing Company, 1981.

Folbre, Nancy. *The Invisible Heart: Economics and Family Values*. New York: The New Press, 2001.

Forsyth, Ann. "NoHo: Upscaling Main Street on the Metropolitan Edge." *Urban Geography* 18 (1997): 622–652.

—, ed. "The Seventh Generation: Special Issue on Feminism," *Planners Network* (July–August 1998).

Francis, Mark, Lisa Cashdan, Lynn Paxson. *The Making of Neighborhood Open Spaces*. New York: Center for Human Environments, CUNY, 1981.

Franck, Karen A. and Sherry Ahrentzen, eds. *New Households, New Housing*. New York: Van Nostrand Reinhold, 1989.

Friedan, Betty. *The Second Stage*. New York: Summit Books, 1981.

Friedmann, John. *Retracking America: A Theory of Transactive Planning*. Garden City, New York: Anchor Press, 1973.

Fromm, Dorit. *Collaborative Communities: Cohousing, Central Living, and Other New Forms of Housing with Shared Facilities*. New York: Van Nostrand Reinhold, 1991.

Gans, Herbert. *The Levittowners: Ways of Life and Politics in a New Suburban Community.*1967. New York: Columbia University Press, 1982.

Gardener, Carol Brooks. "Out of Place: Gender, Pubic Places, and Situational Disadvantage," in Roger Friedland and Deirdre Boden, *Nowhere: Space, Time and Modernity*. Berkeley: UC Press, 1994.

Getzels, Judith, and Karen Hapgood, eds. *Planning, Women, And Change*. Chicago: Planning Advisory Service, 1974.

Gilfoyle, Timothy. "Prostitution," in Kenneth Jackson, ed. *The Encyclopedia of New York*. New Haven: Yale University Press, 1996.

Gilroy, Rose, and Roberta Woods, eds. *Housing Women*. London: Routledge, 1994.

Glazer, Nona Y. *Women's Paid and Unpaid Labor: The Work Transfer in Health Care and Retailing*. Phildelphia, PA: Temple University Press, 1993.

Goffman, Erving. *Gender Advertisements*. New York: Harper Colophon Books. New York: Harper and Row, 1976.

Goings, Kenneth W. and Raymond A. Mohl, eds. *The New African American Urban History*. Thousand Oaks, Calif.: Sage Publications, 1996.

Greed, Clara. *Women and Planning: Creating Gendered Realities*. New York: Routledge, 1994.

Handlin, David. *The American Home: Architecture and Society, 1815–1915* Boston: Little Brown, 1979.

Hansen, John E. and Robert Morris. *Welfare Reform, 1996-2000: Is There a Safety Net?* Westport, Conn.: Auburn House, 1999.

Hare, Patrick, et. al. *Accessory Apartments: Using Surplus Space in Single Family Houses*. Chicago: Planning Advisory Service, 1982.

Hartman, Chester, ed. *America's Housing Crisis: What Is to Be Done?* Boston: Routledge and Kegan Paul, 1983.

Hayden, Dolores. *The Grand Domestic Revolution: A History of Feminist Designs for American Homes, Neighborhoods, and Cities*. Cambridge, Mass.: MIT Press, 1981.

—. *The Power of Place: Urban Landscapes as Public History.* Cambridge, Mass.: The MIT Press, 1995.

—. "Revisiting the Sitcom Suburbs," *Land Lines: Newsletter of the Lincoln Institute of Land Policy,* (March 2001), 1–3.

—. *Seven American Utopias: The Architecture of Communitarian Socialism. 1790–1975.* Cambridge, Mass.: MIT Press, 1976.

—. "What Would a Non-Sexist City Be Like?: Speculations on Housing, Urban Design, and Human Work," *Signs: Journal of Women in Culture and Society* (Spring 1980), 170–87.

—and Gwendolyn Wright, "Architecture and Urban Planning," review essay, *Signs: Journal of Women in Culture and Society* (Summer 1976), 923–33.

Hayden, Tom. *The American Future: New Visions Beyond Old Frontiers.* Boston: South End Press, 1980.

Hemmens, George C., Charles J. Hoch, and Jana Carp, eds. *Under One Roof: Issues and Innovations in Shared Housing.* Albany, N.Y.: State University of New York Press, 1996.

Heresies Collective, special issue. *Making Room: Women and Architecture, Heresies* 11 (1981).

Hertz, Rosanna and Nancy L. Marshall. *Working Families: The Transformation of the American Home.* Berkeley: University of California Press, 2001.

Heskin, Allan. *Tenants and the American Dream: Ideology and the Tenant Movement.* New York: Praeger, 1983.

—and Jacqueline Leavitt, eds. *The Hidden History of Housing Cooperatives* (Davis, CA: Center for Cooperatives, University of California, 1995).

Hirschmann, Nancy J. and Ulrike Liebert. *Women and Welfare: Theory and Practice in the United States and Europe.* New Brunswick, N.J.: Rutgers University Press, 2001.

Hochschild, Arlie Russell, with Anne Machung. *The Second Shift.* New York: Avon Books, 1989; 1997.

Howell, Sandra C. *Designing for Aging: Patterns of Use.* Cambridge, Mass.: MIT Press, 1980.

Hughes, Francesca. *The Architect: Reconstructing Her Practice.* Cambridge, Mass.: The MIT Press, 1995.

Hunter, Christine. *Ranches, Rowhouses and Railroad Flats.* New York: W. W. Norton, 1999.

Institute for Community Economics. *The Community Land Trust Handbook.* Greenfield, Mass.: ICE, 1982.

Jackson, John Brinckerhoff. *Landscapes: Selected Writings of J.B. Jackson.* Amherst, Mass.: University of Massachusetts Press, 1970.

Johnson, Bruce, ed. *Resolving the Housing Crisis: Government Policy, Decontrol, and the Public Interest.* Cambridge, Mass.: Ballinger, 1982.

Jones, Tom, William Pettus, and Michael Pyatok. *Good Neighbors: Affordable Family Housing.* New York: McGraw-Hill, 1995.

Kamerman, Sheila B. *Parenting in an Unresponsive Society.* New York: The Free Press, 1980.

—, and Alfred J. Kahn. *Not For The Poor Alone: European Social Services.* Philadelphia: Temple University Press, 1975.

Kaplan, Temma. *Crazy for Democracy: Women in Grassroots Movements.* New York and London: Routledge, 1997.

Keller, Suzanne, ed. *Building for Women.* Lexington, Mass.: Lexington Books, 1981.

Koebel, C. Theodore, ed. *Shelter and Society: Theory, Research, and Policy for Nonprofit Housing.* Albany, N.Y.: State University of New York Press, 1998.

Kolodny, Robert. *Multi-Family Housing: Treating the Existing Stock.* Washington, D.C.: National Association of Housing and Redevelopment Officials, 1981.

Lake, Robert W. *The New Suburbanites: Race and Housing.* New Brunswick, N.J.: Rutgers University, 1981.

Leavitt, Jacqueline, and Susan Saegert. *From Abandonment To Hope: Community-Households in Harlem.* New York: Columbia University Press, 1990.

Lindsey, Karen. *Friends as Family: New Kinds of Families and What They Could Mean to You.* Boston: Beacon Press, 1981.

Lovins, Amory. *Soft Energy Paths: Toward a Durable Peace.* 2nd ed. Cambridge, Mass.: Ballinger Publishing Co., 1977

Lynch, Kevin. *A Theory of Good City Form.* Cambridge, Mass.: MIT Press, 1981.

Marris, Peter. *Community Planning and Conceptions of Change.* London: Routledge, 1982.

—. *Loss and Change.* New York: Pantheon, 1974.

Massey, Doreen. *Space, Place, and Gender.* Minneapolis: University of Minnesota Press, 1994.

Matthews, Glenna. *"Just a Housewife": The Rise and Fall of Domesticity in America.* New York: Oxford University Press, 1987.

McCamant, Kathryn and Charles Durrett. *Cohousing: A Contemporary Approach to Housing Ourselves.* Berkeley, Calif.: Ten Speed Press, 1994.

McDowell, Linda and Joanne P. Sharp, eds. *Space, Gender, Knowledge: Feminist Readings.* London: Arnold, 1997.

Miliutin, N.A. *Sotsgorod: The Problem of Building Socialist Cities.* Tr. George Collins and William Alex. Cambridge, Mass.: MIT Press, 1974.

Miranne, Kristine B. and Alma H. Young, eds. *Gendering the City: Women, Boundaries, and Visions of Urban Life.* Latham, Md.: Rowman and Littlefield, 2000.

Moore, Gary, et al. *Recommendations for Child Care Centers.* Madison, Wisconsin: University of Wisconsin, 1979.

Montgomery, Roger, and Daniel Mandelker. *Housing in America.* Indianapolis: Bobbs-Merrill Company, 1979.

Morris, David. *Self-Reliant Cities: Energy and the Transformation of Urban America.* San Francisco: Sierra Club Books, 1982.

—and Karl Hess. *Neighborhood Power: The New Localism.* Boston: Beacon Press, 1975.

Muller, Peter O. "Everyday Life in Suburbia: A Review of Changing Social and Economic Forces That Shape Daily Rhythms within the Outer City." Bibliographical essay. *American Quarterly* 34 (1982): 262–77.

Mumford, Lewis. *The Transformation of Man.* New York: Harper and Row, 1956.

National Housing Law Project. *The Subsidized Housing Handbook.* Berkeley.: National Housing Law Project, 1982.

National Policy Workshop on Shared Housing, Findings and Recommendations. Philadelphia: Shared Housing Resource Center, 1981.

Orfield, Myron. *Metropolitics: A Regional Agenda for Community and Stability.* Washington, D.C.: Brookings Institution Press, 1997.

Palen, John J. *The Suburbs.* New York: McGraw-Hill, 1995.

Pawley, Martin. *Architecture Versus Housing.* New York: Praeger, 1971.

—. *Home Ownership.* London: Architectural Press, 1978.

Perin, Constance. *Everything in Its Place: Social Order and Land Use in America.* Princeton, N.J.: Princeton University Press, 1977.

Planning and the Changing Family, special issue of the *Journal of the American Planning Association.* (Spring 1983).

Radford, Gail. *Modern Housing in America: Policy Struggles in the New Deal Era.* Chicago: University of Chicago Press, 1996.

Rapoport, Amos. *House Form and Culture.* Englewood Cliffs, N.J.: Prentice Hall, 1969.

Relph, Edward. *Rational Landscapes and Humanistic Geography.* London: Croom Helm, 1981.

Rendell, Jane, Barbara Penner, and Iain Borden, eds. *Gender Space Architecture: An Interdisciplinary Introduction.* New York: Routledge, 2000.

Rich, Adrienne. *Of Woman Born: Motherhood as Experience and Institution.* New York: W. W. Norton, 1976.

Richards, Janet Radcliffe. *The Skeptical Feminist: A Philosophical Enquiry.* London and Boston: Routledge and Kegan Paul, 1980.

Ritzdorf, Marsha. "Women and the City: Land Use and Zoning Issues," *Journal of Urban Resources* 3 (1986), 23–27.

Rose, Gillian. *Feminism and Geography: The Limits of Geographical Knowledge.* Minneapolis: University of Minnesota Press, 1993.

Rothblatt, Donald N., and Daniel J. Garr, and Jo Sprague. *The Suburban Environment and Women.* New York: Praeger, Holt, 1979.

Rothschild, Joan, ed. *Design and Feminism: Re-Visioning Spaces, Places, and Everyday Things.* New Brunswick, N.J.: Rutgers University, 1999.

Rowe, Peter G. *Making a Middle Landscape.* Cambridge, Mass: The MIT Press, 1991.

Rubin, Nancy. *The New Suburban Woman: Beyond Myth and Motherhood.* New York: Coward, McCann, and Geoghegan, 1982.

Ryan, Mary P. "Gender and the Geography of the Public." *Women in Public: Between Banners and Ballots, 1825–1880.* Baltimore: Johns Hopkins University Press, 1990.

Safa, Helen, and Eleanor Leacock, eds. *Development and the Sexual Division of Labor.* Special issue, *Signs: Journal of Women in Culture and Society* 7 (Winter 1981).

Sandercock, Leonie and Ann Forsyth, "A Gender Agenda: New Directions for Planning Theory," in Richard Le Gates and Frederic Stout, eds. *The City Reader.* London; New York: Routledge, 2000.

Sanders, Joel ed. *Stud: Architectures of Masculinity.* New York: Princeton Architectural Press, 1996.

Sargent, Lydia, ed. *Women and Revolution: A Discussion of the Unhappy Marriage of Marxism and Feminism.* Boston: South End Press, 1981.

Schoenauer, Norbert. *6,000 Years of Housing.* Rev. ed. New York: W. W. Norton, 2000.

Shared Housing Resource Center. *National Policy Workshop on Shared Housing: Findings and Recommendations.* Philadelphia, Pa.: Shared Housing Resource Center, 1982.

Sherman, Roger. *Re: American Dream: Six Urban Housing Prototypes for Los Angeles.* New York: Princeton Architectural Press, 1995.

Shuman, Michael H. *Going Local: Crating Self-Reliant Communities in a Global Age.* New York: The Free Press, 1998.

Sclar, Elliot, Matthew Edel, and Daniel Luria. *Shaky Palaces: Homeownership and Social Mobility in Boston's Suburbanization.* New York: Columbia University Press, 1984.

Siegel, Reva B. "Home as Work: The First Women's Rights Claims Concerning Wives' Household Labor, "*The Yale Law Journal* (March 1994), 1075–1217.

Smith, Ralph, ed. *The Subtle Revolution: Women at Work.* Washington, D.C.: Urban Land Institute, 1979.

Spain, Daphne. *Gendered Spaces.* Chapel Hill: University of North Carolina Press, 1992.

—*How Women Saved the City.* Minneapolis: University of Minnesota Press, 2001.

"Special Issue: Gender and the City." *Historical Geography: An Annual Journal of Research, Commentary, and Reviews,* 26 (1998).

Sprague, Joan Forrester. *More Than Housing: Lifeboats for Women and Children.* Boston: Butterworth Architecture, 1991.

Stacey, Judith. *In the Name of the Family: Rethinking Family Values in the Postmodern Age.* Boston: Beacon Press, 1997.

Stansell ,Christine. *City of Women: Sex and Class in New York, 1789–1860.* New York: Knopf, 1986.

Stein, Peter J., ed. *Single Life: Unmarried Adults in Social Context.* New York: St. Martin's Press, 1981.

Stilgoe, John R. *Common Landscape of America, 1580 to 1845.* New Haven: Yale University Press, 1982.

Stimpson, Catherine, Elsa Dixler, Martha Nelson, and Kathryn Yatrakis, eds. *Women and the American City.* Chicago: University of Chicago Press, 1981.

Stoesz, David. *A Poverty of Imagination: Bootstrap Capitalism, Sequel to Welfare Reform.* Madison, WI: University of Wisconsin Press, 2000.

Strasser, Susan. *Never Done: A History of American Housework.* New York: Pantheon Books, 1982.

Sussman, Carl, ed. *Planning the Fourth Migration: The Neglected Vision of the Regional Planning Association of America.* Cambridge, Mass.: MIT Press, 1976.

Taylor, Lisa, ed. *Housing: Symbol, Structure, Site.* New York: Cooper-Hewitt Museum and Rizzoli, 1992.

Thomas, June Manning, and Marsha Ritzdorf, eds. *Urban Planning and the African American Community: In the Shadows.* Thousand Oaks, Calif.: Sage Publications, 1997.

Todd, John and Nancy Jack Todd. *Tomorrow Is Our Permanent Address.* New York: Lindisfarne/Harper and Row, 1980.

Torre, Susana, ed. *Women in American Architecture: An Historic and Contemporary Perspective.* New York: Watson Guptill, 1977.

Transportation Research Board, National Research Council. *The Costs of Sprawl—Revisited.* Washington, D.C.: National Academy Press, 1998.

Uhlig, Günther. *Kollektivmodell "Einküchenhaus."* Wekbund-Archiv 6. Berlin: Anabas Vertag, 1981.

U.S. Department of Housing and Urban Development. *The Affordable Community: Growth, Change, and Choice in the '80s.* Washington, D.C.: U.S.G.P.O., 1981.

—. *Housing Our Families.* Washington, D.C.: U.S.G.P.O., 1980.

Urban Land Institute. *Affordable Housing: Twenty Examples from the Private Sector.* Washington, D.C.: Urban Land Institute, 1982.

—. *Housing for a Maturing Population.* Washington, D.C.: Urban Land Institute, 1982.

Van Allsburg, Cheryl M. "Dual-earner Housing Needs," *Journal of Planning Literature* (Summer 1986): 388–399.

Van Vliet, Willem, ed. *Affordable Housing and Urban Redevelopment in the United States,* Urban Affairs Annual Reviews 46. Thousand Oaks, CA: Sage Publications, 1997.

Wachs, Martin. *Transportation for the Elderly.* Berkeley: University of California Press, 1979.

Walker, Lester. *American Shelter: An Illustrated Encyclopedia of the American Home.* Woodstock, N.Y.: Overlook Press, 1981.

Weicher, John C., Kevin E. Villani, and Elizabeth A. Roistacher, eds. *Rental Housing: Is There A Crisis?* Washington, D.C.: Urban Institute, 1981.

Weisman, Leslie Kanes. *Discrimination by Design: A Feminist Critique of the Man-Made Environment.* Urbana: University of Illinois Press, 1992.

Wekerle, Gerda. "A Woman's Right to the City: Gendered Spaces of a Pluralistic Citizenship," in E. Isin, ed., *Democracy, Citizenship, and the Global City.* London: Routledge, 2000, 203–217.

—. "Responding to Diversity: Housing Developed By and For Women," *Canadian Journal of Urban Research* (Dec. 1993): 95–113.

—. *Women's Housing Projects in Eight Canadian Cities.* Ottawa: Canada Mortgage and Housing Corporation, 1988.

—, Rebecca Peterson, and David Morley, eds. *New Space for Women.* Boulder, Colorado: Westview Press, 1980.

—, and Carolyn Whitzman. *Safe Cities: Guidelines for Planning, Design, and Management.* New York: Van Nostrand Reinhold, 1995.

Whyte, William H. *The Last Landscape.* Garden City, N.Y.: Doubleday, 1968.

Wilson, Elizabeth. *The Sphinx in the City: Urban Life, the Control of Disorder, and Women.* London: Virago Press, 1991.

Wolfe, Tom. *From Bauhaus to Our House.* New York: Farrar, Straus, and Giroux, 1981.

Women and the City. Special issue, *International Journal of Urban and Regional Research* 2 (October 1978).

Women in the City: Housing, Services, and the Urban Environment. Paris: Organization for Economic Cooperation and Development, 1995.

Women's Expressions on the Environment: A Commentary to the Exhibition På Vej That Shows the Works of Women Architects, Planners, and Artists. Arhus, Denmark: 1980.

Wright, Gwendolyn. *Building the Dream: A Social History of American Housing.* New York: Pantheon Books, 1981.

—. *Moralism and the Model Home: Domestic Architecture and Cultural Conflict in Chicago, 1873–1913.* Chicago: University of Chicago Press, 1980.

Young, Iris Marion. *Justice and the Politics of Difference.* Princeton: Princeton University Press, 1990.

Index